Deadly Affair
A Linn County Scandal

Lorraine Robinson

Deadly Affair
A Linn County Scandal

© 2014 Lorraine Robinson
August 2014

ISBN: 978-1-63110-076-5

All Rights Reserved Under
International and Pan-American Copyright Conventions.
No part of this book may be used or reproduced in any manner
whatsoever without written permission except in the case of brief
quotations embodied in critical articles or reviews.

Printed in the United States of America by
Mira Digital Publishing
Chesterfield, Missouri 63005

Dedication

For my late mother, Kathryn Jean Sims
Thanks for getting me started.

~CHAPTER ONE~

Dawn was breaking over the misty water of the Marais Des Cygnes river as the freight train pulled to a slow jerking stop at the La Cygne station. The hobo occupying the boxcar, third from the end of the train, was jolted awake from a vivid, horrifying dream, and for a few moments couldn't quite realize where he actually was. In his dream, he was watching his drunken father beating his young sister, Meg, mercilessly with a razor strap. As in most dreams, the hobo felt helpless to save his sister. He couldn't move his arms or legs to reach out and stop his father's blows. He could only watch and scream silent screams of horror as the strap ripped through the young girl's skin, blood pouring down her body with each blow. His sister's screams were also silent and the picture of the terror on her face and the pain in her tear filled blue eyes was etched in his mind as he was suddenly awakened.

He shivered as he looked around the boxcar to get his bearings. The boxcar was empty except for a couple of old wooden boxes in a corner where he had propped his head before falling asleep the night before. His neck was stiff, and his right arm was totally useless for a few minutes until he was able to shake life back into it. As he worked to stand he realized his whole body felt like a lead weight. Not yet a man of forty, he felt as if he were ninety. He had been riding the rails most of his life, working odd jobs along the way to meet his meager needs. He never stayed in one place long enough to put down roots of any kind. Most people who ever worked by his side never even knew his name and he preferred it that way. Occasionally someone would ask him his name and he would tell them to call him anything they wanted to, and he ended up with a lot of nicknames over the years. He had always desired to fade into the background, not getting close to anyone. Just stick to his job, get his paycheck and move on, making his life a lonely one.

Years of personal neglect were taking their toll on him, and his body was starting to rebel. When was the last time he had a hot meal? A clean change of clothes? A good night's rest in a real bed, or even a hot bath. He couldn't remember.

Once he got his bearings, the hobo realized he needed to get a move on and get himself off the boxcar before the yard workers made their way down the train on their mandatory inspection. He stretched his body as well as it would allow, trying to awake fully. He picked up his huge leather bag, which held all he owned in the world, threw it over his shoulder and headed for the door. He had to put his whole body weight into his effort to slide the heavy wooden door open. He looked out on a very foggy, hot summer morning. The birds were singing and the bugs were chirping along the banks of the river. He rubbed his tired watery eyes and the scruff of his beard as he bent to sit down on the edge of the boxcar. He moaned as his left knee refused to bend. Once he got seated, he drew in a breath and jumped to the ground, stumbling once as he worked to balance himself on the gravel track. He heard voices and laughter. He turned to see the yard workers were still at the front of the train. They seemed to be involved in a friendly joke among themselves and weren't even looking his way. He sighed in relief and turned to walk toward the river.

Favoring his left knee again he squatted near the water. Once he felt balanced, he cupped his hands in the water and splashed the wet coolness over his face. He repeated this process a few times then sat back on his butt, drawing his legs to his chest. He took a couple of deep breaths of the humid air and rested his head on his knees. "Where am I?" he thought.

He figured he was probably still in Kansas, but he wasn't sure which stop this was. He was on his way to Sedalia, Missouri for a haying job, but wasn't sure when the next train east was heading out. He wasn't even sure what day it was, but knew he had to be in Sedalia by Friday.

His stomach was empty and he knew he would have to buy some food at this stop. It had been over a day since he had last eaten and he was starting to suffer from the effects. He opened his leather bag and pulled out his tattered coin purse. He counted out the two dollars in coins that had to last him, not only until he got to Sedalia, but until he got paid for his first week of work.

He laid his head back on his knees and in a flash the nightmare he was entangled in before he was jolted awake was back in his head. This dream, along with the guilt that accompanied it was a constant companion in his life.

"Meg...I'm so sorry I couldn't save you. Forgive me, Meg!" he moaned to himself.

She had been swinging on the rope swing tied to the old cedar tree in the front yard. It was a beautiful sunny day. She was happy for a change, not a care in the world. Her long brown hair wrapped around her face then flew behind her with each swing. She started singing a sweet little song as she swung as high as she could go.

"Stop that damn singing! The old man bellowed from inside the house.

Meg slowed the swing and quickly became quiet. Fear flushed her face, and she sat still for a few minutes, not wanting to anger her father. She started swinging slowly and methodically for some time and quietly started singing again. Before long her song became loud enough that once again her father became irritated. In an instant, before realizing what was going on, she heard the screen door slam and saw the old man on the front porch, razor strap in hand.

"I'm going to teach you to mind me or else!" he yelled, slapping the strap against his leg.

The child froze. She knew that look all too well. Her tiny body bore healing scars from past encounters with that strap. Before she could get off the swing and run the old man was on top of her, beating her over and over with no regard for her screams of pain.

The boy heard the screams and grabbed the shovel out of the wagon as he rounded the house as a fast run. He didn't even think about what he was going to do, he just knew he had to save Meg. He came up behind the old man, raised the shovel and hit him in the head with all his strength. The old man staggered and raised his hand to the boy, but the boy just kept hitting him, his rage building with each blow. Totally drunk, the old man lost his balance and fell as the blows kept coming. The old man tried to fight back but the boy was insane with anger by now and kept swinging the shovel until his father lay motionless in the bloody grass.

His mother had come out to the porch and watched the whole event in stunned horror, her hands covering her face in disbelief.

The boy stood over the lifeless body, heaving until he finally caught his breath and calmed down. He knew the old man was dead and he was glad. He hated him and he hated his mother even more for putting up with his abuse. His abuse of all of them, but especially his abuse of Meg. She was only eight years old. So tiny, and so frail.

He dropped the bloody shovel and walked over to her. She lay unconscious, her body covered in blood, but still breathing. He picked up her limp, tiny body and carried her back into the house.

He walked past his mother on the porch. She stood frozen, her hands still over her mouth. She was staring at her bloody, dead husband lying in the yard, but couldn't make herself move toward him.

The boy carried the small girl to the couch and gently laid her down. He ran to the kitchen and gathered several rags together. He filled a big bowl with water and returned to the couch where he began to wash and clean the child's wounds. He heard the screen door slam and saw his mother walking slowly into the room. Her face was dominated with shock and fear.

"What have you done, boy...what have you done?" she whispered.

"Shut up!" he yelled at her. His own fear was coupled with anger and he really didn't want to deal with his mother right now. But he knew she wasn't going to leave him alone. He lashed out at her.

"He had it coming and you know it! I should have killed him a long time ago! Look what he's done to Meg! And why?!" He was shaking by now. He laid his head on Meg's tiny chest and wept. Then sobbed. He loved his little sister so.

He looked up at his mother and screamed, "You bitch! How could you let this happen?"

His mother dropped her hands and her mouth flew open as if to say something, but didn't.

This angered the boy even more.

"What's wrong with you anyway? Why have you let him get away with this all these years?! Why didn't you ever try to protect Meg from that son of a bitch?"

His mother crumbled to the floor and the sobs started uncontrollably. The room was quiet for some time as mother and son sobbed in their grief.

"I couldn't stop him, son." She finally said. "He hit me every day for the smallest reasons. Sometimes for no reason at all. Even if he wasn't drinking. But he was always meaner when he was." She folded her arms around herself and started rocking back and forth as if looking for comfort.

He went back to washing his sister's wounds until he was satisfied he could do no more for her. He rubbed the hair away from her forehead, somehow trying to soothe her.

"What am I going to do, son? What am I going to do now?" She looked so pathetic, that for an instant he felt pity for her. He walked over to her and grabbed her arms and gently pulled her off the floor. He held her shoulders firmly in his hands and looked her square in the eyes. In a calm voice he said to her.

"First thing you're going to do is call Doc Joseph and tell him you've got an emergency here. Tell him he needs to get out here in a hurry and patch up Meg. Then, Ma, what you're gonna do is keep taking in washing and ironing regularly. You're gonna keep selling eggs and baking pies for the café. Hell, Ma, you could even sell this spit of a farm and move you and Meg to a small house in town. She could even go to school. It's not too late for her to go to school, she's only eight. You'll be better off, Ma, really. Least now all the money you make you can keep. The old man won't be taking it for his booze anymore!"

She looked at him for the first time. "And you. What about you, son?" Her eyes held fear and hope. He dropped his hands from her shoulders.

Deadly Affair

"I'm outta here, Ma!" I just killed the devil himself and I ain't gonna rot in no jail the rest of my life for that piece of shit laying out there in the yard! You just make sure you take care of Meg. Get her well and move on, Ma. Don't be worrying about me."

He walked back to the little storage closet off the kitchen where he slept on a small cot every night. He pulled the leather bag out from under it and started filling it with a few clothes and anything else he might need. He took his coin purse out of the top drawer of his small dresser and checked the contents inside. He had almost five dollars saved from working odd jobs over the past month. It wasn't much, but it would get him by for awhile. He put a few more things in his bag, knowing he would never be back here again, and threw it over his shoulder as he walked back to the front room. His mother was still standing there the way he had left her. He hesitated at the door. He looked at his mother.

"You call the Doc, Ma. You call him *now!*"

She turned her face to him, tears streaming down her cheeks. She slowly walked to the old box phone on the wall, lifted the receiver and put it to her ear.

He walked out the door and never looked back. He walked past the lifeless body of his old man and didn't bother to look at him either. He just kept walking, his eyes straight ahead, on the grass covered drive until he hit the main road to town and just kept going.

That had been 25 years ago. He had never seen his sister or mother again since that horrible day. He never wrote to them or contacted them in any way over the years. It was best for him if no one knew his whereabouts.

"Oh, Meg," he sighed.

He braced himself as he struggled to stand. Once he was up and straight he reached in his bag and pulled out a canteen filled with water. He drank heartily from it and returned it to the bag. He started walking up the riverbank and headed to a row of trees. He walked into the thick brush and there relieved himself before heading back to the railroad track. He slowly made his way toward the small brick building with a faded green roof that was the train depot. Hanging on a post outside the depot was a sign, which read, **La Cygne, Kansas**. The train had brought him near the Kansas-Missouri border to La Cygne.

Had he ever been here before? He looked around but nothing seemed familiar. He couldn't remember. He didn't know but guessed it didn't much matter. He walked up to the ticket window of the depot and looked to see when the next freight train would be leaving to head east. The date at the top of the schedule read, **Tuesday, June 19, 1923.**

He was glad to find out it was only Tuesday. That gave him a few days to make it to his job in Sedalia. He read down the schedule to find the time of the next freighter's departure, and was disappointed to find it didn't leave until nearly 2 o'clock Wednesday morning. He had a whole day to kill before he could leave, and wasn't sure how he was going to spend it. One thing for sure he did know was he needed to find a grocery. His stomach was starting to rebel, and he was feeling weak. He pulled his watch out of his jacket pocket and flipped the cover open. The watch read 8:30. He closed the watch, returned it to his pocket and hoped by the time he walked uptown there would be a store open. The misty fog had rolled on by now and the sun was bright and hot by the time he made his way to the main street.

~CHAPTER TWO~

    The temperature outside had reached nearly 90 degrees by 9 o'clock that morning but it was very cool inside the J.E. Scott Grocery and Meat Market. There were three ceiling fans running in succession down the center of the store, as well as two fans stationed at the check out counter in front of the store. It was even colder at the back of the store, as that was where the meat coolers ran the width of the room.
    Ellison Scott, the owner and proprietor of the grocery, along with his wife, Ella, had been at the store since 7:30 that morning, stocking shelves from the items in the storage room. Clyde McCullough, the manager of the meat department and in charge of meat deliveries, usually came in the store at 8 o'clock to start cutting and packaging meat for the day's sales. However, today he had taken the delivery truck to the train depot to pick up the new shipment of goods that had arrived on the morning freighter. It was his job to do this every couple of weeks, and he enjoyed the change of pace. It of course meant a long day for him, as he would have to make all his meat deliveries in the afternoon. He was still at the train station when the hobo walked into the grocery.
    At first the hobo just stood there. The store was so cool, so refreshing that he just stood there enjoying the relief from the heat. Ellison was standing at the counter watching him. It didn't take long for Ellison to smell the stench of the man standing in front of him. After a moment he asked the hobo if he could help him find something. Ellison was hoping this man would not be in his store for long.
    "I need some groceries," the hobo smiled. "Just enjoying the coolness for a minute."
    The hobo started walking toward the shelves, looking up and down the aisles at all the items he wished he could afford to buy. His stomach was really growling by now, being tempted by the selection at hand. He reminded himself that he didn't have much money, so he made his way to the bread rack, and picked out a loaf of bread then placed it under his arm. Although not quite following him, Ellison kept a close eye on the hobo. Just because he was a stranger who was filthy and tattered didn't mean he was a thief, but Ellison didn't think he trusted him just the same.
    The hobo make his way back to the meat counter to buy some meat to go with his bread, when he spotted Ella.

She was a very handsome woman with light brown hair, curled up in a bun on top of her head. Little strands of hair that hung down around her face and neck seemed to be damp. Even though it was cool in the store it was obvious that she was hot and sweating from her work. She had just carried in a large bowl of ice to pour over one section of the cooler. She turned around, placed the bowl on the counter behind her and picked up a glass. She turned back around to reach for the pitcher of water buried deep in the ice of the cooler to pour herself a glass of water, when she noticed the hobo standing there. She took a deep, long drink of the water before asking the man if she could help him.

"Are you feeling alright, ma'am?" he asked her with deep concern on his face.

"I'm fine," she said absently. "It's just very hot this morning, I guess." She lifted her glass and finished it off, before pouring herself more water.

She looked intensely hot, he thought, but more than that she didn't look well. Her face was flushed and she kept wiping sweat from her forehead with the back of her hand. She seemed to be sweating more than he thought she should, in spite of her lacy, frilly blouse buttoned high up her neck, and her long heavy black skirt that reached the floor. It was the fashion of the day, however he thought it was much too heavy for such a small woman to be wearing on such a hot day.

She had finished her second glass of water, wiped her forehead with her apron, and asked the man once again if she could get him something.

"Yes, ma'am you can. I need some of that lunchmeat you have there, if you don't mind."

"And how much would you like today, sir?"

He looked at the sign that listed the prices of meat and read:
LUNCHMEATS FROM 15 cents TO 50 cents.

"I'll take 15 cents worth today, I reckon. Can't carry much more than that with me." he said, feeling a little embarrassed that he couldn't afford to buy more.

She took some lunchmeat out of the cooler and laid it in waxed paper before placing it on the scales to weigh it. After taking away a few slices, she decided it was 15 cents worth, and turned to the counter to wrap the meat in packaging paper.

The hobo watched her the whole time, never taking his eyes off her. She reminded him of someone. He couldn't quite put his finger on it. He realized all of a sudden she reminded him of Meg!

She reminded him of what Meg might look like as a grown woman. Same brown hair. Same blue eyes. He didn't know if she reminded him of his sister because his dream was still fresh in his mind, or if she really resembled what his sister might look like by now. He wondered if Meg was still alive, all grown up. He wondered if she ever did move to town with their Ma, if she ever went on to school and learn to read and write. He wondered if maybe she was married, maybe had herself a bunch of kids. He allowed himself to smile a little.

"Will that be all then?" she asked as she handed him his package over the counter.

"Yes ma'am, thank you." She had startled him out of his little daydream.

She was wiping her forehead again, and pouring some more water when he told her he would like something else. He reached into his bag and pulled out his canteen, and asked her if she would mind putting some cool water in it to take with him.

She smiled, took the canteen and started scooping small chunks of ice into the lid. She then went to the faucet and filled the rest with cool water from the tap. She handed the canteen back to him with one hand and started rubbing her temple with the other. She closed her eyes in pain.

"Ma'am are you sure you are alright?" The hobo hadn't felt concern for anyone like this in years, and he wasn't sure he liked feeling this way.

She tried to smile a little. "I'm sure it's just the heat, and I've started to get a headache.

It's nothing to be concerned about, but thank you for asking." She turned around and picked up the big ice bowl before walking in the back room to refill it.

The hobo made his way up the aisle to the check out counter in no special hurry. Ellison had been watching him out of the corner of his eye the whole time he was in the store. He noticed the man looked very tired and old. He also noticed he was favoring his left leg with each step he took.

Where had this man come from? Ellison knew everyone from five counties around, and he had never seen this fella. He decided he must have ridden the rails in early this morning. He found him curious.

The hobo made his way up to the counter and noticed there were bushel baskets full of tomatoes, peaches, apples, and pears. It had been a long time since he had eaten some fruit, and it made his mouth water.

"How much for your fruit, mister?"

"Three for 5 cents mix or match." Ellison said, handing him a small sack to put some in.

The hobo took the sack gladly and picked out a tomato and two peaches. His teeth were in pretty bad shape by now, but he didn't think he would have much trouble chewing on this ripe fruit.

Ellison added up his purchase and it came to 30 cents. The hobo took his tattered coin purse out of his leather bag and handed the quarter and nickel to Ellison's waiting hand. Ellison almost winced at the filthy hand the money came from but instead he somehow felt pity for the man.

"You aren't from around here, are you?" Ellison asked, staring at the man as he put the purchase in a large paper bag.

"Just passing through on my way to Missouri. Got a job waiting for me there," the hobo answered as he took the sack from Ellison and placed it in his leather bag and swung it over his shoulder.

Ellison was curious as to what kind of a job this man could do, as beat up as he appeared to be, but decided not to ask him.

"Are you staying in town long?" Ellison asked.

"I'll be leaving on the next train east," the hobo said, tipping his torn, tattered hat to Ellison as he stepped out the door back into the horrible heat of the day.

Ellison was fascinated with this man. He watched him out the window. At first the hobo just stood there. Then he took a pack of rolling papers out of his coat pocket, licked his fingers and separated one from the rest. He took out a pouch of tobacco and poured it into the paper, licked one side and rolled the paper around the tobacco. He put the other papers and the pouch back into his pocket and pulled out a small box of matches. He lit the cigarette and took a long drag of smoke into his lungs. He stood there a little longer, then headed north on the sidewalk back toward the train station.

Ellison was still watching the hobo walk down the street when he heard Ella scream his name from the back of the store. He rushed around the counter, almost knocking over the basket of apples on his way to her. Ella was laying, head down on the counter, moaning in great pain. Ellison rushed to her and lifted her head in his hands. Her eyes rolled open as she turned her head and vomited all over the floor.

"Oh my God, Ella! Are you okay?!" He exclaimed. He gently laid her down on the floor and at that moment he heard the back screen door slam.

"McCullough! McCullough is that you? Get in here quick!"

Clyde McCullough came rushing around the corner to find Ella on the floor and Ellison in a panic. He at once noticed the vomit on the floor and ran back to the washroom to get rags and a mop. He ran as fast as he could to the meat department. Ella lay with her eyes closed, as if she were passed out. Ellison was unbuttoning her blouse and grabbing ice chips from the cooler to put on her hot chest. Clyde ran cool water from the faucet over one of the rags he had grabbed and placed it on her forehead before starting to clean up the mess. Ellison kept calling her name gently while brushing the hair from her forehead. After a few minutes she started to come to, and color started returning to her face.

A few customers had entered the store while all the commotion was going on, and were now standing quietly near the meat counter, concerned about what was happening to Ella.

"You scared the daylights out of me, you know that?" Ellison said to Ella with a sweet smile on his face. She looked at him for the longest time. He hadn't looked at her in such a loving way in a long time. She was pleased by his smile.

"Maybe I ought to go home and lie down for awhile. I don't know what's wrong with me, but my head is really starting to ache. It must be the heat, I just don't know why I feel so bad." She sat up, and started to stand. Ellison took one arm and Clyde took the other and helped her to her feet.

"I imagine it *is* the heat, Honey. You're right. You need to go home and rest for awhile." Ellison said gently. Ella wasn't sure she totally trusted his kindness at the moment. But she was to weak to question it.

Ella and Ellison, both were trying very hard to blame her illness on anything but the real reason. That being that she was three months pregnant and hadn't been feeling well at all for several weeks now.

When Ella stood up, the crowd of people who had gathered around, began to disperse and go about their shopping.

"I can unload the truck in a jiff and run Miss Ella on home on my way back to the depot to pick up the rest of the shipment, if that's okay with you Mr. Scott."

Ellison didn't care for the idea, but what choice did he have? He looked at Clyde with contempt, but decided Ella needed to go home and he couldn't leave the store unattended. He reluctantly nodded his head in agreement to Clyde, who jumped up to go unload the truck. Ellison very carefully walked Ella up to the front of the store and gently lowered her into the soft chair that sat behind the counter. He had re-dampened the cloth on her forehead and she sat very still in the chair as her husband waited on customers. Soon Clyde had the truck unloaded and was ready to drive her home.

Ellison and Ella Scott lived only three blocks from their grocery and meat market. Ella and Clyde didn't exchange a single word on the drive to her house. She rested her arm on the windowsill of the passenger door and rested her forehead in the palm of her hand. Her eyes remained closed on the drive home. Clyde pulled into the tiny gravel lane, lined with grass in the center that led to the back door of her house. The garage was about fifty feet from the house, but the lane stopped here at the back door.

They both sat in silence for a few moments. Finally Clyde spoke. He cleared his throat and shifted in his seat.

"What did Ellison say? About, well you know?" He cleared his throat again. Ella didn't move, she didn't even open her eyes.

"He has his doubts, Clyde."

"Doubts?"

"He doubts that I could be pregnant because he believes he could never father a child."

There was an eerie silence between them for a moment. Ella opened her eyes and looked at Clyde. He had a very puzzled look on his face.

She sighed, "Ellison knew when we married that I wanted children; that it was very important to me." She sighed again. "We had been married a couple of years and I started to press him about having a baby. It was then that he confessed to me that he had an accident when he was a young boy and the doctor told him he would probably never be able to father a child."

Ella looked away from Clyde and returned her gaze through the truck window. "He never explained the details of the accident to me, and I never asked. For years I refused to believe it, I didn't want to believe that he would deceive me that way. But as the years went by, I realized I would never be a mother. So..." She placed her hands firmly on her lap. "He doubts that I am pregnant. By him anyway." A tear streamed down her cheek. "He believes there must be something else wrong with me."

"Ella." Clyde whispered.

"Clyde, I really need to lie down. My head is pounding!" She reached for the door handle. Clyde placed his right hand over her left. She closed her eyes in impatience.

"Ella, I'm sorry."

"Not as sorry as I," she whispered. "You need to get to the station and get the rest of the supplies to the grocery before Ellison wonders about you." Clyde nodded slowly.

Ella stepped out of the truck and walked up the path to the back door of her house. Clyde waited until she reached the door before backing out of the drive. Ella raised her hand in a short wave before entering the house.

The kitchen was stifling, even though the windows were open. Ella walked to the small floor fan and flipped on the switch. She opened the two windows in the living room and switched on the small table fan next to the couch. She then walked back into the kitchen, opened the icebox door and took out a pitcher of cold water. She poured herself a tall glass of the refreshing liquid, popped an aspirin in her mouth and drank deep from the glass. She stood in front of the kitchen fan while unbuttoning the front of her blouse. She stood still, with her blouse open, soaking in the cool air on her hot skin. Finally she walked into the bedroom where she took off her blouse and lay in neatly across the chair. She then stepped out of her shoes and skirt and sat down on the bed to take off her stockings. She stopped to catch her breath as she felt the lightheadedness coming back. When she thought it had passed, she finished taking off her stockings and walked into the bathroom. Standing only in her slip, she turned on the cold water faucet and cupping her hands under the water, she began splashing it on her face and neck.

Once she felt cooled down, she used the toilet and walked back to the bedroom. She opened the windows as wide as they would go, and pulled the shades down to block out the late morning sun. She adjusted the table fan so it would hit the bed, switched it on and lay back down. For several moments Ella lay very still, only feeling her head pound with every heartbeat.

She tried to control the feeling of nausea that encased her whole body. After some time she started to relax as she began to feel a little cooler. Her headache diminished some and the nausea subsided as she started to doze in and out of sleep.

* * * * * * * * *

The pay phone hung on the wall at the top of the stairs of the college boarding house. The only bathroom on the second floor was right off the stairs where Pauline Potter had just poured herself a warm bubble bath. She was just stepping in the tub when the pay phone began to ring. She hesitated, waiting to hear if the phone call was for her. She heard loud footsteps running down the hall then heard a voice say, "Hello?"

"ARLENE! It's for you!!"

Pauline relaxed herself into the tub. Tuesdays were her favorite day. Classes didn't start until afternoon on Tuesdays, and she enjoyed using the morning to finish homework, to read, or to do whatever she wanted. On Tuesday she liked to take her bath about mid-morning, after the other girls were all finished with the bathroom, so she could relax and take her time.

"Hello…?" Pauline heard Arlene say. Pauline lay back in the tub and closed her eyes. She found herself eavesdropping on Arlene's half of the conversation.

"Hi! I'm doing well! How are you? How's Aunt Ella?"

'Uncle Ellison.' Pauline thought. Seems 'Uncle Ellison' was about the only person who ever called Arlene.

"Oh? Arlene had a touch of concern in her voice. There was a long period of silence.

"Okay," Arlene almost whispered. More silence.

"Okay. Goodbye then. Arlene whispered. Pauline heard Arlene hang up the phone then slowly and quietly walk back down the hall.

She spent another ten minutes or so in her bath, then drained the water and dried off. She picked up her clothes and headed back to her room. She and Arlene were roommates. As Pauline entered the room she saw Arlene sitting in a chair staring out the window, lost in her thoughts.

"Everything okay, Arlene?" Pauline asked as she put her clothes in the closet hamper. Arlene did not respond.

"Everything okay, Arlene?" Pauline asked a little louder. Arlene startled.

"YEAH! Yeah fine."

"Are you sure?" Pauline sat on the bed across from Arlene. She felt Arlene was not being honest with her. They both sat in silence for a couple of minutes and finally Arlene waved her hand at her roommate.

"Everything's fine, Paulie. My Aunt Ella is not feeling well but I'm sure she'll be fine. I'm sure it's nothing." Pauline knew she wasn't telling her the real problem, but she also knew Arlene had a flair for the dramatic, so she decided to let it go. She stood up from the bed and started getting dressed for school, leaving Arlene sitting quietly in the chair.

* * * * * * * * *

The sun had moved to the backside of the house by the time Ella had awakened from her nap. She woke feeling somewhat rested and realized her headache was all but gone. Ella slowly sat up on the edge of the bed. After a minute or two she also realized her stomach seemed settled. Ella looked at the clock on the table and was amazed that she had slept over two hours. As she stood up from the bed, the telephone in the kitchen began to ring. She walked as fast as she could to answer it.

"Hello?"

"Hi Babe, how you feelin'?" Ellison had recently started calling her 'Babe' and Ella didn't think she liked it much.

"I feel quite a lot better I believe. I just woke up from a long nap. That must have been what I needed."

"That's great, Babe. I'm so glad you're feeling better. Do you think you'll feel like going to the tent show tonight?"

The tent show. Ella had forgotten all about the tent show being tonight. Ellison had been looking forward to tonight for weeks!

Uh. Yes, I guess so. It would probably do me good to get out for a little while." She lied.

"What time does it start?"

"We should be there around 8 o'clock or a little before." He sounded so excited.

Deadly Affair

"Ellison-Uh-Are we going with anyone else?" She closed her eyes in hopes he would say no. Sometimes when they got together with their friends things could get out of hand, especially when there was a lot of drinking going on.

"Well, yeah. The Bishops and the Mendenhalls are going to meet us there, Hon."

Ella was silent.

"Don't worry Babe, there won't be any booze there. Not tonight, okay?"

"Okay," Ella sighed. She was reluctant to trust him.

"I'll be home around 6:30 or 7:00, Ella. Do you want me to bring home some meat?"

"There's potato salad leftover and I have tomatoes and cucumbers. If you would like to bring home sandwich meat, that would be good."

"I will then. See you soon, Babe."

Ella hung up the phone. She stood there a moment anticipating her headache coming back. She let out a huge sigh and walked back to the bathroom. She thought maybe a cool shower would revive her mood.

The tent show. Oh well, maybe it would be a good distraction for her. She stripped off her slip and let her hair down. She turned on the water, pulled the curtain back and stepped into the tub. She let the cool water run through her hair and down her body. It felt wonderful. So wonderful in fact she began to cry.

* * * * * * * * *

Ella Holt and Ellison Scott were married in March of 1911. Ella had lived with her parents on a farm near Centerville, Kansas before they married. Ellison grew up on a farm near the trading post of Cadmus, between Centerville and Paola, Kansas. They had known each other through school and church events growing up. After they were married they settled on a small farm belonging to Ellison's father, Charles Scott, who was a major landowner in Linn County and several surrounding counties. While having a few chickens, a large garden and a milk cow, Ellison did not farm the land. He chose instead to work for a local grocery and did so until around 1919. He had lived and worked on a farm all his life, as did Ella, but he had aspired to live in a town and become a successful merchant. It didn't take much convincing Ella to move off the farm to La Cygne. She and Ellison had some wonderful times and wonderful memories living on their farm, but Ella was excited about an easier life in the 'city'. Compared to the small farm town she had known as a child, La Cygne seemed like a real 'city' to her. She felt almost rich when, with the help of Ellison's father, she and Ellison had purchased their small home, complete with running water, electricity, and telephone.

Ellison had taken a position at the J.T. Potter department store where he worked hard learning what he could about the business world and getting to know the men who managed the businesses of the community. Ellison's father, Charles, was of great reputation in La Cygne, as one of the wealthiest landowners in the county, and Ellison gracefully used that reputation to his own advantage as often as he could.

He soon became good friends with a man by the name of L.P. (Lewis) Bishop who took Ellison under his wing and helped him learn the ins and outs of the business world. Ellison really loved the way L.P. could tell a story and make him laugh. When he and Ella settled in their house, Ellison invited L.P. and his wife, Myrtle, over for dinner one evening. Ella was impressed with L.P. and appreciated Myrtle's calm, endearing manner. It wasn't long before the two couples were seen everywhere together.

* * * * * * * * *

Ella stepped out of the shower, wrapped a towel around her hair, and dried herself off with a different towel. She stepped into a lightweight cotton dress and walked into the kitchen to fix herself a glass of iced tea. She took a long deep drink and carried her glass out to the front porch. After setting her glass on a small table next to her wicker chair, she unwrapped the towel from her hair and shook her long curls in the warm breeze. She sat down in her chair and propped her feet on the porch rail, taking another long sip of tea. Relaxing in her chair, she realized she felt extremely peaceful for the first time in a very long time. She very rarely had a moment to herself. Resting her head on the back of the chair, she closed her eyes and let her thoughts take her at will. Her mind wandered through memories, both good and bad, and before long she found herself thinking about Arlene and Leona, her two favorite nieces.

* * * * * * * * *

Ruth Arlene Scott was five years old when her Aunt Ella married John Ellison Scott. Their wedding was a glorious event, and somehow Arlene felt the day was all about her. She and her cousin, Leona were Ella's 'twin' flower girls. Ella had several nieces, but Arlene and Leona were special to her, and the same age, which made them perfect for flower girls. Ella loved and adored both girls and couldn't bear to choose one over the other to be in her wedding, so she decided to have both of them honor her. They were dressed in beautiful white, lacy dresses with colorful flowers and baby's breath in their hair. The little girls were the hit of the wedding and all the guests were happy to make a fuss over them.

Leona, however, was extremely uncomfortable with all the attention. She was painfully shy, and didn't know how to feel about all the notice. She didn't understand and was almost afraid. She sought the comfort of her mother's huge skirt to hide behind.

Arlene, on the other hand was in her element. She loved attention and sought it whenever and wherever she could. While her mother, Bertha, was weaving the flowers and baby's breath in her hair, before the ceremony began, Ella teased the child that after she was married they'd be like sisters because they would have the same last name. Bertha smiled at this, because it was a fun coincidence. Bertha's husband, and Arlene's papa, was Clarence Scott, but he was not related to Ellison. Arlene didn't understand anything about surnames, or that her last name was the same as Ella's would be. She just knew she felt special, and this somehow made her feel even more so.

Over the years, Arlene spent many weekends with Aunt Ella and on occasion, Leona would be able to visit too. Ella and the girls would spend hours entertaining each other, shopping, cooking, and playing dress up. They loved to laugh and tell tall tales to see if they could fool each other. Their visits were always special occasions. Leona didn't always join in the weekend visits as often as she would have liked to. She was always invited, but when her little sister, Wilma, heard of the invitation she would throw a fit until she was allowed to go. Leona and Arlene never had as much fun together when Wilma joined in. Ella either, for that matter. Wilma, too, was a little girl who wanted events to go only her way, and did a lot of whining and complaining if they didn't.

So, on many occasions, Leona would turn down the invitation if she thought her parents were going to insist Wilma tag along. Ella and Arlene developed an exclusive relationship over time that carried a very special bond. It seemed they were truly somewhat like sisters. Arlene worshiped Ella's attention, and since Ella had no children of her own, she loved to lavish her with it.

By the time Arlene was ready to go to high school, it was understood that she would live with Ella and Ellison through her high school years. Not every small farm community in the county could support a high school. Many young people stopped going to school after eighth grade, and started working for their folks, either farming or in a family store. Arlene wanted to be a teacher, and needed to go to high school before going to teachers' college. She lived near the little community of Oakwood, which was a dying town with very little to offer. Oakwood didn't qualify to have a high school, so plans had been made for her to go to La Cygne High School. Arlene wanted Leona to move with her so they could go to school together. Leona liked the idea, but she was set to go to high school in Blue Mound, and live with her parents. She knew better than to argue with her folks about the issue.

It was an exciting adventure for Arlene, to live in a big town like La Cygne. She loved to visit there, but couldn't wait to live there. She already had her own bedroom there, for weekend visits, which she was anxious to move into.

The first three years of school were enchanting for Arlene. She was popular with the other students and was involved with almost all school activities. She loved living away from home. Ella didn't treat her like a child, but rather like an equal, and that meant to world to Arlene.

By her junior year in high school, Arlene started blooming into a handsome young lady. The boys at school started noticing her in a different way all of a sudden, and she soon became addicted to the attention. She loved to tease and flirt, and soon became an expert at it. Her intentions were mostly innocent, but she loved to see the kind of reaction she could obtain from the most popular, or even the least available boy. It became quite a serious game to her. It was only when she started playing this game with her Uncle Ellison that the innocence died, and it became dangerously fatal.

* * * * * * * * * *

Suddenly Ella felt uncomfortable. She shifted in her chair and took another drink of tea. She ran her hand through her hair and was amazed at how fast it was drying.

She started feeling a little guilty about sitting on her front porch in the middle of the day doing nothing. Especially since she was feeling better. 'I should be doing something.' she thought, but she couldn't think what it would be. Her housekeeper, Bessie had cleaned her house the day before and had taken the laundry home to wash and press. Ella had already decided to have a light supper, nothing really to prepare, so she finally convinced herself it was okay to relax on her porch for awhile. She picked up a paddle fan sitting next to her glass and began fanning her face. She once again laid her head on the back of the chair, closed her eyes and continued fanning. She started dozing off-

Deadly Affair

* * * * * * * * * *

The afternoon was hot and muggy, but the young girls reveled in the summer day, as they walked home from the park. Laura Rowley and her friend, Elizabeth, were excited about being on summer vacation from school. As they walked along, they discussed how hard the final tests had been and decided to play 'what if' they didn't pass 8th grade and couldn't go on to high school in the fall.

Neither girl had anything to worry about. They were both straight 'A' students, but being young and full of drama they liked playing 'what if' with the idea of failing.

"I would run away from home!" Elizabeth spurted.

"Oh, me too! But where would we go?" Laura said, playing along.

"Chicago! Let's go to Chicago! I've always wanted to go there!"

"How would we get there?" Laura asked, laughing.

"Hitchhike, ride the rails, join the circus, I don't know." They both laughed hard. The girls wandered down the sidewalk laughing and talking until they came to Elizabeth's house. Laura invited her friend to come to her house for the afternoon, but Elizabeth said she had some chores to do when she got home, and her mother had been adamant about her getting them done. The girls said goodbye to each other and Laura went on her way home. She wasn't in any hurry and decided to walk one block over and take the river road home. She loved to walk by the river. The blooming wild flowers along the banks were not only beautiful to look at, the aroma of their fragrance was intoxicating. As she walked along the sidewalk humming a little tune she noticed something lying on the bank of the river. A couple of steps further and she realized it was a man. She stopped for a moment to watch him. The figure lay on his back, hands folded on his chest, legs crossed at the ankles. He was wearing a faded blue shirt and tattered brown trousers. His coat was folded under his head and a beat up hat lay across his face. Beside him sat a large worn leather bag.

Laura watched him for a few minutes. She was trying to decide if she knew this person. He lay so still she hoped he was just napping and wasn't dead. There wasn't anything about him that looked familiar and since his face was covered, she decided he must be a stranger.

A stranger, an out-of-towner, a hobo.

"A hobo!" she thought to herself. "A rail rider." She thought of her conversation with Elizabeth a few minutes earlier.

'Let's ride the rails to Chicago,' Elizabeth had laughed.

As Laura watched the napping man she fantasized about him. She wondered what an exciting life he must have. Had he been to Chicago?

19

Maybe all the way to the ocean, she thought. She could only imagine what it must be like outside her own little world in Kansas.

Reaching boredom with her little fantasy, she let out a long sigh and headed on down the sidewalk, looking back over her shoulder a time or two at the sleeping man. She stopped at Mrs. Conner's yard and picked some of her flowers to take home. Mrs. Conner wouldn't mind. She had a yard full of flowers and would never miss the few she picked. Old Mrs. Morris was sitting on her front porch and Laura decided to stop and visit with her a few minutes. Mrs. Morris lived alone and enjoyed company stopping by.

Laura reached her house about a half hour later and rushed into the kitchen to fill a vase of water for her now wilting and thirsty flowers. By now the memory of the stranger on the riverbank had long left Laura's mind.

She would, however, remember him, and remember him well before the night would end.

* * * * * * * * * *

Ella was in her garden picking green beans. When her basket was full she walked back to the house. Upon entering the kitchen door she saw Arlene leaning backward over the kitchen stove, Ellison on top of her kissing her passionately and groping her under her blouse.

Ella let out a faint scream, dropped her basket and ran out the door.

She ran... and ran... and ran... not recognizing the scenery she was passing. She just wanted to get away. She finally reached a rocky cliff and realized too late that she couldn't slow down fast enough.

* * * * * * * * * *

Ella startled awake, sitting upright in her chair, gasping for air. Ellison was standing in front of her with a puzzled look on his face. Her first thought was to run then she realized she had been dreaming.

"You okay? Ellison cautiously asked.

"I think so. Bad dream." Ella replied, trying to get up out of her chair. She realized her foot had fallen asleep and reached out her hand for Ellison to help her.

She went into the bathroom and combed her long hair into a loose bun on top of her head.

She then turned on the cold water and generously splashed it on her face and arms. Once she felt refreshed she grabbed a towel and started drying off.

She hated Ellison!!! She hated Arlene!!! The two people she loved the most had betrayed her! Had betrayed her in her own home! Right under her nose! She didn't know if she could ever forgive them. She did know she was tired of pretending everything was fine. *She hated them!*

Arlene was now gone. Going to teaching school in Pittsburg. Maybe it had been nothing really. Just a tryst. Now that she was gone, maybe that would be the end of it.

Ella let out a long sigh, finished drying her face and went to the kitchen to start preparing supper. Ellison took a shower while Ella got supper on the table. He was so excited about the tent show that was all he had talked about since he had arrived home from work. They talked about it while eating their meal and Ella decided she was kind of looking forward to it after all.

The tent show came to the county two or three times a summer. This year it was stopping in La Cygne, which made it even for appealing. La Cygne didn't have a theater, so occasionally Ellison and Ella, along with friends would plan a trip into Kansas City for a weekend get away to take in some entertainment. It had been a very long time since they had done anything like that. They both decided over supper that a night out would do them good.

Ella decided to wear the dress she had on, as the evening would probably stay warm after such a steamy hot day. She pulled on some light colored stockings and her white shoes. She grabbed a light weight shawl to pull over her shoulders in case the evening air did turn cool. Ellison wore dress pants, a starched white shirt, opened at the collar, and brand new suspenders. A recent gift from Ella.

When they arrived at the tent show there was already a huge crowd gathered. Ellison spotted his good friend, Lewis Bishop, who was vigorously waving for Ellison's attention. Bishop was sitting with his wife, next to the Potters, and the Mendenhalls in a row of chairs close to the stage. They had saved two seats for Ella and Ellison, who excitedly joined their friends. The women hugged Ella and the men shook Ellison's hand with slaps on the back. They all sat down, laughing and talking to one another until the show began.

The small orchestra and band started the show with an intensive flair and before long the crowded audience started clapping their hands and tapping their feet in time to the music. Everyone was transformed in the mood for an evening of entertainment.

After the music ended, the host appeared from behind a curtain and announced to the audience, the four act comedy 'THE MEN FROM ARIZONA'. The play was humorous from the very beginning and indeed entertaining. Ella and Ellison soon found themselves lost in the comedy of the story. Laughing so hard at times, they had to wipe tears from their eyes.

There was a fifteen minute intermission before the last act, and while the band played, people moved around to purchase cold drinks, use the facilities, and even to smoke cigars. The crowd was a buzz with elated spirits. The night air was perfect, and no wind to speak of, made the event very enjoyable. Ella and her friends decided to get a cool drink, while Ellison and his buddies decided to smoke cigars.

Ella hadn't felt so giddy in ages and she was glad she had come. She was really enjoying herself. When the group of friends sat down in their seats for the rest of the show, Ellison put his arm around his wife and gave her a big kiss on the cheek. She smiled at him. A genuine, warm smile.

The play ended with a comic twist, which brought the crowd to their feet with applause.

After the play, there was an improv act by Vivian Vetter, a famous comic, whose narrative was hilarious. Ellison was slapping his knees and Ella was holding her sides from pain of laughter. Vetter's act was followed by Skeet Molleston, who was a famous Charlie Chaplin impersonator.

By the time the show was over Ella, her husband, and their friends were worn out and yet their adrenaline was flowing from an evening of extreme comedy and laughter. The couples stood around visiting with each other for awhile, waiting for the crowd to thin out. Some of the men finished their cigars. They finally decided to go to the concession stand and get some ice cream while they waited. The group walked to their cars together, eating their ice cream, laughing and recanting highlights of the show. They all were only about a mile from home, a very short ride, so they were in no hurry.

Eventually Ella and Ellison said goodbye to their friends and got in their Studebaker to head home. Ellison placed his hand on Ella's left leg and gave it a squeeze. She placed her hand over his and wrapped her fingers tightly through his. She smiled at him. He smiled back at her then they both burst out laughing.

"That was so much fun!" Ella blurted out.

"Yeah, I needed some good laughs!"

Ella looked hard into her husband's eyes. She longed to see the Ellison she had fallen in love with. The man that she had given her whole life to be with. She didn't want to see any signs of the man who had betrayed her. She cupped his face in her hands and kissed him sweetly and passionately. He

Deadly Affair

returned her passion, and that pleased her. She smiled at him, as he slowly started the car to head for home.

As Ellison down shifted the car to turn off the highway onto Main Street, they both heard a groaning noise come from the front of the car.

"Dang!" Ellison exclaimed, as he appeared to be struggling to engage the clutch to down shift the gears. "I think I'd better pull the clutch on this thing soon and get some oil on it. It's really dragging." He smiled at Ella, as he pulled in the drive, past the house and parked in the garage. Ella squeezed his hand again before reaching for her purse on the floor of the car. "I really had a good time tonight." She kissed his cheek. He kissed her back, but he had a strange look on his face when he did, and it unnerved Ella.

"I think I'm going to go ahead and pull this clutch now and get it ready to oil," Ellison said as Ella got out of the car. She looked back at him, both surprised and disappointed. She believed they had a spark together this evening, and that maybe they would go in together, go on to bed and make love to each other. Something they hadn't done in a very long time.

"How long before you will be in, then?"

"In a few minutes," he replied.

There was a street light on the corner, two houses away from the Scott house, but it didn't provide much light on the narrow sidewalk leading from the garage to the kitchen door. Ella walked slowly, watching her steps as she went. Her mind wasn't on the broken sidewalk, it was on her husband, and the evening they had shared together. She so hoped they could work things out and become close again.

Upon reaching the kitchen door she heard a loud humming noise coming from inside. As she reached for the door handle, she realized she had left the fan on in the kitchen when they left.

She walked in the door, into the dark room, and cautiously walked across the kitchen in the direction of the table. An eerie feeling came over her as she slightly bumped into the table. She sat her purse down, and reached up fishing in the dark for the pull chain on the light.

She had an instant feeling of relief in finding the chain, and also an instant feeling of fear she couldn't place. She heard a shuffle behind her, and thinking it was Ellison, her fear dissipated. She turned around. Two gunshots rang out. Two bullets hit Ella's chest.

She looked into the eyes of her killer before her body fell in a heap on the floor.

Those eyes would be the last Ella would ever see in this world again.

* * * * * * * * * *

The boarding house was quiet and dark as everyone inside was asleep and had been for awhile. When the telephone in the hall rang out, breaking the silence in the air, Pauline Potter startled awake.

"What?!" she screamed. The phone rang again and she came fully awake, realizing the phone was ringing. Pauline threw off her covers and jumped out of bed.

"Go see what it is!" Arlene, her roommate, cried. "I'm afraid that call is for me and I'm afraid it is very bad news!" As Pauline scrambled out of the room, Arlene put her face into her pillow and wept.

~CHAPTER THREE~

THE LA CYGNE JOURNAL VOL 54 - No 2, DATED FRIDAY, JUNE 22, 1923

MURDERED IN HER OWN HOME

PROMINENT LA CYGNE WOMAN IS SHOT DOWN IN COLD BLOOD

MRS. J.E. SCOTT VICTIM OF INHUMAN FIEND

Arriving home late from the show she entered the house
Alone while the husband was putting the car in the
Garage..when she turned on the light the
Assassin fired two bullets into her breast
And fled..dead when husband arrived.

The most atrocious crime ever committed in La Cygne was the murder of Mrs. J. Ellison Scott, who was shot to death in her own home at about 11 o'clock Tuesday night. Mr. and Mrs. Scott had been to the show and upon returning home Mrs. Scott had gone into the house while Mr. Scott took the car to the garage, located about fifty feet north of the house. About the time he drove into the garage Mr. Scott thought he heard the report of two pistol shots, but did not think much about it and after looking around to see that things were all right in the garage, went to the house and found his wife lying on the floor dead with two bullet holes in her breast. The body was lying just beneath an electric light and it is believed that the assassin shot just as she turned on the light. One bullet entered the right breast and the other pierced her heart, causing instant death.

Mr. Scott was horrified at the sight and called for help. Nightwatchman Ireland, Deputy Sheriff Lindsey, and dozens of neighbors were soon at the scene and the sheriff, county attorney and coroner notified. Every effort was made to find the murderer, but he had vanished without being seen and left little or no clue by which his identity may be established. A posse was organized and roads, motor cars, and outgoing trains were watched and searched for traces of the slayer, but without result.

The sheriff, county attorney and coroner arrived on the scene in a short time and took charge of the investigation. Bloodhounds were sent from Kansas City and arrived about 5 o'clock Wednesday morning. The dogs followed a scent twice to the home of Tom Smith, a Negro, about three blocks from the scene of the crime. Mrs. Smith did the washing for Mrs. Scott Monday and helped with the housework. Tom Smith is an industrious man with good reputation and no one believes he had any connection with the affair.

For two hours Wednesday morning Mr. Scott was questioned by County Attorney Edeburn and Sheriff Ellington, assisted by Harold Kendricks, a Kansas City, Kansas detective; George Eaton, owner of the bloodhounds brought here from Kansas City, Kansas and W.A. Lindsey, Deputy Sheriff.

The conference resulted in no tangible clues. For two hours the heartbroken husband reiterated his story that he went driving with his wife last night. Upon returning she got out of the motor car and went into the house. He took the motor car to the garage at the rear of the house, and soon after heard the two shots which fatally wounded Mrs. Scott.

Ellison Scott is a son of Mr. And Mrs. Charles Scott of Cadmus. He was born and grew to manhood in the Cadmus neighborhood. About four years ago he located in La Cygne and became an employee at the J.T. Potter store. Two years ago he went into business for himself, his place being known as Scott's Cash Grocery and Meat Market. Mrs. Scott assisted in the store and they had a prosperous business.

Mrs. Scott was before her marriage Miss Eleanor Myrle Holt, daughter of Mr. And Mrs. J.W. Holt of Centerville. She was born April 29, 1891, at Oakwood, Kansas. She was married to Ellison Scott, a son of Mr. and Mrs. Charles Scott of Cadmus March 22, 1911. They lived for a time at

Cadmus, but have lived in La Cygne the past few years. They have no children, but a niece, Miss Arlene Scott, has lived in their home the past four years and attended high school.

Mr. and Mrs. Scott were very popular with the young married crowd in La Cygne. They were members of the Methodist church, where Mrs. Scott taught a class of girls in Sunday school. She was also guardian of the Campfire Girls.

Her father and mother, and five sisters live near here, and all came soon after her tragic death, except the father who is at an advanced age, and is in feeble health.

The funeral will be held at the Christian Church Friday and 3 o'clock.

* * * * * * * * *

Ellison was exhausted. His nerves were frayed and his emotions were spent. He sat in a chair in the middle of the kitchen watching, as if in a dream, men walking around him taking notes and asking questions. He watched with horror as Dr. Morrison and Coroner Kennedy worked on his wife's lifeless body. It was hard for him to realize what was really going on around him. He tried to answer questions asked of him as best as he could. At times he would break out shaking and sobbing and at other times he sat as if sedated.

About 30 minutes into the investigation of his wife's murder, Charles Carnegey, Ellison's neighbor from across the street, walked slowly into the kitchen. He walked up to Sheriff Ellington and asked if he might have a word with Mr. Scott. The sheriff recognized Mr. Carnegey and nodded toward Ellison sitting in the middle of the room.

Mr. Carnegey walked over to Ellison, squatted down beside him, and after a moment offered Ellison a bed for the night at his house.

"I thought maybe it would be hard for you to rest here tonight, Mr. Scott. Mary and I would love to have you stay with us. You know, to get away from all this for the night. His voice was soft and comforting. Ellison looked at the man with gratitude through watery eyes. He reached out his hand and Mr. Carnegey helped him out of his chair. Mr. Carnegey led the emotionally broken man out of the kitchen and across the street to his house. His wife, Mary, met them at the front door.

"Mr. Scott...I am so sorry." she spurted. He nodded to her. "Would you like a little something to eat?" she asked him. He shook his head. "Let me show you to the bedroom so you can lay down, then." She led him upstairs.

She walked into the room ahead of him and turned on a small lamp on a table next to the bed. Charles entered the room behind them carrying a clean pair of his pajamas.

"I don't know if these will fit you, Mr. Scott, but you are welcome to wear them." Charles handed them to Ellison and he took them saying nothing.

"The bathroom is downstairs just to the right of the stairway. There are clean towels and washcloths. Please let me know if you need anything...if there is anything I can do, Mr. Scott."

Ellison nodded to the woman and sat down on the bed. Charles and his wife looked at each other and turned and left the room.

* * * * * * * * * *

Twelve year old, Ellison was driving his father's new tractor in the deserted field. He was so afraid of this machine and he didn't like being in this field, so far from anyone, alone. The tractor seemed twice the size of his father's old Ford and his foot barely reached the clutch even though he was sitting on the edge of the seat. It was hard for him to shift the gears and steer the front tires at the same time. Sweat was rolling down his face. The field was full of rocks and boulders, and he really had to concentrate on steering around them. A big pile of brush and tall grass was in the path just ahead of him. He tried to steer around it, but the front tire hit a huge rock hidden in the grass. The tractor stalled and started leaning to the right. Ellison lost his balance and was thrown from the tractor, the gearshift knob cutting into his groin as he went.

He landed hard in the dirt, writhing in pain. Blood filled his trousers and ran down his leg.

He blacked out for short time and when he came to, he heard laughter, faint at first, but it kept getting louder. He looked up and saw Ella and Arlene standing within arms length of him. He tried to reach out but couldn't quite touch them. They had their arms around each other throwing their heads back then bending over in hilarious laughter. They were laughing at him!

"Help me..." he tried to say, but the words wouldn't come out. They laughed harder, pointing at him, mocking him.

"Help me, please!" he cried, hot tears stinging his face. Their faces turned harsh, and their laughter stopped. They started shaking their fingers at him, scolding him. "Shame on you,

Ellison Scott! Shame on you!"

"Please!!" He begged. He was sobbing, his groin was on fire and he was scared.

They turned and walked away from him, and they never looked back. He pleaded with them, as they kept walking until they were out of his sight.

* * * * * * * * *

Ellison sat bolt upright in bed. *Had he screamed!* Sweat was pouring off his face, and his pajamas were soaked. He was frightened. Nothing looked familiar to him. He couldn't figure out where he was for a minute, and the dream was still fresh in his mind. Slowly reality came to him. His wife had been murdered, he was in the Carnegey's guest bedroom and he was all alone.

He pulled the pillow from behind his head and buried his face in it and sobbed hysterically. He thought about Ella, *His sweet beautiful Ella.* He thought about Arlene, and he cried even harder.

Stupid girl! Stupid, stupid girl!! His heart was suddenly filled with anger. He wished he never knew Arlene. He wished she had never come to live with Ella and him. She had been such a flirt, such a tease.

He felt she didn't understand what she was doing. It was all innocent at first. She was practicing her *womanhood* on someone she believed she could trust. He knew she didn't understand what it was doing to him. She was so annoying. So constant! He couldn't take it anymore. He had finally called her bluff. Then she understood. He made her see what flirting does to a man. How it can turn him inside out. He wished he never knew her.

When did Ella know? Just when was it that she found out about him and Arlene.

He sobbed into his pillow awhile longer. When he had calmed down some, he sat up and peeled off his shirt, then lay back down. He didn't think he could go back to sleep, but as he dozed in and out he heard the faint whistle of the train leaving the La Cygne station. The next thing he knew the sun was up and the birds were singing.

His heart was pounding. He felt weak and spent. What sleep he had obtained had not been restful. He had no idea what time it was, but he slowly pulled his clothes on and wandered downstairs to the bathroom. He thought about taking a shower, but decided to just wash up in the sink. He saw a comb lying on a shelf and reluctantly ran it through his hair a couple of times.

When he felt presentable, he hesitantly walked to the kitchen. The smell of coffee was enticing him.

Mary Carnegey was standing at the kitchen counter taking fresh baked biscuits off a baking pan and putting them on a plate. She turned to put the plate on the table and saw Ellison standing in the doorway.

"Good Morning, Mr. Scott." she said trying to sound cheerful. "Were you able to get any sleep?"

"I think I was able to sleep some, yes." He tried to smile at her. He felt very uncomfortable in this woman's house. Yet he was really grateful for her kindness and hospitality.

"Sit down there at the table and I'll get you some breakfast. You must be hungry."

"A little, I guess." he agreed.

She poured him a cup of coffee and motioned toward the cream and sugar on the table. She then filled a plate of bacon and eggs and sat it down in front of him.

"This smells wonderful." He said to her, again trying to smile.

"Do you mind if I sit here with you, Mr. Scott?" She didn't want to intrude, or make him feel uncomfortable, but she felt he might not want to eat alone.

"Not at all, sit... sit down." He motioned to a chair. She poured herself a fresh cup of coffee first and sat down next to him.

The Carnegey's had been good neighbors, in a sense, yet he and Ella hadn't really taken the time to get to know them. He felt sorry about that now.

"Where's Charles? And your girls?" Ellison asked, trying to make conversation.

"The girls are on summer vacation, and are still asleep. Charles left for work a few minutes ago."

"What time is it anyway?" Ellison asked.

Mary looked at the clock on the stove. "7:30 already!" She said, kind of surprised.

"I guess I did sleep, then." Ellison said with a little humor. Mary smiled at him as she sipped her coffee. They sat in silence for a while as Ellison ate heartily of his breakfast. Mary got up at one point and refilled his coffee cup. When he finished eating he sat back and sipped his coffee. It really was the best coffee he had tasted in awhile and he was really enjoying it. Mary got up from her chair and took his plate to the sink. "Is there anything else I can get for you, Mr. Scott?"

"I really don't know what it would be, Ma'am. That was a great breakfast and I really appreciate your kindness." He raised his arms high over his head and stretched the wrinkles out of his tired body.

Deadly Affair

"Mr. Scott," Mary sat back down at the table. "You're welcome to stay here as long as you need to. We would love to help you all we can." Her look was genuine, and he almost started crying, but controlled himself.

"Thank you, Mrs. Carnegey." She reached over and squeezed his hand before getting out of her chair. She walked over to the sink and started washing the breakfast dishes. Ellison took a last sip of coffee before standing up. He pushed his chair under the table. " I think I'll go on home and get a shower. Get some fresh clothes and try to collect myself. I'm supposed to meet with the sheriff and those Kansas City detectives later on this morning and I want to get cleaned up some."

Mary smiled at him. "I imagine it will be a pretty tough day for you."

"Perhaps it will... perhaps it will." He said absently. He thanked her again and slowly walked out of her house and headed across the street to his own.

* * * * * * * * * *

Forensics was not a word commonly used in 1923, Linn county, Kansas. Nor did many people even know the meaning of the word. There were few tools available to law enforcement when investigating a crime. Fingerprinting was in its infancy in 1923, and was only being studied as a viable investigative tool in the big cities back east. For the most part, all investigators had to go on was a 'smoking gun' and eyewitness accounts. There was not a smoking gun and eyewitness accounts were suspect in the murder case of Ella Scott.

Sheriff Ellington entered the small building off Main St., in Mound City, that housed his office and the small jail. It was early Wednesday morning and he had been up all night. As he entered the building, Deputy Lindsey was pouring himself a cup of coffee, while Night-watchman Ireland was snoozing across the room. Slouched in his chair with his feet on his desk, he immediately jumped to attention when the sheriff entered the office. The sheriff gave him an amused smile and motioned for Ireland to sit back down and relax, which he did immediately. Deputy Lindsey carried his newly poured cup of coffee over to the sheriff's desk and walked back to pour himself another cup.

The sheriff sat down hard on his chair and the leather seat sighed at the weight. He took off his hat and ran his hand through his hair a couple of times before dropping his hat on his desk.

"It's the darnedest thing I've ever seen," he said sipping his coffee. After pouring another cup of coffee for himself, the deputy walked over and sat sideways on the edge of the sheriff's desk. The deputy and the night-watchman said nothing, waiting for the sheriff to continue. None of the men had had any real sleep the night before. They had been called out to the home of Ella and Ellison Scott, in La Cygne, where they found Mrs. Scott lying dead on her kitchen floor with two bullet wounds to her chest. Ellison was sitting in a chair in the middle of the kitchen with his head in his hands. Dr. S.D. Morrison was there attending to Ella and there were a few neighbors milling around the crime scene.

The sheriff sipped on his coffee, staring at the floor as if there was something interesting there.

"Nothing really adds up, he went on to say, shaking his head. "What's the motive here?" He looked at Ireland and Lindsey, hoping they would chime in with some revelation. Neither man spoke.

The sheriff sighed. "Okay," he said rubbing his face. "Ellison said he and his Missus came home around 11 o'clock. She gets out of the car, goes to the house. He stays in the car, he hears gunshots, hesitates in the garage for a short time before going into the house where he finds his wife on the floor with gunshot wounds to her chest.

"Ellison said he was working on the car in the garage before going in the house." Deputy Lindsey spoke up. "I went out to the garage and looked around. The car hood was up, and there was a can of kerosene on the shelf. But the clutch had not been removed as Ellison said."

"A man can get confused," the sheriff said, almost as if to himself. He was still staring at something on the floor.

Ireland pulled his chair closer to the sheriff's desk and sat down. "Ellison said the door on the west side of the house was always locked, but when he checked it, it was unlocked. When did he check it?" The night watchman gave the men an exacting look, waiting for an answer. However the sheriff and the deputy just stared at him.

"Well, Ellison said he immediately ran to the doctor's house when he found Ella, and he was in the kitchen with the doctor while he attended her wounds when we all got there." The men were silent.

"Okay, what I am saying is I walked into the living room," Ireland went on, and it was very dark in there. The light from the kitchen didn't carry into the rest of the house. If a *stranger* ran through the house to escape out the west door, as Ellison had suggested, he would have hit furniture, knocking over tables and lamps before getting to the door. Nothing was out of place when I walked in the living room. Could Ellison have been mistaken about the door being locked? 'Cause I really don't think anyone went out that door last night."

Sheriff Ellington wrote something down in a small notepad he pulled out of his desk drawer.

Deadly Affair

"Lindsey, check all around the house near that west door for footprints and any other clues of disturbance near that door, the sheriff said while writing. "We need to get that cistern drained soon, as well, since cartridge shells were found near the cistern. Perhaps the killer threw the pistol in there.

"It's strange," Ireland spoke up, "but I checked around the area between the kitchen door and the cistern with my flashlight and I didn't see any footprints anywhere there. "Course I'll check again this morning in the daylight.

"No you won't!" The sheriff looked him in the eye. "You are going straight home and get some sleep! We all are eventually, but you have duty again tonight and you need some rest. We can check for footprints all around the house when we get back out there."

"Now, what about eyewitnesses?" The sheriff asked, looking back and forth between his deputy and night watchman.

Ireland spoke up, "Everyone I talked to said that after they heard the gunshots and looked out they saw no one running from the Scott house. That is until Ellison ran to get the doctor. One neighbor said he saw, through the kitchen window, Ellison walking back and forth and in and out of the kitchen before running out of the house for help."

"Laura Rowley saw someone," Deputy Lindsey chuckled. "I took her statement," he went on to say, "but it seemed skeptical to me. She said she saw a stranger walking down the street right after the gunshots fired. She said he was wearing a long coat and cap and she had never seen him before. She said she asked him what was going on and he said Mrs. Scott had been murdered. She said he never stopped walking, he just spoke as he walked by."

The men stared at him in silence. "Well, come on," he said. "I just thought it a little suspect. If he was a stranger, how would he know it was Mrs. Scott who was murdered?"

The sheriff started writing in his notepad again. "It's worth checking into, I guess."

The deputy rolled his eyes as he poured himself another cup of coffee. "I guess," he said mockingly. "It sounds pretty skeptical to me, though. A guy just walks down the street nonchalantly and says, 'Mrs. Scott was just murdered!'"

Sheriff Ellington just nodded his head slowly as he kept writing on his note pad. We'll need to question her again. What else do we have here?" the sheriff asked, putting his pen down and reaching for his coffee.

"Well, let's see..." Ireland spoke up, rubbing his chin. "Ellison said he believed Ella must have frightened a burglar in the act of robbing their house, due to the fact the silverware drawer had been pulled out and laid on the floor. While you were talking to him," he said nodding at the sheriff, "I counted the silverware, the knives, forks, and spoons, and other pieces and it looked to me like nothing was really missing. Ellison didn't indicate there was hidden money or jewelry there, did he?"

The sheriff shook his head, as he kept writing on his pad.

"Nothing else in the house seemed to be disturbed. Not to me anyway." Ireland added, and the deputy nodded in agreement.

Sheriff Ellington took his watch out of his pocket, checked the time and looked at the clock on the wall to confirm. "I've got a meeting with Attorney Edeburn in a little over an hour. I think those Kansas City detectives are going to be there, too. Kendricks and Eaton, I think are their names."

"The ones with the hounds?" Night-watchman Ireland chuckled. "What a waste of time that was! And to think we had to wait until 5 o'clock this morning for them to get here! Who called those jokers anyway?"

Sheriff Ellington didn't share in his humor. "County Attorney Edeburn sent for them." He said sternly.

"Yeah, well. All those dogs did was follow Ella's scent to poor ol' Tom Smith's house. I thought the dogs were supposed to follow the scent of the killer, not the victim!" he laughed right out loud.

"Did you see poor Tom's face when those dogs ran into his yard?!" the deputy exclaimed. "The poor guy was scared to death! I guess I would have been scared too, come to think of it," he said, shaking his head.

"Wait a minute..." the sheriff sat back in his chair and started chewing on his pen. "Wait just a minute," he said again, deep in thought. "The dogs followed the scent they found in the Scott house, right?"

The men were silent.

"Okay," the sheriff sat up in his chair. "Think about it. Ellison's laundry was *also* in that basket that Bessie took home. Perhaps the only two people in that kitchen at the time of the murder were Ellison and Ella. Perhaps the dogs didn't pick up the scent of a stranger, because there was no *stranger.* Maybe those dogs know more than we think."

Night-watchman Ireland and Deputy Lindsey looked at each other and nodded in agreement with the sheriff. The sheriff continued to write on the notepad.

"Anything else, boys?" he asked rubbing his face. He was exhausted.

"Nah, I can't think anymore." Ireland yawned and the deputy waved his hand in agreement.

"Okay then," the sheriff said slapping his thighs and standing up from his chair. He placed his hands on the small of his back and stretched his

Deadly Affair

body to relieve the tension he felt. "Lets go get some breakfast, boys. We need to eat, after which you," pointing at the night-watchman, " go home and get some sleep. And you," pointing at his deputy, "Will come with me to meet with the attorney."

Deputy Lindsey unplugged the hot plate under the coffee pot, the sheriff picked up his hat and put his notepad in his shirt pocket, and the three men left the office. They walked down the street for breakfast at Lucy's Café.

~CHAPTER FOUR~

In the center of La Cygne lay one of the most majestic homes in all of Linn County.

The massive structure was two stories high. The first and second stories housed huge paned windows with massive shutters that would close over the windows in case of bad weather. Huge ornate pillars lined the wrap around porch, supporting the delicate gingerbread lined roof. White wicker chairs, benches and small tables sat invitingly on the wide front porch. Huge pots of beautiful flowers were set in eye catching areas near the chairs and benches, giving an air of peace and tranquility. Each table had a fresh cloth and its own vase of flowers. Enormous pine and oak trees stood guard on all sides of the house and precisely manicured shrubs lined the front porch and sides of the parking area. Beautifully groomed flower beds lay in front of the line of shrubs. The first impression one felt when reaching this impressive estate was one of peace, hospitality, and even safety.

The home was owned and occupied by the Mangold family and had been for several generations. The home was not only a residence but was also the local funeral home for La Cygne and the surrounding area. Inside the beautiful, beckoning house lay the fragile, wounded body of Ella Holt Scott.

The wake for Ella was set from 7 o'clock to 9 o'clock on Thursday evening. Ella's parents, John and Sarah Holt, arrived in the parking lot of the Mangold Funeral Home around 6:30 that evening. They rode there with their daughter, Maude and her husband, Robert Rogers. They wanted to be there early to meet friends, family and neighbors who would be coming to pay respects to Ella.

It took the 85-year-old John, a few minutes to get out of the car. His legs had quit working for him years ago and he now needed help getting around. Robert took his arm and helped him get his cane in position for support. Maude took her mother's arm, both to support her, but also for her own support as well. They all walked together up the wide, freshly painted steps to the porch. Beautifully carved wooden doors beckoned them to enter. It was a very hot evening outside, but a cool breeze met them upon entering the massive foyer on the other side of the wooden doors. John was winded by the time they reached the inside of the house. They all stood there for a few minutes taking in the beauty around them. The floor they

Deadly Affair

were standing on was marble with wood inlay. To their left stood double curtained French doors, standing open. Behind those doors lay a large parlor where family and friends would gather to mourn the loss of their loved one. On the right side of the foyer stood closed curtained French doors. At the end of the foyer stood a massive carved wooden staircase. A rich green, carpeted runner lined the center of each stair. Brass posts stood on each side of the bottom stair, holding a red velvet rope, gently reminding visitors that the stairs led to a private residence. To the right of the staircase, the marble inlayed floor led to open paned French doors and a view of more flower beds in the back of the house. As John was catching his breath, and attractive middle aged woman entered the foyer from the closed French doors. She wore a tailored gray dress and short black pumps. Her light brown hair, with streaks of gray, was attractively pulled back in a bun. Her face showed warmth and compassion and Sarah instantly liked this woman.

She held out her hand to John, and after asking him if he was alright, she introduced herself as Mrs. Mangold, and welcomed them all to her home. Mrs. Mangold took Sarah's arm and led them to the parlor, expressing her condolences as they went. Her demeanor was sincere and John, Sarah, Maude, and Robert felt comforted in her presence.

"There is coffee or iced tea here for you and your guests. Feel free to help yourselves," she said, pointing to a white clothed table standing in front of the only window in the parlor. "Let me know if there is anything I can do for you. I'll be in the foyer to greet your guests."

There were velvet lined, wood carved chairs and couches sitting throughout the length of the parlor. Two huge landscape paintings adorned the walls, one on either side of the room. Small pots of flowers were scattered here and there around the room, along with floor fans circulating the air. An arched doorway at the far end of the parlor led to a small viewing room, where Ella's body lay in her satin-pillowed casket. The room was filled with sprays of flowers from family and friends. The smell was overwhelming even though the window was open and the floor fans were running full speed.

John quickly found a large chair near the middle of the parlor and sat down. He took his handkerchief out of his pocket and wiped his face over and over again. His body had been quivering since he had entered the house, and he was starting to feel nauseous. Robert quickly poured a glass of iced tea, walked over to John and offered it to him. John drank a little of it and handed it back. He took his handkerchief, wiped his face again then rested his forehead in his hand to try to steady himself.

"John...?" Robert asked.

John waved him away with his handkerchief. Tears filled his eyes. His heart was broken. He would rather be anywhere but here, and he was worried that he might loose his composure in front of everyone. He had served three years fighting in the Civil War when he was a younger man, suffering harsh weather, horrible illness and near starvation. He watched friends and fellow soldiers being blown apart by guns and cannons right next to him, all the while fearing he would be next. His spirit was often broken, and very rarely did he allow himself to look forward beyond the day ahead of him. He had experienced many losses and tragedy in his long life, but nothing had prepared him to bury his youngest daughter before her time. He broke down in sobs. Sarah sat down next to him and wept on his shoulder. Maude, still standing near the doorway, broke out crying as well. Her parent's heartache was devastating to her. Robert put his arm around his wife and led her to the nearest couch to sit down. All the while wondering if any of them were going to make it through the next couple of hours.

Within a few minutes, other family members began to arrive. They were greeted by the lovely Mrs. Mangold, and led to the parlor. John and Sarah's oldest daughter, Blanche and her husband, George, arrived first, followed by Maude's twin sister Mabel, and her husband Earl. Soon after, a tall handsome man came into the parlor. He was wearing a dark gray suit with a light gray tie and satin handkerchief in his breast pocket. His hair was totally gray, yet his face looked young. He caught the attention of everyone in the room. He introduced himself as Mr.

Mangold, the undertaker and proprietor of this funeral home. He sat down next to John and visited with him a few minutes, then got up and greeted others in the room, offering sincere condolences to each of them. Like his wife, his manner was calming and comforting.

Shortly Maude's sister Bertha arrived with her husband, Clarence and their daughter, Arlene. Arlene was the only grandchild there. She had arrived at her parents' home mid-afternoon on Wednesday, after learning about her aunt's death. She attended all her classes that day, but headed home after the last class was over. Her eyes were red and swollen from crying. She was beside herself with grief. Her Aunt Ella was like a second mother to her and she could not believe she was gone. Ellison's parents, Charles and Mollie Scott, were the last of family to arrive soon after Bertha and her family. Mollie and Sarah hugged each other for a long time and wept. The two women were good friends and had been since their children had first been married.

It was nearly 7 o'clock and the women decided to go in the viewing room and spend some time alone with Ella before the crowd of people arrived. Maude took her Mother's arm and guided her through the parlor.

Deadly Affair

The other women followed. Ella lay still and coldly peaceful before them. Her skin, pale and waxy, brought the realization to her mother that she was truly gone. Ella was wearing the beautiful dress that she had worn on her wedding day and she held her favorite hanky between her lifeless hands. Her sisters gazed upon her, paralyzed in their own grief and disbelief. Her mother, sobbing, only stayed for a few minutes before walking back to the parlor to be with her husband.

After a few minutes, Clarence and George decided to join the women. Robert sat down next to John and fiddled nervously with his hat. Earl found himself talking to Charles Scott while he poured himself a cup of coffee. He didn't really want a cup of coffee, but he didn't know what else to do with himself.

A little before 7 o'clock, people started arriving. They stood in line to sign the guest book then slowly entered the parlor to greet the waiting family. For the next hour a steady stream of people came through the parlor and on to the viewing room. Some stayed to visit with the family, some stayed a few minutes and left quickly. The conversation was quiet and the look on every face was of shock and disbelief. Just a few days before, no one would have expected to be attending a wake for Ella Scott.

At about 8:15, Ellison arrived at the Mangold funeral home. He was wearing his best suit and starched collar. His hair was combed to perfection, but he looked gaunt and pale. His eyes were red and swollen from hours of crying. He looked ill. The room had become warm, in spite of the many blowing fans, due to all the people coming and going, but Ellison seemed to be burning up, his face was flushed. He walked into the room wiping his forehead, face and neck constantly with his handkerchief. Family and friends were stunned to realize that in their own grief, they hadn't missed his presence until now.

He held his handkerchief in his right hand and a small wooden box, about the size of a cigar box in his left hand. A few people crowded around him to offer their comfort. His mother Mollie came to him and hugged him for a long time. Ellison broke down and cried. He was kind to everyone, as he worked his way to the far end of the parlor, but he seemed distracted as well.

The crowd of people had thinned out by this time and there was no one in the viewing room when Ellison made his way there. Arlene, who was sitting next to her mother the whole time, sipped from a cup of coffee, and watched his every move intently. Ellison stood in the doorway, wiping sweat from his face. He looked in the viewing room at a glance, but never entered the room. He did not look at his wife one last time. Mr. Mangold greeted him at the arched doorway and shook his hand. They talked for a few minutes and Ellison seemed to be telling the undertaker about the box he was carrying.

John too, was watching Ellison, curious about the box in his hand. He was also curious about Ellison's behavior. Ellison didn't seem to be displaying grief, as much as he was displaying nervous anxiety.

The undertaker put his hand on Ellison's shoulder as Ellison handed him the small wooden box. They went on talking, but John couldn't make out what they were saying. The undertaker shook his head slowly as he hesitantly took the box from Ellison.

"Mr. Holt?" a soft voice came from nowhere. John had been so intent on watching Ellison, he startled at the interruption.

"Mr. Holt?

He looked up to see Mrs. Proctor standing in front of him offering her hand. He took her hand politely and she patted it with her other hand. Tears welled up in her already wet eyes as she tried to find words that could express her grief without sounding cliche.

"I will pray for you and your family," was as much as she could muster before breaking into sobs. She released his hand and quickly walked out of the parlor.

So many people had come to him this evening, sharing their grief with him, and their love for his daughter. He realized at that moment that many people had been hurt by Ella's murder. Not just him, not just his family, not just Ellison and his family, but a whole community of people were nearly as devastated as he was. He felt pride and appreciation, but mixed with grief in his heart, it only made his stomachache and his head hurt.

By the time John glanced back at the arched doorway, Ellison was standing there talking to someone John didn't recognize. He noticed Ellison no longer had the box in his hand and Mr. Mangold had disappeared. Ellison seemed uncomfortable and distracted as the man he was talking too was trying to hold his attention. Suddenly Mr. Mangold walked up behind Ellison, from the viewing room and put his hand on Ellison's shoulder. Ellison jumped in surprise, and Mr.Mangold shook his hand briefly and walked to the front of the parlor and out the door.

Ellison excused himself from the man he was talking to and started working his way back through the parlor. His demeanor seemed to instantly change. He seemed calmer, less distracted and more attentive to those he spoke to as he went through the room.

John watched him with deep intensity. The man's wife had just been senselessly murdered and John's heart broke for him. He wondered about the gambit of emotions the young man must be trying to cope with. Even

Deadly Affair

though his own grief was more than he could bear, he wished he could offer Ellison a true form of comfort somehow.

At one point Ellison spotted John sitting alone and walked over and sat down next to him. For a few seconds neither man spoke or even looked at each other. Finally John reached out and rested his hand on Ellison's leg. Ellison laid his hand on top of John's.

How are you doing, boy?" John finally asked.

Ellison looked into the eyes of his murdered wife's father and couldn't take the heartache he saw there. He dropped his head and started to slowly nod, as if to say he was doing okay.

"Are you eating, son?" John asked.

Ellison continued to nod his head. "Yeah, I've been staying with neighbors and people have been bringing food by the house."

"You need to keep your strength." He knew Ellison might not feel like eating much.

The two men sat in silence a few minutes longer.

Out of the blue, John suddenly asked, "What's in the box?"

"What?" Ellison looked confused.

"The box you brought in here. What's in it?" John asked bluntly.

Ellison just stared at him. John asked him again what was in the box, and Ellison started to rub the palms of his hands on his thighs as if trying to dry them off.

"Some of Ella's favorite things." He said softly looking down at his feet.

John nodded his head slowly. 'Some of Ella's favorite things.' That rolled around in John's head for several minutes.

"What happened to it?" John wouldn't let it go.

What do you mean?" Ellison asked. "What did you do with it, boy?" John asked impatiently.

Now Ellison was really fidgeting in his seat. "I gave it to Mr. Mangold. I asked him to put it in Ella's casket. I wanted it to be with her." He took his handkerchief out of his pocket again and wiped sweat from his forehead. He patted John's hand nervously before standing up and walking away, before John could ask him any more questions about the box. He walked over to Blanche and Clarence and gave his sister-in-law, Blanche a hug and shook Clarence's hand. John watched them then his eyes started scanning the room.

Some of Ella's favorite things.

All of a sudden, reality hit John hard. He looked around the room and saw his beautiful daughters and their husbands and thought about all their children. His grandchildren. Just five days earlier they had all been together at the farm for a picnic and what turned out to be a wonderful day together.

Just five days earlier.

Blanche and Bertha had come early on that Saturday morning to help Sarah kill and dress four chickens to fry up for dinner. Maude and Mabel arrived a little later with their families. Maude had baked two cakes for the picnic and took them into the house while everyone else went to the garden. They all spent about 45 minutes picking vegetables from the garden, then set their harvest on the front porch where the men worked at shucking ears of corn while the women snapped and prepared green beans, laughing and gossiping as they worked. The oldest granddaughters, Leona, Arlene, and Cleo washed and cut radishes, tomatoes, and cucumbers, as they laughed and told stories on the other side of the porch.

Mary and her family arrived late morning. Mary was famous for her delicious cole slaw, and she had spent the morning preparing a huge bowl of it for the picnic. Her husband, George, joined the men working on the corn, but didn't offer to help. He was not a very sociable person, and only came to the picnic to keep the peace with his wife. Their children joined the other grandkids either helping out or playing in the yard. Mary kissed her father's forehead on her way in the house to put the cole slaw in the icebox. John had been rocking in his favorite chair, watching his family enjoying each other while preparing a common meal they would all soon share together. The sun was hot, but the porch was comfortably cool with a slight pleasant breeze blowing through. His heart was full of love and peace that morning surrounded by his family.

Shortly after Mary and her family had arrived, Ella and Ellison drove up the driveway. Arlene looked up from her work and watched as they drove in. She smiled as they got out of the car then went back to what she was doing.

Ella had prepared a big container of vanilla ice cream and a bowl of ripe fresh strawberries to go with it. All the young boys were excited to see the ice cream freezer arrive. They stopped their play and ran to greet Ellison, who carried the freezer to the porch. Each boy couldn't wait for his turn at cranking the handle to make the ice cream freeze. Ellison sat the freezer down and went back to his car for the bag of rock salt needed to start the process of freezing the ice cream. Ella greeted everyone on the porch, but walked straight to her Papa for a big hug and kiss.

John's day was complete when Ella arrived. He loved all his girls, and even though he always thought he wanted boys to help with farm chores, he wouldn't trade any one of them for the world. They each brought him a special joy, but no one brought him more joy than Ella. She was his favorite and everyone knew it. Ella had been born to him late in his life and by that time John was very settled. He was an established farmer, and had moved beyond the stresses of raising a young family and putting food on the table. When Ella came along his other daughters were old enough to help out with chores and up keep and he had time and desire to spend with his youngest child.

Ella, like her sisters, Maude and Mabel, had been born a twin, but her sister Elsie had been frail from the beginning. Her short little life was plagued with illness and she succumbed to death when she was only three months old. John and Sarah both became overprotective of Ella after they lost Elsie, and Ella grew up with the privilege of being a free spirit. She was always a good girl, helpful and obedient, but she knew she was special somehow, and felt free to express herself. Her sisters had grown up stoic, always aware of their place and their duties. Ella had grown up charmed. Free to be silly, tenacious, and able to question everything around her. Her lighthearted personality was contagious and everyone loved to be around her.

When the men finished shucking the corn they started setting up tables and chairs in the shady part of the yard. Sarah finished frying the chickens, and Blanche put the corn in the boiling pot. Bertha finished making potato salad, and everyone pitched in to get the tables set for dinner. The adults and older children ate at the tables while the younger kids sat with their plates on the front porch, eating, laughing and throwing food at each other. The boys took turns eating and churning the ice cream, hoping the faster they churned the quicker the ice cream would be ready to eat.

The summer meal was luscious and everyone ate beyond their limit. Men unbuttoned their trousers and sat back in their chairs, full and content. The women removed their aprons to relieve a little pressure on their full stomachs. They laughed, joked and told stories as they fanned their faces and fanned the flies away from the food.

Finally, Ella got out of her chair and grabbed Leona's hand. "Come on!" she said. "Let's go see if there is a ripe watermelon in the garden!"

Everyone groaned at the thought of eating another bite of food. Ella raced Leona to the garden and everyone else took that as their cue to get up and start clearing the tables. Blanche went to the porch to check on the children and clean up the messes they left there. Most of them were already back to playing, their empty plates long forgotten. Blanche hollered to them to come and help clean up, but they all pretended not to hear her and went on playing. She single handedly cleaned up the porch then poured herself a glass of iced tea and sat herself down in the most comfortable chair on the porch.

After the tables were cleared the other women joined Blanche on the porch while the men wandered off to the barn to smoke cigars and play a few rounds of horseshoes. John and Sarah laid down for a short nap, as did some of the youngest children. By the time everyone had rested some, the boys announced that the ice cream was frozen and ready to eat!" Most everyone was still stuffed from dinner, but a few adults and most of the children had a piece of Maude's cake with ice cream and strawberries.

As the afternoon grew late and their daughters started gathering their families together to leave and go home, Sarah realized she was exhausted. It was a good exhaustion, but she and John both realized they were tired and needed some quiet and rest. As they said their goodbyes, watching their children drive off, neither of them knew then that today would be the last day there would ever be a Holt family picnic again.

Just five days ago.

* * * * * * * * *

John couldn't take it anymore. His body ached with weariness and he just wanted to go home. He got Sarah's attention from across the room and she immediately came over and sat down next to him. He told her he needed to leave and without hesitation she told Maude her father needed to go home. Robert walked over to help John out of his chair. Ellison realized what was going on and ran over to help. They got the old man on his feet and Robert helped John with his cane.

Once John was on his feet and stable, Ellison left them and walked over to Arlene, who was standing by her mother. He whispered something in her ear and she nodded, not looking at him. He then turned to see if Robert needed anymore help with John.

With Robert's help, John slowly walked out of the parlor leaving Sarah with the duty of saying goodbye to everyone. It was a cumbersome process to get him down the stairs and loaded in the car. John was exhausted, as was Robert, and it took them both a few minutes to catch their breath. John didn't know how he was going to make it through tomorrow. His heart was so heavy, his body so weak, he didn't know if he could get through the burial of his favorite daughter. Ellison followed them out of the funeral home, and walked to his own car. He hollered goodbyes to them as he went.

The sun was low in the west but there was perhaps half an hour of daylight left in the evening. Maude asked her parents if they would like to go by and see the girls for a minute. Leona and Wilma had decided not to go to the wake so there would be more room in the car for their grandparents.

"I just want to get home." was all John could say, rubbing his forehead.

Deadly Affair

Maude said no more and turned around in her seat. They all drove to the Holt farm in silence. Once John and Sarah were in their house, John gave Sarah a grief filled hug and asked her to help him get ready for bed. He just needed to lie down. Sleep came upon him quickly and as he began to doze off his thoughts were of Ella.
Some of Ella's favorite things...
Just five days ago...
Some of Ella's favorite things...

* * * * * * * * * *

Ellison drove straight to the Carnegeys' house after leaving the funeral home. They were sitting on their front porch enjoying the evening air. Ellison walked up the sidewalk and sat down on the porch steps. Nobody said anything.

About ten minutes later, Arlene drove up in her car. She walked up the sidewalk and said 'hello' to everyone.

"Hello, Miss Scott." they all replied in unison. Arlene sat down on a step across from her uncle.

"How is your school going?" Mary Carnegey asked her, trying to avoid any conversation about Ella.

"It's going well," Arlene answered politely. "In fact, I already have a teaching position waiting for me in the fall when I finish school." she said cheerfully, not like someone in mourning.

"How wonderful!" Mary said. "Where will you be teaching?"

"At Cemetery School just east of my parent's home. Where I went to school, actually," Arlene answered enthusiastically.

The conversation kind of dropped off there. Finally Arlene spoke up, "It's so kind of you to let Uncle Ellison stay here."

"We're glad to have him." Mary said without hesitation.

"Ellison stood up and asked Arlene if she would like to go for a short walk. She nodded that she would. They walked down the sidewalk as if they were on a first date, rather than a man who had just lost his wife to murder, and a young lady who lost her aunt. Mary Carnegey and her family watched the two walk away.

* * * * * * * * * *

Earlier that evening after eating supper with her family, and before going to the wake, Arlene had driven to La Cygne to see Ellison. She had arrived at the Carnegey's home around 6 o'clock.

Ellison had gone to his room shortly after supper to lie down for awhile. He had suffered a long day of interrogation from the sheriff and the Kansas City detectives. When Arlene arrived, Mary went up to Ellison's room to tell him Arlene was downstairs to see him. He rose from the bed and walked to the hallway. He hollered for Arlene to come on up to his room.

Mary was taken aback. Horrified, really. Her first thought was that it was very improper for him to call a young lady to his bedroom. She had expected him to go downstairs to greet his niece. When she thought about it for a second, she felt a little embarrassed. They were, after all family, for goodness sake, and he probably only wanted privacy to talk.

Now Mary watched them walk down the street and shook her head. "I think I'm going in and get ready for bed, she said to no one in particular, as she got up and went in the house.

* * * * * * * * *

At around 11 o'clock Friday morning, several ladies from the Centerville Methodist Church arrived at the Holt farm with many dishes of food to feed the family before they left for Ella's funeral. John and Sarah's children and grandchildren started arriving around noon.

John's brother, Jonah came to dinner with Mabel and Earl. John was so grateful to have him there. Jonah, like John was old and not in good health. He rarely left his home, so the brothers saw very little of each other. They sat together and visited while they ate.

Ellison and his parents arrived soon after Jonah got there, just in time to start eating. John and Sarah's modest dining table was too small for the family to all sit together, so everyone found a chair, couch, or stair step to sit on while they ate. There was constant conversation going on in the house, but no laughing. No joking or story telling. Not today.

* * * * * * * * *

Sheriff Ellington got out of his patrol car after he pulled in the drive at the Scott home.

Deadly Affair

There were a couple of farm boys and their fathers working at draining the cistern near the house. "Morning, Carl, Emery. How's it going?" The sheriff nodded to the men.

"Morning, sheriff," Carl answered. "We got her about half empty, I'd say."

"The sheriff stood and watched as the boys worked at drawing the water out. He took his hat off and ran his hand through his hair a couple of times, then returned his hat to his head. "How long you guys been at it?" the sheriff asked to anyone who would answer.

Emery pulled his watch out of his pocket and after looking at it he answered, "'bout an hour and a half, two hours maybe."

The sheriff nodded disappointedly. He was hoping they would be further along. He decided to have a look around, even though he and many others had already combed every inch of this property. He walked to the garage and took a look around. Ellison's car was gone and except for a few shelves on the front wall the building was empty. No clues here. He walked to the back of the property and absently looked around bushes and tall grasses for the possibility of a gun. This area had also been thoroughly searched, but he was here and had time to kill, so he kept looking around.

'Even if they found the gun, how are they going to tell who it was that used it to shoot Ella?' he thought. He had asked Ellison if he owned a gun and Ellison had told him that he didn't. There had been no footprints anywhere around the house. There was no evidence anyone had come or gone from this house except from the sidewalk leading to the house from the driveway or garage. If someone had come to the house to rob the Scott's, what did the Scott's have that was valuable enough to take a life for? The Scott's made a good living, but they were far from wealthy.

Sheriff Ellington knew just about everyone in this town, in this county for that matter, and he knew of no one capable of this kind of crime. It could have been a stranger, he guessed, but there were no clues. He took his hat off again, and again ran his hand through his hair. He stood there holding his hat in his hand and began shaking his head. He was beginning to come to the same conclusion the Kansas City detectives and Attorney Edeburn had come to. Heck, the conclusion his deputy had come to. This crime was *personal!!*

The sheriff found he had walked the entire property while deep in thought. He walked back to the men working on the cistern. "I'm going back to my office, to try to get some paperwork done. Will you men let me know the minute you find the gun? Or if you don't." I need to let Edeburn know what I find out as soon as possible."

47

"You bet, Sheriff," Carl said, waving. The sheriff got in his car and backed out of the drive.

* * * * * * * * *

The morning had started out hot and muggy. The air was thick with humidity. The river held a thick fog until mid-morning. By afternoon however, a cool breeze started to blow gently and the air became drier. "There must be a storm rolling in," thought John Holt. But it was as if God had taken mercy on the people of La Cygne in their grief and gave them a cool afternoon to bury their dead.

About 2:15 the Holt family loaded into their automobiles and headed to the Christian Church in La Cygne. Leona rode with Arlene and stayed close to her throughout the funeral. John and Sarah again rode with Robert and Maude and their daughter, Wilma. The family was the first to arrive. The first five pews in the church were dedicated to family members and they were all soon filled. Robert helped John sit on the far side of the first pew, next to an exit door. He wished to leave through that door when the service was over. He didn't feel he could walk the length of the church and out the back door, and he didn't wish to see Ella in her casket. It had already taken a lot out of him just to get to this seat. When Robert got John settled, he went out and moved his car near that door.

Over the next half hour the church started filling up with the townspeople of La Cygne and people of the county. Within a short time the pews were full and people crowded in any space where they could stand.

Ella's casket sat peacefully at the front of the church. A beautiful spray of pink roses and white carnations covered the top. The pastel flowers were a reflection of Ella's delicate spirit.

The pastor started the service right on time, knowing the sanctuary would soon become too warm with so many people crowded in there. He delivered a moving eulogy about Ella's life. Sobbing and sniffling could be heard throughout the room. This woman had been taken too soon.

The choir sang three of Ella's favorite hymns and during the last hymn, the pallbearers moved Ella's casket to the foyer in the back of the church. They gently laid the spray aside and opened the casket, so anyone who wanted to could say their last goodbye. The ushers led the family out first then slowly guided the crowd from the room.

John and Robert sat silently where they were until the building was nearly empty. Robert helped John as he struggled to walk out the side door and on to the car. Once John was in and comfortable, Robert pulled his car up behind the hearse, allowing Maude and Wilma to assist Sarah into the car

Deadly Affair

before climbing in themselves. Ellison and his parents soon pulled in behind him. Ellison's estranged brother, Walter had sent condolences from Kansas City, but had never planned to come to Ella's service.

About half the people who attended the funeral lined their cars behind the hearse to go to the cemetery. It took about twenty minutes for all the cars to get in line, after which the pallbearers loaded the casket into the back of the hearse. Then shortly after, the hearse pulled away from the church and the procession slowly headed to Oaklawn Cemetery on the outskirts of La Cygne.

Maude turned in her seat and looked at her father. "Are you doing okay, Papa?" she asked, concerned.

He nodded his head looking out the window.

"Mama?"

Sarah nodded as well, dabbing her eyes with her hanky. Maude could tell her parents were barely holding up and she was worried about them.

Her eyes connected with her young daughter sitting next to her Mother.

"Wilma?" Maude asked mockingly.

Wilma was sitting with her arms folded across her chest. Her eyes were full of tears, but they weren't tears of grief, they were tears of anger. She had wanted to ride to the cemetery with Leona and Arlene and she hadn't been allowed to. She was used to getting her way and could pull the best of tantrums when she didn't. Maude rolled her eyes at her and turned back in her seat.

'Leave it to Wilma to add more misery to the day.' Maude thought with a huge sigh.

There was a canopy set up by Ella's open grave, guarding ten chairs setting under it. Not near enough chairs for the entire Holt family, but enough for those who needed to sit down. Robert pulled his car as close to the canopy as he dared to, so John wouldn't have so far to walk on the uneven ground. Ellison pulled in behind him, and quickly left his car to help Robert guide John to the nearest chair. Jonah had ridden to the cemetery with Mabel and Earl, and once he made his way to the canopy, he sat down next to John. John took his hand and squeezed it hard. Sarah sat on the other side of John and Ellison sat between Ella's parents and his own. The rest of the chairs stood empty.

Once most of the people had settled around the grave the pallbearers unloaded the casket from the hearse and carried it to the platform over the grave. The pastor stepped to the front of the casket and said a few more words about Ella before reading a few verses of scripture. Then he asked everyone to bow with him in prayer. When he had finished he asked the crowd to join him in saying the Lord's Prayer aloud.

"May you all go in peace," he said signaling the end of the service.

Blanche walked to the casket and starting pulling roses and carnations from the spray. She lined up all the children and handed them each a flower. As the platform slowly descended in the ground the children walked by and tossed their flower into Ella's grave.

As people mingled around saying goodbye and offering their last condolences to family members, no one noticed the sheriff's patrol car pull up on the other side of the gravel lane. Sheriff Ellington and his deputy sat quietly in the patrol car, watching the crowd of people. Many people quickly left the cemetery when the service was over, but several close friends and family members stayed on as if they couldn't let go of Ella. John decided to sit right where he was until someone told him it was time to go. He watched the children pass by the grave dropping in their flowers. He had made it. He had made it through this horrible day. He didn't know how he would make it through tomorrow, or the next day... or the next day... or the next. But he had made it through today. At least he thought he had.

* * * * * * * * *

"I really hate this," the sheriff said quietly.

Yeah... me too, his deputy sighed, opening his car door.

The sheriff and his deputy walked slowly through the crowd of people, stopping occasionally to speak to townspeople. They worked through the people until they reached Ellison. He was standing next to his parents near Ella's grave talking to his good friend Lewis Bishop.

"Afternoon Ellison," the sheriff said taking his hat off.

"Afternoon Sheriff," Ellison replied.

"Ma'am," the sheriff nodded to Mollie Scott.

"Ellison, I know this is a hard time for you. But I have my orders." he sighed. "I hate to do this but I'm here to arrest you for the murder of Ella Scott.

Deputy Lindsey pulled handcuffs out of his pouch and cuffed Ellison's hands behind his back.

Mollie let out a feeble scream and fainted. Sarah was standing next to her and tried to grab her, but Charles caught her on her way down. The crowd stood in stunned silence as Ellison was led handcuffed to the back seat of the patrol car.

"Don't worry, Scott!" Lewis Bishop hollered after him. "We'll have you out before nightfall!"

Several other men hollered in agreement and ran to their cars to follow the sheriff to the county seat, in Mound City.

~CHAPTER FIVE~

THE LA CYGNE JOURNAL VOL 54 - No 3 DATED JUNE 29, 1923

SCOTT ACCUSED OF WIFE'S MURDER

Arrested Last Friday on Complaint of County Attorney

RELEASED ON $15,000 BOND

Search for Revolver Continues Unabated And
Confidence is Expressed that Missing
Weapon will be Found-Every Clue
Being Traced.

J. Ellison Scott was arrested late Friday afternoon, charged with the murder of his wife, Eleanor Myrle Scott, on Tuesday night, June 19, on complaint issued by County Attorney Edeburn. The complaint charges first-degree murder and was issued only after diligent effort by the county officials to discover the identity of the assassin, whoever it may be. The county attorney said he had failed to find evidence to support Scott's story of the tragedy, but said he had evidence indicating Scott's possible guilt.

Scott was taken to the county seat, Mound City, and arraigned in the court of Judge D.C. Potter. He was accused of first-degree murder. He pleaded not guilty. He was ordered held and his preliminary hearing set for July 5. He was released on bond of $15,000 provided by I. Glucklish, Charles W. Scott, L.P. Bishop, A.T. McMichael and B.W. Mendenhall.

About forty friends of Mr. Scott, many of them among the most substantial farmers and businessmen of Linn County, accompanied the sheriff and the accused to the county seat in automobiles, all anxious to be permitted to be one of the bondsmen.

The bond was filled out and signed in a few minutes time and Mr. Scott returned home with his friends.

"I did not kill my wife," Scott said to his friends. "There has been gossip several days and the trial will give me a chance to show the rumor I killed Ella is not true."

Several cartridge shells similar to ones that encased the bullets that killed Mrs. Scott were found on the ground near a well at the Scott home.

Friday afternoon every drop of water was bailed out of the well and every inch of the premises searched thoroughly in an effort to find the revolver with which the crime was committed, but no trace of the missing weapon could be found. Failure to locate the revolver strengthens the belief that the crime was committed by some person surprised in the act of robbing the house or one who had a grudge against the Scott's.

One citizen expressed the sentiment of the entire community when he declared, "You never will make me believe Ellison Scott killed his wife, unless he admits it in court."

Apparently the mystery of the killing is no nearer a solution than it was a week ago. Practically every person one meets has a pet theory of his own concerning the affair, but those who know the real facts are carefully guarding their secret. When it comes to theories and guessing the field is open with the sky for the limit and one opinion is worth just about as much as another.

Whatever clues the officers have followed and any evidence they may have obtained they are very careful to keep to themselves until the preliminary hearing of the case, which is set for next Thursday, July 5.

Several detectives (near and real) have been here since the crime. Apparently they were working on their own initiative. They looked around, asked questions, learned what they could and as silently departed as they came. If any one of them learned anything of importance he is not telling it. There may be sensational developments at the preliminary and there may not be. Anyway there is nothing for an anxious and curious public to do but wait and see.

Deadly Affair

* * * * * * * * * *

Sheriff Ellington and his deputy escorted the handcuffed, Ellison Scott, through the Courthouse doors and down the hall to the office of Justice D.C. Potter. The clerk to Judge Potter had been expecting them and had already started the paperwork for the arrest of Ellison Scott. Within minutes the hallways of the courthouse broke out in chaos as the men rushed through the doors, pushing, shoving and each man hollering he would be the one to bail Ellison out of jail. L.P. Bishop, the towns most prominent banker, put up most of the $15,000 bond, but Ellison's father, Charles was one of the bondsmen as well, along with several others. Within half an hour, Ellison was walking out of the courthouse a free man until his preliminary hearing, set for July the 5th. He was surrounded by all his business friends, who had come to his rescue and he couldn't help but feel blessed to have such good friends. Actually the feeling was more pride than anything. He had worked hard to be a part of the business community, to be part of the elite in La Cygne, and today he felt like he was being assured he had reached that position.

As he reached the doors he looked around for his father, who was walking alone behind the crowd. Ellison waited at the doors for him and waved the other men on through. When his father reached the doors both men stood face to face alone. Charles Scott looked like he had aged twenty years in this one long afternoon. He had buried his daughter-in-law, watched his son handcuffed and taken to jail, and had helped bail him out. He stood looking at his youngest son in total disbelief that he had just been arrested for murder. He had just been arrested for murdering his *wife!*

Charles was so torn. He loved Ella like a daughter, and his grief over her murder was immense. The grief he felt for his son's loss was equally immense. But now he had to face the fact that he was being told that his son was suspected to be responsible for Ella's murder and Charles just couldn't wrap his mind around it all. It was like he had awakened in a different world just a few short days ago and nothing made any sense to him. He stared helplessly at his son and Ellison could see the pain in the old man's eyes. Ellison broke out in sobs and threw his arms around his father. The two men, father and son, held each other tightly as they sobbed for what seemed like forever.

Charles let go of Ellison first and tried to compose himself. He realized he had left his wife, Mollie, in the car and opened the door to leave the building. Lewis Bishop was sitting at the base of a pillar smoking a cigarette when the two men came out of the courthouse. Ellison nodded to Lewis, and asked him to wait there for him, and Lewis nodded in reply.

Ellison and his father walked to Ellison's Studebaker where Mollie Scott sat sobbing into her handkerchief. When she noticed them coming down the sidewalk she threw the car door open and ran to Ellison. She threw her arms around him and sobbed into his neck. His father's pain and disappointment were hard for Ellison, but his mother's heartache was beyond what he could bear. He held her tight and whispered over and over that everything was going to be alright.

Mollie pulled away from her son. "Come home, boy, it's not good for you to be alone right now."

Ellison wiped his eyes with the heel of his hand and nodded his head. "I've got to go by the house and get some clothes. I'm going to see if Lewis will take me by there and then I'll be out later, Ma."

Charles had driven Ellison's Studebaker from La Cygne to Mound City, after the arrest.

Ellison told him to take the car on to the farm, and he would see if Lewis would mind taking him out there later.

Mollie kissed her son's cheek and hugged him tight one more time before getting back in the car.

Lewis Bishop pulled his car slowly up to the curb of Ellison and Ella's little house at the end of the block. It was strange that the house and the whole block did not look the same as it had just a few days ago. Lewis turned off the ignition, and sighed.

"You want me to go in with you, man?"

"No. I'm just going to get a few things to take out to my folks. I really don't want to stay here any longer than I need too."

Lewis nodded his head. "Take your time, buddy, take your time." he said, lighting another cigarette.

Ellison got out of the car and slowly walked up the tiny walk to the kitchen door. His heart was heavy. He felt such grief. His wife was really gone. Never again would he hold her, talk to her, laugh with her.

Suddenly his grief took on a tone of anger. A few short days ago life had been normal. His days had been ordinary and routine. Now his future was uncertain and out of control.

It wasn't supposed to be like this!!!

He walked through the kitchen door into a surreal emptiness. He had been here a couple of times the past week to pick up fresh clothes, but he hadn't stayed more than a few minutes. As he stood in the silent, stale room he looked around and realized the room had been left as it had been on the night of Ella's murder. The drawer from the chest was still on the floor with the contents sprayed all over. His eyes settled on a small pool of dried blood on the floor where his wife's body had lain dying. For a moment he couldn't

Deadly Affair

catch his breath. He thought about getting a washcloth and wiping the blood off the floor, and realized he didn't have the heart for it.

He walked slowly into the small living room. He was very aware of the heat and stuffiness in the house and it occurred to him it didn't even seem like his house. It seemed all of a sudden like he had invaded the home of a stranger.

Reality hit Ellison hard when he entered the bedroom he had shared with his young beautiful wife up to a few short days ago. His eyes fell on her side of the bed where the spread and pillow held the imprint of her body where she had napped the afternoon before her murder. He sat down on his side of the bed and ran his hand slowly over the bedspread where her body had been. Tears filled his eyes. He looked away and his eyes fell on her petite dresses hanging in the room's small closet. He slowly got up from the bed and walked to the closet. He took several dresses in his hands and pressed his face into them. He couldn't hold the tears back now.

He could smell her perfume all over the dresses. For a moment he pretended to be holding her. He pretended the past few days had been a horrible nightmare.

He collected himself after a few minutes and started removing his own clothes from the closet. He put them in a suitcase he removed from under the bed. He also took clothes from his chest of drawers and toiletries from the bathroom. The whole time he was packing his things he felt like he was in a dream. He kept thinking to himself, *'I've got to wake up from this!!'*

When he felt he had everything packed in his case he locked it up and headed back through the house to the kitchen. He looked back one last time before heading out the door.

It wasn't supposed to be like this!!

* * * * * * * * * *

John Holt sat stunned as he watched the sheriff walk his handcuffed son-in-law to the waiting patrol car. Sarah ran to sit in the chair next to him and buried her face in his chest sobbing. He patted her head absently as he watched Ellison being helped in the back of the sheriff's car.

Once Mollie Scott collected herself, she went with her husband, Charles, to their son's car. They pulled into the caravan of cars that were following Sheriff Ellington to the county seat.

John knew nothing about the investigation of his daughter's murder, what the detectives had or had not discovered. But he couldn't wrap his mind around the possibility that Ellison could be responsible for the murder of his precious Ella.

Arlene sat paralyzed on the other side of her grandfather. *What had just happened!*

She knew there had been a lot of tension between her aunt and uncle for sometime now, but nothing so severe as to merit murder. Yet Ellison had been calling Arlene a lot lately saying some crazy things and making senseless threats. Things she couldn't believe, and didn't want to believe. She felt scared... She felt *really* scared. Arlene slowly got up from her chair and walked over to her mother who was standing and talking to her sisters.

"I am so worried about Mama and Papa right now, I don't think they should be alone.

Papa is so fragile and I'm not sure Mama can take care of him by herself," Bertha confided to her sisters.

They all nodded in agreement, sharing in the same concern.

"What should we do?" Mary chimed in.

"Well, I was thinking," Bertha went on "That maybe we could all take turns staying with them and helping out. At least for awhile." Mary shook her head. Unlike her sisters, she was married to a mean man, who had no use for or patience with children and she couldn't envision leaving him in charge of her nine children even for a short time while she was gone helping her parents. Taking her children with her would be no help at all. She thought a moment about offering her oldest daughter, Glenora's help once in awhile, but she needed her help at home most of the time.

Bertha immediately read the look on Mary's face and realized and understood that Mary would probably not be participating in their plan. She hugged her sister. "That's okay Mary, we all know you have your hands full as it is. We'll all manage."

"I'll stay with them tonight," Maude spoke up. "It only makes sense, since Rob and I drove them here today and will be taking them home. I'm sure Rob won't mind if I stay tonight. Then we can all talk later and work out a schedule. We are all so tired now and I know Mama and Papa probably just want to get home."

"That sounds good," agreed Mabel and Blanche as Arlene was walking up to her mother. She gave her a heartfelt hug.

She apologized for interrupting their conversation. "Mother, I am going to head back to Pittsburg now."

Bertha started to protest but Arlene stood firm.

I am so tired and I have some important tests coming up that I really need to study for and I really need to get my mind away from all this.

Her mother saw the pleading in her daughter's eyes and withdrew her protest. Arlene hugged her mother once more and then hugged each of her aunts before walking to her car. She stopped on her way to talk to Leona

Deadly Affair

and the two young ladies hugged each other hard. Leona walked Arlene to her car where they talked a little while longer before Arlene drove off.

The sisters gathered their husbands and told them their plan to each take turns staying with John and Sarah. All except Mary, whose husband wasn't even there. The men were all in agreement and felt it was a necessary plan. Everyone was worried about the well-being of the elderly couple.

Robert walked over to John and helped him up out of his chair. Maude took her Mother's arm and helped her up. On the way to the car, Maude explained to her parents the plan she and her sisters had to stay with them and help out for as long as they were needed. Sarah patted Maude's hand and tried to smile at her as they walked slowly along. She appreciated the support and concern from her girls and was relieved to have them offer to help with taking care of their father.

The family gathered together and followed John and Sarah to the parking area. They all hugged the old folks warmly before heading to their own cars.

No one noticed the old wreck of a pick-up truck that pulled in across the lane. Two men got out of the cab and walked around to the bed where they each lifted out several shovels. The grave diggers stood respectfully silent at the back of the truck waiting for the last person to leave the cemetery before going to work backfilling Ella's grave.

* * * * * * * * * *

Maude made a small supper for her parents and herself out of the leftovers from the food the church ladies had prepared for them earlier that day. There was little to no conversation while the three of them sat and ate together. After cleaning up the dishes, Maude helped her Mother get John ready for bed. She walked her father down the short path from the kitchen door to the outhouse. She supported him on one side as they walked; his cane supported the other. Once she got him settled in the small, smelly building, she patiently waited for him on the other side of the door. Getting him to the outhouse and back to the kitchen again seemed to take forever. Maude found herself winded and realized just how hard taking care him must be for her elderly mother. She made a mental note to talk to her sisters about getting a chair toilet for their parent's bedroom.

She walked him to the bedroom and supported him as he slowly sat down on his side of the bed. She left the room as her mother helped him undress and put on his nightshirt. Once Sarah was done, Maude helped her lift his legs onto the bed, settle him in and adjusted the covers over him.

She kissed her father on the forehead. "Goodnight, Papa," she said as she walked out of the room.

The two women sat quietly in the living room for quite some time. Both women were exhausted and each was lost in their own thoughts. Sarah picked up some crocheting she had been working on, but soon lost interest in it. The flickering light from the kerosene lamp pained her swollen eyes. She dropped the thread and hook back in the basket next to her chair. She laid her head back, closed her tired eyes and gently started rocking in her chair. Maude watched her mother, and she sincerely wished she could impede the anguish she saw in her face.

"I'm so grateful for your help today, sweetheart." Sarah said, eyes still closed, still rocking in her chair.

Her mind started to wander through memories of years gone by. Of when she was young and her babies were little. She remembered how frightened she had been when Maude and her twin sister, Mabel were born right here in this house. She hadn't known she was carrying twins, and they came early. The babies were too small. They weighed less than three pounds each, too small to survive. It had been a hard labor and delivery and Sarah wasn't able to do much for weeks after. Blanche, Bertha and Mary had tried to help as best as they could but they were just children. Neighbors came and stayed around the clock to help out. They wrapped the newborns in several warm blankets and placed them in small shoe boxes. They laid the boxes on the hearth of the cook stove to keep them warm. No one thought the babies would survive. The odds were against them, but somehow they did survive. They grew strong and healthy, and Sarah thanked God everyday for sparing their lives.

When Ella and her twin, Elsie were born, Sarah had to relive her fear of losing one or both of them all over again. Elsie had been sick from the beginning, and Sarah knew she wouldn't make it. However, it didn't make it any less heartbreaking when she died at three months of age. Now both Elsie and Ella were gone. A stray tear ran down Sarah's cheek.

"How long has Papa been such a handful to take care of?" Maude found herself asking her mother. She knew he was crippled and her husband helped him all the time when they were out, but she had no idea how much strength was required to help him. "How do you do it, Mama?"

Sarah sat up a little in her rocker, and cleared her throat. "I just do what I can, dear. Sometimes it takes a long time to get something done with him, but we work on it together. I can't always lift him, but we do what we can, take a breath, and try again."

"Mama, I had no idea he was so disabled. I feel so bad, why didn't you say something about needing help before now?"

Deadly Affair

"Well, Honey, he's been hard to take care of for sometime now, but it's just been in the past few days, since Ella... that he's been so bad. His heart is broken you know, and I think he might be giving up..." she broke out crying. She blew her nose on her handkerchief and slowly stood from her chair. "I'm getting sleepy sitting here rocking," she said trying to smile. "I think I'm going on ahead to bed."

Maude stood as well. Sarah gave her daughter a hug and kissed her forehead before walking on to the bedroom. John and Sarah had never been openly affectionate with their children, but the events of the last few days had brought a need for closeness to them all.

John's body ached from exhaustion. He was physically and emotionally spent. He summoned sleep but it did not come quickly. His mind would just not shut down. It kept playing over and over, thoughts, events conversations, emotions...

Before long, however, his thoughts became dreams as he drifted in and out of consciousness. His last thought before drifting off to sleep was... *Some of her favorite things...*

When Sarah entered the bedroom, John was peacefully and softly snoring. She was grateful he was able to sleep. She only hoped she would be able to as well.

Maude decided to sleep in the small bedroom off the kitchen rather than upstairs, in case her parents called for her help during the night. She didn't feel like making the trek to the outhouse and decided to use the porcelain commode in the corner of the bedroom. She slipped her clothes off and pulled on a nightgown her mother had loaned her. She crawled under the covers of the small bed and lay there for some time staring at the ceiling. She tried to pray, but the words wouldn't come. She couldn't concentrate on sleep. Her mind couldn't leave the part of the day she and her mother couldn't talk about. Ella did not die. Ella was murdered! And now the man who was her husband, a man Maude knew and loved as a brother, was being accused of that murder.

Maude had hoped this morning when she woke up, that once Ella was laid to rest, the family could possibly begin to work on healing. It was hard to imagine a total stranger killing Ella for nothing more than a little silver or money, but to try to believe Ellison was responsible was more than a nightmare! Ellison was *family*. Ellison was a *son, brother, friend...*

What evidence did the detectives have that implicated him? Why would they believe Ellison to be guilty?

Healing from Ella's murder would not now be possible until Ellison was found innocent.

But what if Ellison were really guilty?

Maude could not control her emotions. She buried her face in her pillow and cried herself to sleep.

~CHAPTER SIX~

Clyde McCullough and Tom Peters were taking inventory in the grocery and meat market storeroom, early Monday morning before the store opened. Tom was a part time employee, but had been working full days the past week. Clyde himself had been putting in a lot of hours a day, but he couldn't make deliveries and keep the doors open all on his own. He was grateful for Tom stepping up and helping out. In spite of Ella's murder and Ellison's arrest, business in the grocery had not slowed and the men were constantly busy.

Tom seemed exceptionally tired, yawning and stretching every several minutes. He worked only part-time at the grocery because he worked full-time on his dad's farm. His dad had a lot of livestock, and depended on Tom's help taking care of them daily. For the past week Tom had been pushing himself hard to keep up with both jobs, working late into the night and up early in the morning.

Climbing down the ladder after counting the last row of canned goods, Clyde noticed Tom rubbing the back of his neck.

"You gonna be okay, Buddy?" he asked Tom.

"Man, I don't know!" Tom shook his head. "I'm exhausted! Have you talked to Scott lately?" he asked, taking the inventory sheet from Clyde.

Clyde hesitated. "Yeah. He called me... let's see... He called on Thursday, I think."

"What did he have to say?" Tom asked.

"Not much really. He sounded weary, asked how things were going, thanked us for holding down the fort and said he'd keep in touch. That's about it, I guess."

Tom was leaning against the doorway with his arms folded across his chest. He started slowly shaking his head.

"What?" Clyde asked.

"I don't know... It's all so unbelievable, you know?"

"Yeah," Clyde shook his head as well.

"What do you think, Clyde?"

"What do you mean?"

"Come on Clyde, I mean do you think Scott murdered his wife?"

The two men were walking back to the tiny office behind the storeroom where Tom set the inventory sheet on the small dusty desk. Clyde sat down in the worn desk chair, and rubbed his hands over his face. He looked Tom in the eye.

"It's possible, Tom. Not to say I think he did, but...." His mind started drifting. Clyde held secrets that he couldn't share with Tom. He had witnessed many battles between Ella and her husband over the past couple of years and he knew more than he cared to about their problems. What he didn't know was that Tom had also witnessed his own share of their differences.

"Yeah...." Tom sat down in the only other chair in the room. "Clyde, I know for a fact Ellison was abusive to Ella."

Clyde just stared at him.

"She showed me bruises more than once that she said Ellison had inflicted on her," Tom hesitated. "One day, I walked in on them while they were arguing and I heard her say to him,

"If you had caught me as I caught you, you would kill me." I don't know what they were talking about, but Ellison gave me such a look, that I walked out of the room as fast as I had walked in."

Clyde continued staring at him. A chill ran down his back. "Have you been subpoenaed yet, Tom?"

Tom startled. He hadn't even thought about it. "No have you?"

"Not yet." Clyde sighed, sitting back in the old chair. "But I'm sure I will be. You too, probably."

Tom just nodded his head. After a moment he said, "Guess we better get back to work, huh?" He was ready to move on from the subject of Ella's murder.

"Yeah, guess you're right!" Clyde slapped his hands on the desk and stood up quickly from his chair.

The two men were working at cutting meat when they heard a key tumbling in the front door. It was still about half an hour away from time to open the store. The two men stared at each other. Clyde picked up a towel and wiped his hands as he walked out into the main room of the store.

"Good mornin', Clyde!" Ellison blurted. "Good to see ya!"

Morning, Boss." Clyde replied reluctantly. Clyde had not talked to Ellison since his arrest and wasn't aware he had been bonded out of jail. He was really surprised to see Ellison and couldn't think of a single work to say to him.

"Clyde, you look as if you've seen a ghost, man! You okay?!" Ellison chuckled as he walked over to the store counter.

"I wasn't expecting you, is all," was all Clyde could think to say. He thought Ellison a little to chipper for a man accused of murdering his wife.

"Yeah, I'm sure. My hearing isn't until the 5th, so I thought I'd work for a few days. Catch up on things around here. Give you guys a little break, if I can."

The look on Clyde's face told Ellison he was offended that Ellison didn't trust him to handle taking care of the business. He suddenly felt out of place in his own store.

"Sure, Boss," Clyde tried to smile. Tom and I were just cutting some meat and getting ready to stock the coolers."

"How's the inventory?" Ellison asked.

"Pretty good for today. There's a shipment coming in tomorrow."

Ellison nodded. "Sounds like you guys are doing a great job. Thank you," he said sincerely and humbly. "How's business been?"

"Good," Clyde said. "Deliveries haven't dropped off, and in store customers have been constant."

"Thanks, Clyde. I'll work the register today, if that would help you guys out." Again, a wave of feeling out of place hit him hard. He was asking his employee if it was okay to work in his own store.

"Great, that would help a lot." Clyde said turning to go back to the cutting room. Ellison stood at the counter for several minutes, looking around at his store. The grocery and meat market was the only stable part of his life right now. He needed to be here. He needed something familiar to fill his time.

Ellison had grown up a farm boy, but from a very early age he had wanted to be a businessman. It had always been his dream, to own his own business. In Linn County, Kansas you were either a farmer or a businessman. There wasn't much in between. Ellison had memories of going to town on Saturday nights with his folks to socialize. He was always impressed with the store owners. They were always dressed in nice suits, with white starched shirts, and polished shoes. Their fingernails were always clean and filed smooth. There were no signs of calluses on their well-groomed hands. What fascinated him most at an early age was the gold chain they all had hanging from the small pocket in their vests attached to their pocket watches. They seemed so glamorous to him.

The farmers, on the other hand, wore their least worn Key overalls over their least dingy white shirts. A well used handkerchief usually hung out of their back pocket. They wore cowboy boots that had never been introduced to a can of polish. If they had been able to get the mud scraped off the soles of their boots, they were good to go.

Ellison loved the farmers. They were good, solid people, but he desired the status the businessmen seemed to possess. His father, Charles, had always hoped Ellison would work with him on his farm and take it over someday. Charles had taken over his father's farm, who had taken it over for his father, and that was the way it was supposed to be, from father to son. Charles had two sons, Walter and Ellison, and it was always his dream that his sons would inherit his land and carry on the legacy of farming. However, Walter hated farming! He always got the bulk of the chores and his father worked him hard. He couldn't leave home fast enough after graduating high school. He headed to Kansas City, where he went to college and settled in. Charles was furious with Walter, and the animosity between them eventually destroyed their relationship. Walter had not visited home for years and never bothered to write or call.

Charles was heartbroken over his son's decision to leave, but Mollie was devastated! She never forgave her husband for his relentless stubbornness. Years later, when Ellison approached his father with his idea of owning his own business, Charles was once again heartbroken. Ellison had been his last hope.

Unlike Walter, Ellison had a decent relationship with his father, and tried hard to convince Charles he would see to it the farm would always stay in the family, and never be sold to strangers. Ellison had grandiose plans of becoming very wealthy someday and would be able to hire enough people to take care of the farm when his father was gone.

Charles decided not to count on Ellison becoming wealthy, but did decide to let Ellison follow his dream. He didn't want to lose Ellison the way he had Walter. Eventually he even gave his son three thousand dollars toward buying his own business.

Ellison walked back to the cutting room. "Hi, Tom! How ya doin'?"

Tom acknowledged him as he worked on cutting a slab of meat on the block in front of him.

"Is the register ready for the day, Clyde?"

"Not yet, Boss. I was getting ready to do that when you walked in," he lied.

No problem," Ellison waved as he walked into his office. He walked over to the safe and turned the tumblers. He took out thirty dollars in a ten, fives, ones and change. He then went to his desk, wrote the amount of money on a slip of paper and placed it under his favorite paperweight. One Ella had given him when they first opened the grocery. He glanced at the clock on his way back up to the counter at the front of the store. The clock read 7:57 and he decided to go ahead and unlock the front door. He deposited the money in the register. Suddenly he felt a wave of anxiety spill over him. He hadn't been in the store since Ella's murder, and hadn't even really been out in public. How were people going to treat him? Would the community still support him or would they take their business elsewhere?

Deadly Affair

Ellison's thoughts were suddenly interrupted by Clyde and Tom laughing heartily at a joke told between them as they carried trays of meat to the cooler. He watched the men as they worked and felt a twinge of jealously at their friendship.

Ellison liked Tom, but he felt contempt for Clyde. He had no real reason for this feeling, but something in his gut kept him from totally liking the man. He was a good employee, a hard worker, dependable and always on-time to work. Ella always liked Clyde, and they would at times joke and laugh together and that was maybe why Ellison was leery of him, maybe even a little jealous of their friendship.

Ellison had decided to walk the aisles and see if any of the shelves needed to be straightened or restocked, when the bell over the front door rang as a little old woman pushed her way through the heavy door.

"Mr. Scott!" she exclaimed. "How wonderful to see you here!"

Ellison couldn't help but smile. Irma Mitchell was one of his very regular customers, and it was great to see her smiling face.

"How are you, Mrs. Mitchell? Good, I hope!"

"I'm just fine, young man. It's you I want to know to be doing okay!" She patted his arm. "How are you doing, son? What a horrible, horrible thing you have been through!" Tears were welling up in her eyes. "I know you didn't kill your beautiful wife, son. The shame of it, to arrest you an innocent man of such a horrible crime. It's an outrage!" she said, shaking her head.

"Such a shame!"

Thank you, Mrs. Mitchell, but I'm sure I will be exonerated and the true killer will be brought to justice. Is there anything I can help you find today?" he asked her, wanting to change the subject.

"I have a list, son. I'll just walk the aisles until I find what I need. Thank you, though." She grabbed a cart and slowly headed down an aisle on her shopping quest.

Before Ellison could collect his thoughts and try to remember what he was doing, the bell on the front door rang again.

"Ellison! Hey! Great to see you, man!!"

"Good to see you, too, Harvey!"

He reached out his hand to the big burly farmer, and Harvey Schmidt grabbed his hand and shook it hard. The two men made small talk before Harvey headed down an aisle to look for the few items he needed. By the time Ellison remembered he was going to stock shelves, he noticed Clyde was already doing that. He decided to go back behind the counter and take care of the register.

Throughout the day a steady stream of customers flowed in and out of the store, all seemed glad to see Ellison back to work, and all offered support and best wishes for him. All seemed sure that an innocent man had been wronged, and he would surely be found not guilty. Most were glad to see him at work again, so their own world would feel a little bit more normal as well, after the murder and all. By the end of the day, after the store was closed and Tom and Clyde had gone on home, Ellison sat at his small desk in his small office going over the day's receipts. Sales had been good that day. He was very encouraged that his business had not suffered harm from the recent events of his life.

He sat back in his chair, locked his hands behind his head and smiled. He felt naively confident that everything was going to turn out all right. He didn't have a doubt in his mind that his lawyers defense would override the prosecution and that he would never go to trial. What evidence could they possibly have of his guilt? None that he could think of. He was sure that he would be a free man the minute his preliminary was over and he could get on with his business and his life. As far as he was concerned, the detectives could look elsewhere for the killer. He didn't feel like going home, to his parents' house just yet. He liked the feeling of just sitting here in his own space. He felt a sense of control in this small office, something he hadn't felt in several days.

He went to the tiny janitor's closet and found a rag and dusting oil on a very dirty shelf. He shook the dust out of the rag as he walked back around the corner to his office. He started removing things from the desktop and rearranged the papers and items that were there. He then wiped the top of his desk with the oil and rag until it shined the way he wanted it to. He spent about an hour and a half working in his office, cleaning and arranging things he hadn't thought about in years. It lifted his spirits, and he really didn't want to finish. But when he did, he was pleased with the way his office was organized. He stood at the door, taking in a panoramic view of his office several times before he turned out the light.

He walked through the store, checking the lock on the back door, and then turning off all the lights, except those over the cooler, before locking the front door as he left. He headed home to his parents' farm, a very self-assured man.

~CHAPTER SEVEN~

The sun peeked through the small east window of the lean-to room off the barn, signaling the start of a new day. The hobo sat up on the side of his bunk, yawning awake. He set his elbows on his knees and started aggressively massaging his neck. After two weeks of daily hard work his muscles were finally starting to loosen up. He walked over to the washstand, stretching his arms and back as he walked. He poured some water from the pitcher into the basin, cupped the water into his hands and splashed some on his face. The cool water felt good. The day was young, but already very warm, and it promised to get much warmer before it was over. He grabbed his shirt off the chair next to his bunk and slipped his arms through the sleeves then slipped his legs into his trousers.

He walked out the screen door, where there was a light cool breeze blowing through. He opened the door gingerly so it wouldn't squeak and awaken the other two hired men who were still sleeping in their bunks. He took his tobacco pouch and papers out of his shirt pocket and rolled himself a cigarette. As he smoked, he enjoyed the coolness of the morning air. He heard the rooster in the hen yard welcoming the morning and soon after the cows started bellowing. Needing to be fed and milked, they were growing impatient. He stepped behind some bushes to relieve himself, and by the time he walked back, he saw Oliver rushing out of the kitchen door, hooking the strap of his overalls as he grabbed a couple of milk buckets near the kitchen door.

"I'm coming bossy!" Oliver hollered toward the barnyard on his way to start the morning chores.

Harold came charging out the door after him, stumbling on something that made him curse as he worked to regain his balance. The hobo chuckled as he threw his cigarette butt on the ground and walked back into the bunkroom.

Oliver and Harold McGruder were the adult sons of Evan McGruder, known as 'Mac' to most who knew him. Evan McGruder had been farming his whole life and had inherited a pretty large spread of land from his father. He owned an abundance of livestock, and raised many different crops on several acres of land. During the summer months he always hired extra hands to help him and his sons keep up with all that needed to be done.

The hobo had a standing job every June and July with Evan McGruder for the past several years. This job was one constant thing in his life he enjoyed and looked forward to. Mac was an honest and fair man and the hobo appreciated that he never pried into his personal business. Mac knew the hobo was a rail rider, but he never asked him about his past or personal affairs. The hobo gave him a good days work and that's all Mac expected from him. The hobo never gave him a reason for concern and the two men seemed to share an honest respect for each other.

When they met for the first time and Mac had asked the hobo his name, he was kind of amused when the hobo told him he could call him whatever he wanted. Mac thought for a minute, then smiled and said, "Okay, I'll call you 'Bo'. "Short for hobo, how's that?" The hobo grinned, reached out to shake his hand and said that would be fine.

For a couple of months a year, on a large farm in Missouri, the hobo had a name and he kind of liked that.

As he walked into the bunkroom the other two men were stirring awake. The hobo sat down on his bunk, picked up his pillow and whirled it at Jesse, hitting him in the face.

"Rise and shine, boys," he chuckled.

Jesse threw the pillow back as he sat up scratching his head.

Jesse was McGruder's nephew from St. Louis, and always spent the summer working on his uncle's farm. Mort, a man of few words, rolled out of bed and headed straight for the screen door. The hobo pulled on his socks and boots as Jesse started to get dressed. Soon the three men walked together toward the main house. As they came closer, they could smell the enticing aroma of breakfast cooking.

Mac was sitting at the head of the table sipping his coffee and reading the newspaper in front of him, as the hired hands walked through the kitchen door.

"Mornin', boys," Mac said, without looking up from his paper.

"Mornin', Mac," they returned in unison as they sat themselves down at the kitchen table.

"Ma'am," they all also acknowledged Mac's wife, Mildred, who was at the stove dishing up their plates of food.

She said good morning to them without turning around. She set plates of eggs, bacon, and biscuits in front of each hand then poured them each a cup of coffee. Once the men were served, she fixed herself a plate of food and a cup of coffee then sat at the opposite end of the table from Mac.

There was little to no conversation around the table as the men devoured their meal. One of the things the hobo liked the most was the wonderful food he ate while working here.

As soon as breakfast was over, Mildred would pick up her basket and head to her garden for fresh vegetables to prepare for the noon meal. After three or four hours of morning work in the fields the men would sit down to a huge spread of wonderful farm fresh food. The regular meals and schedule worked wonders to restore the hobo's health. He usually always gained a few extra pounds and muscle during the weeks of work here. The time spent here most likely sustained his life for the rest of the year.

Once his plate was clean, the hobo sat back to sip on his coffee. Mac was still hiding behind his newspaper engrossed in reading an article. The hobo glanced at the back of the paper briefly when a headline caught his eye.

"Prominent La Cygne Woman is Shot Down in Cold Blood..." The article caught his eye because he had just traveled here from La Cygne. He read on as he sipped his coffee, and realized the murdered woman was the same woman who had cut lunchmeat for him in the meat market the morning he had arrived there a few short weeks ago. He read she was shot dead in her own kitchen. It had been suspected she had walked in on a burglar. Several witnesses told of a stranger, a rail rider, who had arrived in town that morning, that they suspected as being involved.

The hobo froze in mid sip of his coffee.

Mildred finished her last bite of food and picking up her plate, walked to the sink. "You boys want some more coffee before heading out?"

Mac folded the newspaper and set it on the table between him and the hobo. He laced his hands behind his head and stretched his back from side to side. "I've had enough, Hon., thanks."

hands behind his head and stretched his back from side to side. "I've had enough, Hon. Thanks."

"I'll take a little more, Ma'am," the hobo said. Mort also asked for another cup, but Jesse stood up, walked his plate to the sink then headed out the door to smoke a cigarette.

"Thanks for breakfast, Aunt Mildred," he hollered back.

Mildred poured the hobo more coffee as she took his empty plate then did the same for Mort.

The hobo took a sip of his coffee as he slyly picked up the newspaper. He flipped it to the back page to finish reading the article about the murdered woman. It said the husband had been charged with the murder but that he held to his innocence, saying a 'stranger' burglarized his home and killed his wife.

The hobo felt the 'stranger' might refer to him. The hot coffee he sipped didn't take away the cold chill running up his spine. The part of him who had been running from trouble all his life wanted to jump out of his chair and run. Run and keep running! But his common sense soon took over and calmed him a little. He knew he hadn't been involved with the crime against that poor woman and there would be no evidence against him. No one saw him leave town and no one knew where he was going. He had not left a trail and no one would be coming to Missouri looking for him. Being on the move all his adult life for a murder he *had* committed kept his nerves raw, and the idea of any trouble heightened his anxiety.

"That's really something, huh?" Mac said, pointing to the article the hobo was studying.

"A woman shot in her own kitchen," he said shaking his head. "What's the world coming to? I hope they catch the guy and string him up from the highest tree!"

"Yeah, me too," was the only reply the hobo could muster.

Mac stood up from his chair and took his coffee cup to the sink. "Time to get after it boys. Bo, you drive Jesse and Mort to the bean field and I'll meet you there later."

Mac tossed him the keys to the truck. Still shaken, the hobo almost missed catching them.

He rose from the table and scooted his chair in, then picked up his coffee cup and set it in the sink, before walking out the door. He stood on the porch long enough to roll a cigarette, then slowly walked to the truck. His nerves were starting to relax some. He had a few more weeks of work here then he would be on his way to Texas for the crop-picking season there. He assured himself several times throughout the day that no one was looking for him here.

~CHAPTER EIGHT~

The week had passed by quickly and work around the grocery and meat market had fallen smoothly back into a defined routine. Around 10 o'clock, Friday morning the bell rang on the front door as Sheriff Ellington entered the store. He was carrying several envelopes in his hand. Ellison was in the office and Tom and Clyde were in the storeroom. Upon hearing the bell, Ellison headed to the front of the store.

"Morning, Mr. Scott," the sheriff said, taking off his hat. He was surprised to see Ellison there.

"Morning, Sheriff." Ellison was taken aback.

"I need to speak to Clyde McCullough and Tom Peters if they are here this morning." The sheriff felt a little awkward being here, talking to Ellison. He started running his fingers back and forth across the envelopes.

"Yeah, sure, Sheriff. They are both in the storeroom, I believe."

The sheriff pointed toward the back of the store, as if to ask if that was where he could find the men. Ellison nodded, and headed to the front of the store. Clyde and Tom were both taken off guard when the sheriff entered the storeroom.

"Morning, boys."

"Sheriff?" Clyde offered.

"I have a couple of subpoenas to serve, one for each of you," he said direct and to the point. He really didn't want to have to do this in Ellison's store. Clyde reached for his envelope first then reluctantly Tom reached for his envelope. Sheriff Ellington returned his hat to his head.

"Gentlemen," he nodded, and left the room.

Clyde and Tom stared at each other in silence.

"Damn," Clyde whispered, and walked out of the room.

* * * * * * * * * *

The day started out overcast, which allowed a cool breeze to blow through the open windows of Ellison's childhood bedroom. He woke to the smell of fresh coffee, sausage frying, and biscuits baking in the kitchen. He had been looking forward to today. His preliminary hearing was this morning, and Ellison, being a very arrogant and self-absorbed man, believed there was no one in his community that would hold him responsible for

Ella's murder. He had received a lot of support from the community the past few weeks and he felt sure most everyone thought him innocent. There was no evidence he could think of that they could hold him on. 'Yes!' he thought to himself. 'Come tomorrow I can start getting on with my life!'

Of course Ellison wasn't thinking that it didn't matter what the community thought, it only mattered what the court thought. He crawled out of bed and poured water into the basin on the washstand. He washed himself as best he could. He missed the shower he and Ella had shared in their little house in La Cygne.

When he was washed and dressed, he ran down the stairs to the kitchen where his Mother was standing over the stove. He ran up behind her and hugged her around the waist, kissing her over and over on both cheeks. It made her laugh. She loved to see him happy. The past many weeks had been so heartbreaking, that a moment of folly raised her spirits.

She turned around and kissed his forehead and told him to sit down for breakfast. She filled him a full plate of food and poured each of them a cup of coffee. While he ate she sat across from him chatting and laughing while she drank her coffee. Ellison and his mother shared a lighthearted breakfast together on a day they both thought would be the beginning of good things.

* * * * * * * * *

The courtroom of Justice D.C. Potter was overwhelmingly warm by 9 o'clock that morning as people crammed into the room. Besides the witnesses, a large crowd of citizens started out early Thursday morning for Mound City to attend the hearing. By 10 o'clock when the hearing was to start, Ellison could feel the tension mount in the courtroom as his attorneys and the prosecution were consulting with the judge for what seemed like a long time, if things were going well. He sipped nervously on the glass of water setting on the table in front of him.

Finally the pow-wow between the lawyers and the judge broke up and the attorneys returned to their chairs.

"What's going on?" Ellison whispered to his attorneys. His eyes darted back and forth between them.

Charles Trinkle didn't even acknowledge him, but John Hall put his hand on Ellison's shoulder and tried to assure him things were okay.

For several minutes Judge Potter sat reading papers on his desk as the people in the court- room sat silently. The only noise in the room came from the whir of the blades on the four ceiling fans working hard to take the edge off the heat in the packed room.

Deadly Affair

Finally Judge Potter looked up from his papers and addressed the attorneys for the prosecution." Mr. Edeburn, are all your witnesses for the prosecution present for this hearing?"

Mr. Edeburn stood. "No Your Honor. Many of our witnesses were out of town for the 4th of July holiday and many were not available to be served subpoenas, sir."

"Mr. Hall, Mr. Trinkle. Are all your witnesses present for this hearing?"

Mr. Hall stood quickly, "No, Your Honor, and for the same reasons, sir."

"Your Honor, with the absence of witnesses and also the absence of evidence against my client, we wish to make application for Mr. Scott's discharge on Habeas Corpus proceedings."

"Very well," proclaimed Judge Potter. "I will release the defendant, Ellison Scott, on ten thousand dollars bond, and set a new hearing for July 26th in Judge Gates' courtroom, at which time evidence is to be produced by the prosecution to hold Mr. Scott over for trial." The judge slammed his gavel once. "Court is dismissed.

Everyone stood as the judge walked into his chambers.

"What just happened?!" Ellison asked his attorneys, who were shuffling papers into their briefcases.

"We just got here! What the hell just happened?!" Ellison was almost screaming.

"Calm down!" John Hall took Ellison by the arm and guided him out the side door of the courtroom.

"I was supposed to be exonerated today!!" He was screaming by now as the men walked into a vacant room near the hallway.

Trinkle and Hall stared at Ellison in disbelief.

"Look, Ellison," Hall said as calmly and carefully as he could, as if trying to calm an hysterical child, "This was not a trial, man, this was a *hearing* to determine if there will be a trial! Sometimes it takes time to get the evidence gathered to get through the preliminary hearing. And as you heard, most of the witnesses to this case aren't even here."

"But they don't have any evidence against me!" he yelled. "They have evidence of a burglar, of a break in, what evidence do they have against *me*?! There was no weapon! They didn't find a weapon."

"Calm down, man!" Mr. Hall said firmly, grabbing Ellison's shoulder. He went on to say, "Edeburn claims he has quite a bit of evidence that has been presented by those detectives from Kansas City. The only reason they didn't go into that evidence today was again, because not all the witnesses were here to testify"

"Look, man," Trinkle added, "by applying Habeas Corpus we were able to get another hearing on the books in a couple of weeks instead of months from now." Trinkle gave Hall a wink and Hall gave a short smile in return.

"Come on, Scott," Hall said, leading him toward the hallway. "Murder is a serious charge, and the State is going to do all it can to find fault with you!"

Fear gripped every muscle in Ellison's body. Why were they not certain that a burglar had committed this horrible crime. Why were they so sure that he was the culprit. Anxiety welled up in his chest. Since his arrest he had been scared, but now he was terrified. Under his confident demeanor he was really terrified!

"Yeah, Scott," Trinkle added. "We're going to do the best we can to defend you, but we have to let the State make the first move." He took Ellison's arm. "We need to go work out your bond with the judge, c'mon."

The three men walked together to the bailiff's office, where they were informed Ellison's bond had already been posted by his father. Ellison instantly felt shame and grief run through his veins at learning his father had once again bailed him out of trouble.

* * * * * * * * * *

Arlene had not been her usual bubbly, cheerful self in the weeks since her aunt's funeral.

She had become reclusive, studying alone, going for long walks alone, even eating alone. The girls at the boarding house had become very worried about her. They knew she was grieving for her aunt, but they were concerned about her self-isolation. No one more than her roommate, Pauline. Pauline felt Arlene was suffering from more than grief.

Late one afternoon after returning from class, Pauline walked into her room at the boarding house and found Arlene sitting on her chair looking absently out the window. A math book lay forgotten across her lap. Pauline walked over to her and gently started massaging her shoulders.

"I'm worried about you girl," Pauline said quietly.

A tear fell down Arlene's cheek. Pauline had become her best friend over the summer, and Arlene cherished that friendship.

"Talk to me," Pauline pleaded.

After some hesitation, Arlene let out a short sigh. "I've been contacted a few times by detectives from Kansas City," Arlene said without removing her gaze from the window.

Pauline walked over and sat down on the edge of her bed facing Arlene.

Deadly Affair

"They think because I lived with my aunt and uncle for four years, I might have some information for them about Uncle Ellison." She never took her eyes from the window.

"What kind of information?" Pauline asked.

Arlene turned her gaze toward Pauline. "Like if he had a motive to kill Aunt Ella, Arlene said harshly.

"Did he?" Pauline gasped. "Have a motive, I mean."

Arlene stared at her for what seemed like the longest time. Pauline thought Arlene might jump out of her chair and go for her throat for asking such a question. However, Arlene was thinking of the possibilities that her uncle was guilty. She sighed and turned back toward the window.

"I don't know," she whispered. "I really don't know. Arlene slowly stood from her chair and announced she was going for a walk.

"Arle...." Pauline started to say.

Arlene held up her hand in protest. "I'll be back in about an hour.

Arlene had taken many walks in the past few weeks and had favorite streets lined out in her mind. Streets with trees that would shade her from the sun's heat. The affair of her aunt's murder had been all she thought about, day and night. As she walked the cracked sidewalks, she played it all over and over in her mind.

Could Uncle Ellison really do such a horrible thing?

Was she herself partly to blame? That's what really was haunting her. Was she herself partly to blame? Her relationship with her uncle had not been so straightforward and over time had become horribly complicated. It had been a little game to her at first. Flirting to get a reaction. To make herself feel special. To have the attention of an older man. At first, he ignored her awkward advances for what they were, a young girl testing the waters. But by the time Arlene was a senior in high school he had started flirting back. At times he would even make the advances, which she couldn't resist. And before long they had crossed a forbidden boundary.

~CHAPTER NINE~

Ellison had been in a profound depression since his first preliminary hearing. He couldn't keep his mind occupied with any thing other than his up coming trial. His life was on hold, not at all what he had planned it would be. Plans were something he didn't feel he had the privilege to even think about now until the murder of his wife had been solved. He felt his friends were still supportive of him, and that was important to him, but his greatest worry and concern was what evidence the detectives had against him.
There was no evidence!
His attorneys were confident his case would be solved in his favor, but he just didn't understand why this nightmare couldn't be over with now!
He still went to the store everyday, but he didn't have the same outlook and enthusiasm he'd had before his hearing. He spent many days in his bed nursing severe headaches. He only ate when his worried mother insisted he eat something. Ellison's next hearing was on July 27th, which seemed like an eternity away to him. On many occasions he would call his attorney, John Hall, for any updated information and Mr. Hall usually had none to share.
About a week and a half before his new hearing, Ellison nearly had a breakdown. His nerves were shattered. He couldn't abandon his obsession with his situation. He became disenchanted with his legal council and decided to divert his diligence to finding a new attorney.
He called his friend, Lewis Bishop, for advice on possible defense lawyers who might take his case with more promptness and perseverance than Hall and Trinkle had demonstrated. Lewis hadn't really talked to Ellison for some time. He, as well as Ellison's other friends thought him innocent and vowed to support him, but they didn't go out of their way to spend time with him as they once had. They had their business reputations to think about. Ellison missed the companionship with his friends. With everyone really. The isolation he felt was a huge part of what fueled his obsession and headaches. Lewis instantly recognized the strain in Ellison's voice and felt immediate concern for him.
"Ellison! How are you, man?!"
""Not good... not good... I need a favor if you can."
"Sure..." Lewis answered reluctantly. "What's up?"

Deadly Affair

I need new representation. Do you know any dependable defense lawyers who would serve me well?"

"What's wrong with Hall and Trinkle? They seem to be doing all they can for you."

Ellison let out a heavy sigh of impatience. "I don't think so, Lewis. They act like I'm a bother to them or something. I thought they were going to get me out of this and they did nothing at my hearing to defend me!" Ellison was starting to sound a little insane.

Lewis let out a sigh of his own. He tried to think how he would feel if he were being accused of murder, but he felt Ellison was being overly unreasonable.

"Man, this whole thing is just getting started really. There are formalities and a process the courts have to go through and abide by. This is all going to take time and I think they are doing their best," Lewis tried to reason.

"I want this over!" Ellison screamed. Then After a few seconds of silence, Ellison apologized.

"I'm sorry, Man." It's so hard to sit and wait with all this hanging over my head, day in and day out... I'm sorry." He sighed.

"Look, Ellison, I can't even imagine what you are going through. I've heard tell of a pretty good lawyer from Fort Scott. He might be able to help you. His name is Edgar... uh... Stone, I think. Edgar Stone. I really don't know much about him personally, but I've heard his name tossed around from time to time. He is the only person I can think of right off hand."

"Thank you," Ellison whispered. "Thank you."

"No problem, man. Please try to take care of yourself. You really don't sound good."

"Yeah..." Ellison hung up the telephone and wept.

* * * * * * * * * *

Ellison poured some water in the wash basin and splashed some on his bearded face, and thought for a moment about shaving, but didn't. He put on a clean shirt and trotted out of the house to his car. He drove to the Centerville telephone office and asked the operator if she would ring Edgar Stone's number in Fort Scott. After a few moments she signaled the call was ringing through and for him to step into the privacy booth.

"Mr. Stone's office." a woman's harsh voice stated after Ellison picked up the receiver.

"Yes, this is Ellison Scott from La Cygne, and I wish to speak to Mr. Stone, if I may."

His voice was shaking, he was so nervous.

"One moment..." the harsh voice said, and then there was silence for what seemed like forever to Ellison.

"Edgar Stone, speaking." Ellison almost let out a scream, he was so startled. He nervously explained his situation to Mr. Stone and asked if he would be interested in meeting with him for counsel.

"Let me check my calendar," he said, distracted. I might have some time on Wednesday morning, July 18th, but other than that I'm pretty booked."

"That will be fine. I'm looking forward to meeting with you." He sounded over anxious.

"Well okay, perhaps around 10:30 that morning. Would that work for you?"

"Yes sir!" Ellison almost shouted. That will be great. I'll see you then." Ellison bounded out of the telephone booth, feeling a small ray of hope.

"Thanks, Mrs. McGee," he hollered at the operator, as he left the building.

* * * * * * * * *

Ellison had looked forward to meeting Mr. Stone for over a week. The meeting was the only thing that helped him maintain his sanity from day to day. He really believed if he had the right representation his problems would just go away, and he hoped that Mr. Stone was the man to solve his problems. He was being unreasonable, of course. With each new day, he lost a little bit of his grip on reality. Ellison always believed himself to be above reproach, a model citizen, one of the good guys. Someone who should never even be considered a criminal, much less actually arrested for murder.

Why didn't the court, the judge, and the prosecution believe his account of Ella's murder? What was so unbelievable about it? Why didn't they all believe his account of a burglar killing his wife? His mind played these questions over constantly, eating up any chance for any other thought to give his mind some peace and rest.

In the days that followed his phone call, Ellison bought a train ticket in La Cygne, to travel to Fort Scott the morning of his appointment with Mr. Stone. He thought about driving, but really didn't want to put the miles on his Studebaker, and he didn't want to drive that far.

As he drove from his parents' farm to La Cyne on the dusty gravel roads, he allowed his mind a reprieve to a fantasy of sorts. It centered around meeting Mr. Stone. He fantasized Mr. Stone having some sort of legal 'trick up his sleeve' that would put an end to Ellison's legal

Deadly Affair

obligations, and deliver an instant exoneration for him. Once he boarded the train, he settled in and enjoyed his ride. It was a sunny day, but not yet horribly hot or humid.

The train station was several blocks away from Mr. Stone's office, but Ellison managed to walk the distance and arrive within five minutes of their scheduled appointment. He decided to take advantage of the time and use the restroom and wash a little of the dust off his face, and comb his hair.

As he entered Mr. Stone's office he was met by a middle aged, heavyset woman with her red hair tied on her head in a loose bun. She was sitting behind a very old wooden desk concentrating intently on her typewriter. She looked up when Ellison walked over to her desk and a look of embarrassment crossed her face.

"May I help you, sir?" she said, with that same husky voice he had heard on the telephone.

"Yes, I am Ellison Scott and I have a 10:30 appointment with Mr. Stone," he said, smiling for the first time in weeks.

She briefly looked at her calendar then looked back at Ellison.

"Mr. Scott, I'm very sorry. Mr. Stone was called away from town very early this morning, an emergency in Joplin. I couldn't reach you in time to cancel, as you had already left home. I am ever so sorry you made this long trip for nothing." Her expression was one of true sympathy.

Ellison stood in front of the desk, motionless, with such anger on his face, he began to scare the secretary with the bright red hair and husky voice.

"Would you like to reschedule another appointment, sir?" Her voice was just above a whisper.

Ellison only stared at her. After a moment his hands started shaking at his sides. He simply turned around and quietly walked out the door. He was furious!

~CHAPTER TEN~

Arlene had been wrapping up a lot of her courses and doing some final testing, as there were only a couple of days of school left. She had finished her morning schedule and decided to go back to the boarding house for a little nap, as she hadn't slept well the night before.

As she ascended the stairs to the second floor, the telephone on the wall rang out loudly and startled her. She reluctantly answered it. She hated answering the telephone at the boarding house. She hated trying to hunt people down.

"Hello?"

"Arlene?"

"Ellison? Is that you...?"

"Yeah, it's me."

"What's wrong, Ellison? You sound terrible!"

"Are you busy this afternoon?" he asked, ignoring her question.

"Well, no. Not really, why?" she hesitated. She recognized the mood in that voice, and she really wasn't interested in dealing with it this afternoon.

"I'm in town. I took the train to Fort Scott. I had a meeting with someone, but it didn't really work out. I thought as long as I'm this close maybe we could meet up. I was able to get a train here right away, but have to wait until this afternoon to catch one back to La Cygne. So what do you think?"

She noticed he had tried to lighten the dread in his voice some, and thought maybe she was over reacting. "Okay, I guess so. Where and when?"

"Well, how about Miller's Drugstore? I'll buy you a malt if you like."

She smiled at that. "Sounds good. When?"

"How about in a half hour?"

"Sounds good."

* * * * * * * * * *

He did buy her a malt. Chocolate. She had to stifle her reaction when she first walked in the drugstore and saw him. He looked just as terrible as he had sounded on the telephone. He was pale and there were deep dark circles under his eyes. He must have lost twenty pounds since she had last seen him, she thought to herself. She tried to smile like she was glad to see him, but she was really horribly concerned.

"How ya doin', kiddo?" he said, trying to be lighthearted, as he gave her a hug.

"How are *you*, Ellison. Are you well?!" she became emotional.

"Here, here...!" he said, walking her over to the counter where they both sat down.

As they sat and drank their malts, he tried to explain to her how he was really struggling to cope with the events in his life the past few weeks, and how he wasn't handling it well.

They sat and talked for over half an hour, all the while Ellison massaged his left temple with his fingertips. He wasn't aware he was doing it, but Arlene noticed and she also noticed the grimace on his face.

"Do you have a headache?" She finally asked him.

He kind of chuckled. "Sweetheart, I've had an on going migraine since this whole nightmare began! It would help a little, I think, if I could lie down for awhile. He started rubbing both temples aggressively.

"We could get a room at the Wick and you could lie down there for awhile, since you have a few hours until your train departs." Arlene said sincerely.

He smiled at her. That was exactly what he had in mind.

The afternoon was hot and muggy. Before they walked a block, they both had sweat beads popping out on their foreheads. By the time they reached the Wick Hotel, Ellison's head was pounding unbearably. Arlene wrapped her arm around his and steadied him as they walked in the front doors of the building.

* * * * * * * * *

A black Nash sedan was parked across the street from the Wick Hotel, and behind the steering wheel sat a man in a black suit. He was wearing dark glasses and wiped the sweat from his forehead as he watched the couple walk arm in arm through the front doors of the Wick Hotel. He looked at his watch then wrote something down in a note pad. He looked in the rear view mirror then looking around him, he exited the car and walked across the street and into the hotel.

"Good day, sir," he said to the man behind the counter as he removed his badge from inside his jacket pocket and flashed it in front of the gentleman. "I am involved in a little investigation on a murder case, and I need to see the register for the past couple of days."

"Certainly sir," the desk clerk said as he turned the register book right side up for the detective to see.

He pretended to look at several pages, but what he was really interested in was the last entry in the book, and the name written there, Mr. and Mrs. Bowman.

The detective smiled at the clerk, tipped his hat and walked back out in the very hot sun to sit in his hot car and wait for 'Mr. and Mrs. Bowman' to leave the hotel.

* * * * * * * * * *

Sheriff Ellington was sitting at his desk going over paperwork when the man in the black suit entered the office. He folded his dark glasses and placed them in his front jacket pocket. The man was tall and slender, probably around thirty years old, and carried an air of arrogance about him. As he approached the desk, Sheriff Ellington looked up from his papers and asked the gentleman if he could help him in any way. The man reached in his other jacket pocket and pulled out a small wallet containing a badge and identification.

"I'm a detective with the Kansas City Crime Unit. I have some information for you, Sheriff, concerning the murder case of Ella Scott," he said, handing the sheriff a large envelope, thick with papers.

"Thank you," the sheriff said as he reached for the envelope. He watched the man walk out of the office as quickly and quietly as he had walked in. The sheriff sat for a moment contemplating the envelope, it's contents, and what it might mean to the case. Deputy Lindsey sat quietly at his desk watching the sheriff, dying to know what was inside that envelope. Finally, the sheriff turned the envelope over and ripped the flap open with his pocket-knife. He sat back in his chair and started reading the information on the papers. Once in awhile he would run his hand over his hair as he slowly rocked back and forth in his chair. Finally when he was finished reading, he sat forward and sighed as he tossed the papers on his desk. He propped his elbows on the arms of his chair and started rubbing his face hard with the palms of his hands. The deputy couldn't take it anymore. "Bad news, Boss?"

The sheriff sighed deeply and locked his fingers behind his head. "I don't know. It's definitely a new development," was all he would say.

~CHAPTER ELEVEN~

Arlene had allowed herself the luxury of sleeping in an extra hour since she had graduated teachers college and moved back home with her folks. She was happy to be back in her old bedroom. She was looking forward to relaxing for a few weeks before she started teaching at her childhood grade school the first of September.

She had gotten dressed for the day and was finishing her breakfast when Sheriff Ellington's car pulled into the drive near the house. Bertha went to the front door to greet the sheriff as he climbed the stairs to the porch.

"Mornin', Ma'am," he tipped his hat.

"Mornin', Sheriff. What brings you out this way?" She pushed the screen door open and motioned for him to enter the house. He removed his hat and stepped inside.

"I'm sorry to bother you all this morning, but I'm afraid I need to talk to your daughter, Arlene, if I may?"

"Well of course, Sheriff," she said reluctantly. "What's this about."

"Well... it has to do with the case surrounding your sister's murder, I'm afraid," he said, twirling his hat in his hands.

"Of course." She felt unease rush through her body. "Excuse me, then," she said before leaving the room. She returned shortly with Arlene by her side.

"Morning, Sheriff!" Arlene greeted him with a flirtatious smile. "How can I help you today?"

"Miss Scott, I need to ask you some questions. Some... uh... rather personal questions," he stuttered. "I need for you and your Mother," he nodded at Bertha, "to come down to my office at your earliest convenience where we can talk over some things.

The two women looked at each other, confused. Finally Bertha spoke up. "Would around 2 o'clock this afternoon be okay?" she asked, looking from her daughter to the sheriff for confirmation.

"They all agreed on 2 o'clock and the sheriff thanked them both before leaving the house.

Bertha and Arlene stared at each other in silence. Finally Arlene walked off to her room and Bertha sat down in the nearest chair. Tears started to fill her eyes. She really missed her little sister, and she was scared of why and how her daughter was being questioned in her murder.

* * * * * * * * *

Around 2:05 that afternoon, Arlene and her mother entered the building that housed the sheriff's office and the jail. Sheriff Ellington stood up from his desk and walked over to greet the ladies. As Bertha entered the room she noticed the sheriff's wife, Stella, sitting in a chair next to his desk. She felt apprehensive when she saw Mrs. Ellington there. Why was she here?

"Ladies, I believe you've met my wife, Stella," he said as she rose from her chair. The ladies all nodded to each other, and said hello.

"Let's go to the little conference room in the back here as we will have a little more privacy, should my deputy walk in."

Bertha and Arlene followed the sheriff and his wife into the small room in the back of the building. There was a small window left open on the shady side of the room, providing a gentle breeze. There were three fans placed at different angles in the room to provide ample comfort for everyone from the heat of the day. The sheriff motioned everyone to take a chair around a rickety wooden table in the center of the room.

Although the room was cool, Bertha had broken out in a sweat. Her nerves were standing at the edge of her skin. She did not feel comfortable with all the formality the sheriff was displaying, and perceived this meeting was not going to be pleasant.

Arlene sat in a chair next to her mother, and Stella Ellington sat in a chair on her other side. The sheriff sat across the table from all of them. Unlike her mother, Arlene was very composed and appeared oblivious to her surroundings.

As tactfully as he possibly could, the sheriff asked Arlene about her relationship with her Uncle Ellison. Arlene lightheartedly started telling of her high school years living in La Cygne with her Aunt Ella and Ellison, until she went off to teachers college the previous May. She told of a very congenial relationship between all of them. Bertha sat quietly listening to her daughter talk, telling a tale of a joyous four years living in her aunt's home. Bertha had been made aware of tensions between her daughter and her sister, but didn't really think too much of it. At least... not until now. Bertha suddenly realized the sheriff was asking to hear a different side to her story. One that included the *whole* story that she wasn't telling. "Arlene, the sheriff said clearing his throat. "I imagine it was nice to kind of be on your own living away from your folks for awhile. But, well... uh... Are you

Deadly Affair

keeping any information back. Are you telling the whole story about your relationship with Ellison?"

Bertha was becoming anxious. "Yes dear," she asked her daughter as she rested her hand on Arlene's arm. "Are you leaving anything out?"

Arlene glared at her mother with huge doe eyes, then at the sheriff. She even shot an ugly glance at Stella. She had a sense the sheriff knew something she didn't want him to know, but she was going to play her innocent card as long as she could, and hope he would buy it.

"Just what do you mean?" she said as convincing as she possibly could. Her face was flush and she knew everyone noticed, but she felt they were all trapping her in a corner. They were making her feel uncomfortable. "What do you mean?" she asked again in her sweetest voice.

Sheriff Ellington cleared his throat again, and let out a distressing sigh.

"Arlene... this isn't easy for me, but it has been brought to my attention that on... uh..." he looked at his papers a minute, "On July 18th of this year, you spent several hours at the Wick Hotel in Pittsburg with your Uncle Ellison, registered as man and wife under an assumed name. Is this true, Miss Scott?"

Arlene was devastated. How did he know that? When you said it like that it sounded very scandalous. But then again, she realized her behavior with her uncle had been scandalous for some time now, and the truth of it all was now falling down around her. How was she going to explain her way out of this.

Arlene put her head on her arm and sobbed. She became very angry that she had been found out, but after a few moments, she knew she had to tell the truth. The real story. She straightened up, wiped her eyes, and started calmly talking.

"Yes, she said, looking down at the table. "I've been keeping something back all this time. She admitted there had been improper relations between her and Ellison at the Wick Hotel in Pittsburg.

"Arlene... When did this relationship start with your uncle?" the sheriff asked, again clearing his throat.

Bertha sat with her handkerchief over her mouth. Her eyes looked as if they were ready to pop out of her head. Her body was trembling and it was all she could do to remain calm.

"About a year ago... In my Aunt Ella's house," she hung her head as she quietly spoke.

Upon hearing her daughter's confession, Bertha's eyes filled with tears and she couldn't catch her breath. 'Horrified' does not even describe the depth of emotion running through her Christian soul.

She grabbed Arlene's arm with such a grip, fingernail marks left bruises in her skin. Arlene's eyes grew large with alarm.

"ARLENE!" her mother screamed. "You can *never* tell anyone about this! *Not anyone! Not ever!!*"

The sheriff started to say something to Bertha, but the look she shot back at him stopped his words cold.

Bertha couldn't conceive of dealing with her daughter's reputation being so vulgarly tarnished in the eyes of the family and the community. In her mind she could only accept that this 'truth' must go away. *It must not exist!* The final thread to her sanity had just been snapped. Her sister's murder, her father's poor health because of it, and now she was being told her daughter was a tramp, and probably the reason her brother-in-law had killed her sister. Bertha looked at her daughter as if she were a stranger, someone she didn't know. She could not believe her beautiful, Christian, naive, 'good girl' could ever *think* about sexual relations with anyone, much less her own sister's husband.

Before she knew what she was doing, she slapped Arlene hard across her face, knocking her out of her chair to the floor. The sheriff was across the room in a heartbeat grabbing Bertha's arms and pulling her away from Arlene. Stella jumped to Arlene's aid and helped the girl to her chair. Arlene's nose was pouring blood, and her eyes were already starting to blacken.

"You are nothing but a *whore!* You are not my daughter! My daughter is not a whore! You have shamed your father's name, and you have shamed your family. How *could* you!?" *How could you!!?"*

She started to step toward Arlene again, but the sheriff had a good grip on her and led her back in the office. He sat her down hard on the metal chair next to his desk and asked her if she thought he needed to cuff her to it. With that, the realization of the events of the last few minutes crashed in on her and she began wailing. Her hair had fallen around her face, and her top knot was unrecognizable. The top three buttons of her blouse had popped open, and her hand was throbbing from hitting her daughter's face so hard. She was devastated. She was now a broken woman, without a plan for recourse.

What am I going to do? was all she could think to herself.

"What am I going to do?" she whispered aloud. How would she ever face her family? She wailed louder! Losing her little sister to murder was a nightmare she had not been able to wake from. Learning of her daughter's nasty involvement with Ellison definitely took her sanity over the edge. She was never the same.

* * * * * * * * * *

Arlene sat in shock as Stella tenderly worked at cleaning blood from her face. The pain was immense and the fact that her eyes were swelling and already turning color, meant her nose might be broken. Arlene had no idea her mother could hit anything that hard!
What have I done? Arlene thought to herself. *What have I done!* Warm tears started streaming down her cheeks.
I'm sorry, Arlene. I'm trying not to hurt you." Stella said, thinking she was the source of the tears. Arlene closed her eyes and began sobbing hot tears of embarrassment at the thought of this woman being so nice to her after having just learned of her perverse behavior with her uncle.
The revulsion her mother exhibited, broke her heart. She never thought there would be anything she could do to make her mother hate her so. She harshly realized their relationship would forever be changed by this.
Her tears, however, were not of remorse for her behavior, but for getting caught.

* * * * * * * * * *

Mother and daughter sat in cold silence on the drive back to the farm. By now Arlene had a screaming headache and her eyes were nearly swollen shut. Clarence was in the yard pulling weeds from the flower garden when the car pulled in the drive. After shutting off the key, Bertha exited the driver's side of the car, slammed the door hard and rushed into the house. Arlene continued to sit quietly in the car.
Her father slowly walked over to her and the closer he got the more he realized her face had been damaged. He was horrified when he reached the car and saw the extent of her injury. He stood silent, waiting for his daughter to explain, but she just sat staring straight ahead.
"Arlene?" he finally said softly.
She hung her head and softly sobbed. He opened the car door and carefully helped her out. He supported her arm as they climbed the steps to the porch. He was devastated to see his little girl in such pain and misery. He couldn't even imagine what had happened to her. He helped her to her bedroom and to her bed. She sat down slowly and he removed her shoes for her before she lay down. He left the room and shortly returned with a cold compress, which he gently placed over her eyes. She winced slightly then began to relax as the compress started to relieve her pain some. Clarence left the room and quietly closed the door behind him. He slid his

hands in the pockets of his overalls and stood in the hallway by the door for several minutes, trying to sort it all out in his mind. His daughter lay in one bedroom, beaten up, and his wife lay in the other bedroom sobbing. Finally, he walked down the hall to the bedroom he shared with his wife to see if he could get some answers. The door was closed, but Bertha's sobs could be heard throughout the house. He calmly opened the door and entered the room. He felt sickened as he listened to his wife's account of the day's events.

* * * * * * * * *

After her trip to the sheriff's office, Arlene didn't leave her room anymore often than she needed to. Her father brought her meals to her room, and anything else she might need. She and her mother purposefully avoided each other.

Three days after the altercation, a car pulled into the driveway late in the morning. An elderly man stepped out of the passenger side, and Clarence could not see who was driving as he stepped off the porch and approached the car. The elderly man standing by the car with the help of a cane was John Holt's brother, Jonah. The driver was a neighbor of Jonah's and a good friend of his.

Clarence invited both men into the house and after a short conversation, he offered them both some ice cold lemonade. The driver was grateful for the refreshment, but Jonah declined the offer. "I have come to talk to Arlene, if I may, Clarence."

"Sure, Jonah," Clarence said reluctantly. He slowly led the old man down the hall to Arlene's bedroom door, where he knocked gently.

"Arlene, honey, Uncle Jonah is here and has asked to talk with you. Do you feel up to a little company?"

"Okay," Arlene answered him with little enthusiasm.

Clarence opened the door and found Arlene sitting in a chair looking out her bedroom window. A small chair sat on the opposite corner of the room and Clarence moved it near Arlene. He helped the old man across the room and into the chair then he left the room.

"How are you doing, child?" Jonah asked Arlene, after sitting in silence for a moment. She did not respond. He cleared his throat, "I've been concerned about you the past few days, dear. I heard about you... uh"

She shot him an ugly look from the corner of her eye.

"Perhaps this isn't any of my business, but I'm worried about you. I've heard of your confession to the sheriff and was wondering if... Well, if you were okay. If maybe there is something you aren't saying." He wiped his forehead with the sleeve of his shirt. He was very uncomfortable asking his young great niece these questions. "Are you involved in this case in anyway? Is there more to this story?"

Damn gossips! Arlene thought to herself. She rolled her eyes in response to her uncle's question. She wished he would go away, but knew he wouldn't, just the same way this whole mess with Ellison was not going away. She was going to have to deal with it all one way or the other, so she decided to answer her uncle's question. She looked him straight in the eye and said,

"Uncle Ellison told me, that if I told anything there would be more trouble!"

Jonah was stunned. "What do you mean, 'more trouble,' child?" he prodded.

"He meant there would be more murder!" she snapped at him angrily. "He said he would kill me, and I know he would," she said flatly, turning her gaze back to the window.

Arlene wasn't sure if Ellison had killed her aunt, but she did know he had become a very angry man that was no longer familiar to her. She felt he had betrayed and used her, and she wasn't sure how to process that. She had never had to suffer such an emotion, at least not until her aunt's death. Her loss had been, and still was hard for her to accept. The loss of her trust in her uncle was beyond comprehension to her. She no longer cared what happened to him.

Her uncle Jonah slowly stood from his chair and walked his way out of the room and out the door. He didn't know if what Arlene had told him was the truth or the rambling of a very angry vengeful young woman, but he was shaken by it.

* * * * * * * * * *

Ellison awakened early Friday morning, July 27th, feeling a sense of dread. He woke in the middle of the night to claps of thunder and lightning and the noise of rain pounding on the roof and window of his room. Sleep was not his friend these days, but somehow he had been able to drift back off. It was still raining softly when daylight broke. He sat up in bed and decided the gray gloom of the weather perfectly matched his mood. Attending his preliminary hearing this morning was the last thing he wanted to do today.

"Ellison, it's time to get up." A voice hollered from downstairs.

"I know, Ma, thanks. I'll be down soon," he said rubbing his face.

Mollie was pouring herself a cup of coffee when Ellison walked into the kitchen, adjusting his suspenders. He was carrying his shoes and sat down in a chair at the head of the table to put them on.

"Morning, dear," Mollie said, sipping her coffee. "Want some breakfast?"

He shook his head. "A cup of coffee... Maybe some toast." He didn't look up.

She fixed him toast and set some jam and butter on the table. After she poured him a cup of coffee, she sat down next to him at the table. She continued to sip her coffee, but remained quiet while he silently ate his toast.

~CHAPTER TWELVE~

The hearing started at 9 o'clock and Ellison had been in the courthouse, counseling with his lawyers long before that. They met in the little side room off the main courtroom. He learned from them that testimony about his indiscretion with Arlene at the Wick Hotel was going to be the prosecution's bombshell evidence.

Ellison was shocked and overwhelmed. He had not left his home since his trip to Fort Scott and then to Pittsburg. He hadn't been aware of the status of his case, or the communities' knowledge of it until today.

When Hall told him what would probably happen at the hearing today, Ellison's face turned ashen. His ears started ringing and he felt nausea come over him. Trinkle rushed a chair under him before he fell and hit the floor. Ellison was visibly shaken. Mr. Hall poured Ellison a glass of water and insisted he drink it. He drank half the glass and worked at collecting himself.

"How would anyone know of such an event? If it were true, I mean?" he asked, arrogantly. His mind instantly thought of Arlene and he started blaming her blabbing mouth in his mind.

"Cut the crap!" Trinkle said, unsympathetically. "Seems there have been several detectives following both you and your niece around since the murder of your wife. Seems they know a lot about what you two have been up to." He got right in Ellison's face. "Do you think maybe it's about time you were straight up with us, old man!?" Trinkle said unkindly, his face flushed with anger.

Before Ellison could defend himself, Trinkle continued to jump down his throat. "We can't defend you, Scott, if you aren't honest with us! Maybe you are guilty of killing your wife. But we can't defend you if we don't know what the prosecution is going to throw at us!"

"Therefore, Mr. Scott..." Hall went on the say, "Because we aren't as prepared as we should be, because the prosecution just decided to share this news with us now, today might turn out pretty unpleasant for all of us."

Ellison sat frozen in his chair. "We didn't do anything! I had a bad headache, and needed a place to lay down, *that's all!*" Ellison protested.

"Let's see if I have this straight then," Trinkle mocked him, rubbing his chin. "You had a *headache*... so you traveled all the way to Pittsburg to call upon your niece to go lay down with you at the Wick Hotel because you needed a place to rest your head!! Is that about right!?"

Ellison sat ashamed. It all sounded so absurd. But he didn't want his attorneys to know the reason he was in Pittsburg in the first place was because he had gone looking for a new lawyer to represent him. Now he just felt like a fool. He sat there and sighed, shaking his head.

* * * * * * * * *

Rumor was out that sensational developments in the Ellison Scott hearing were going to be revealed. Everyone who could buy, beg or steal a ride headed for the county seat that Friday morning for the hearing.

It was becoming the most exciting and dramatic case Linn County had ever dealt with. Everyone in the county knew of or were, good friends with Ella and Ellison, and the community just wanted justice to be rendered concerning Ella's murder.

The small courtroom was filling up by 8:30 and people were beginning to worry they wouldn't get a seat. Ellison could hear the muffled roar of people crowding down the hall and into the courtroom. The excitement in the building was electric. By 9 o'clock the room was packed. The ceiling fans had been turned on as high as possible, and even with the windows open, the heat was already starting to become uncomfortable.

Mr. Hall and Mr. Trinkle escorted their client into the courtroom and straight to the defendant's table. In unison the people gasped as Ellison entered the room. Soon after, the people fell silent.

Attorney Edeburn entered from the judge's chambers and sat down at the prosecution's table. Within minutes Judge Edward C. Gates entered from his chambers and all who could, stood in his honor. After he sat down in his big leather chair, he instructed everyone in the court-room to be seated.

The judge summoned the attorneys for the defense and prosecution to approach the bench. After a few minutes of conversing in low voices, the attorneys returned to their tables.

Judge Gates cleared his throat and began to explain to the assembly that there would be delicate testimony presented today, and that all persons under the age of eighteen years were to leave the courtroom at this time. A few people did leave the room and this excited the crowd all the more, knowing the hearing was going to be sensational after all. Judge Gates slammed his gavel hard and demanded silence.

Ellison sat motionless. He scanned the room to see who had come to witness his public humiliation. That's the way he felt about it. He instantly noticed, not all, but many members of the Holt family sitting directly to his right. His gaze immediately fell on Arlene sitting at the aisle end of her row. She sat next to her grandmother, Sarah. She sat very straight, her legs and ankles were firmly set together and her hands were planted in her lap, fingers twined together.

She had on a mustard colored sleeveless dress, belted at the waist. Her shoes and purse, both an off white color, were a matching set. Her dark brown hair was combed up in a bun, which was covered by a stylish white pill box hat. Her face was almost healed and the dark circles under her eyes were all but gone. She stared straight ahead as if she were the only person in the room. She did blink her eyes on occasion. Other than that, she sat as a stone.

* * * * * * * *

The hearing started with the testimony from the detectives on the case and it didn't take long for the prosecution to present the sensational developments of their case. The testimony was of course about Arlene and Ellison's meeting at the Wick Hotel in Pittsburg, but it was also about Ellison registering them as man and wife under an assumed name.

The hearing took all day Friday, several hours Friday night, and until about 11 o'clock Saturday morning. Witnesses and on lookers came and went. Almost all in attendance had developed an opinion of Ellison they hadn't had before, by the time the hearing was over.

Arlene had left the courthouse about mid-afternoon Friday, and didn't return until Saturday morning when she was scheduled to testify.

She was again smartly dressed and made a positive impression on most people in the courtroom. Her posture was stoic as she stepped up to the witness stand. She placed her right hand on a well-worn black Bible and vowed 'to tell the truth, the whole truth, and nothing but...' However that was not at all what she did.

Attorney Edeburn wasted no time getting right to the reputation-damning question. "Miss Scott, have you ever had intimate sexual relations with your uncle John Ellison Scott?"

The room was so quiet you could hear a pin drop.

"No sir, never." she said coldly, looking at her hands in her lap. There were murmurs in the room"

"Miss Scott, are you saying you did not meet with Ellison Scott at the Wick Hotel in Pittsburg on July 18th of this year?"

"I met with my uncle in Pittsburg, but nothing of an intimate nature took place between us there." Her voice projected throughout the room, but her eyes stayed focused on her hands in her lap.

Ellison had been tensely sitting at the defense table, nervously twirling an ink pen between his fingers. The sweat from nerves poured from his face, and wiping it away had become constant in the past day and a half. When Arlene lied on the stand, a gush of relief rushed through his body and he allowed a little smirk to cross his face. They hadn't talked to each other since Pittsburg, but he had hoped she would be smart enough to keep her mouth shut. Being the arrogant man he was, he didn't even think that she was lying to try to save her own reputation, not his.

Arlene's mother hung her head. She took a hanky from her purse and gently started wiping tears. Her sisters and their families sitting near her were stunned, not knowing what to think about this new information. Arlene's father twirled his hat in his hands, looking straight ahead, emotionless. Sheriff Ellington sat with his arms across his chest shaking his head, and his wife, sitting next to him, let out a disappointed sigh.

Attorney Edeburn continued his questioning, trying to get Arlene to incriminate herself, but she remained steadfast. Finally, he rested his case. Hall and Trinkle thought it best not to ask her any questions, since her testimony served their client well. Arlene left the witness stand and walked out of the courtroom, her dark brown eyes staring straight ahead with her head held high.

She left the building before anyone could testify that she had lied.

Sheriff Ellington was the next witness called to the stand and his testimony destroyed Arlene's testimony and her reputation. He told of the meeting with Arlene, his wife, and Bertha Scott in attendance. He not only testified that she had confessed to an indecent sexual affair with her uncle, but that it had been going on for over a year while she lived in his house with her aunt.

Before the sheriff was done with his testimony, Bertha left the courtroom quickly, holding her hanky over her mouth. She could not take the shame from her family or anyone else. She knew her family was going to blame her for Ella's death. They were going to think she was a bad mother, and it was all her fault. She spent a long time just walking around town, alone in her own thoughts.

Upon hearing this demoralizing news, mumbling, shuffling, and shifting in chairs began and did not stop until Judge Gates hammered his gavel a couple of times and demanded order.

Stella Ellington followed her husband on the stand and corroborated his testimony.

Ella Scott's family and loved ones sat stunned in their chairs. *What on earth had just happened? It couldn't possibly be true! Arlene? Ellison? It couldn't be true!*

Judge Gates decided there was enough evidence, all told, to hold Ellison over for trial and set a date for September 16th. At that point people began trickling out of the courtroom, realizing it was entirely possible Ellison Scott *did* murder his wife. His friends and supporters began to desert him, not looking at him as they left the room. When it was time to post bond, not a person could be found to help him out. His bond for trial was now twenty thousand dollars. Scott, himself, was unable to post bond and was turned over to Sheriff Ellington. He was placed in the county jail in Mound City and remained there until his trial in district court in September.

~CHAPTER THIRTEEN~

The weeks between the hearing and the trial dragged on slowly for everyone involved. Arlene and her mother were still avoiding each other and only spoke to one another when absolutely necessary.

Bertha stopped going to her parent's house to help take care of her father. She couldn't stand the fact that her own daughter had helped cause the grief and depression she saw in them. She couldn't deal with the guilt and their coldness toward her.

John Holt spent his days either sleeping in bed or in his rocking chair. It was true that he was depressed, but his body had become weaker with each passing day, making it practically impossible for him to move around or do anything productive. Sarah tried to keep her routine and worked long morning hours in her garden preparing to start canning vegetables for winter storage. Her daughters were doing the same at their homes when they weren't helping her. Their husbands were busy with harvest, and worked late into the evening some days. However, the death of Ella and the drama of Ellison's trial were always in the forefront of their minds.

Arlene started teaching school the first of September. She had spent the previous weeks preparing lessons and getting her classroom cleaned and ready. She was so grateful for this diversion in her life.

The days probably passed the slowest for Ellison, who was spending his days in a 6 by 6 foot cell in the county jail. The first few days were the hardest for him, because he refused to accept so many of his friends now believed him guilty of murder and adultery. He knew that even if he was eventually exonerated of his wife's murder, his reputation would never recover from the allegations. The longer he sat in his cell, the angrier he became.

About a week and a half into his stay, the sheriff marched a man by the name of Edward Lee into the small cell next to Ellison's, his hands cuffed behind his back. Ellison watched as the sheriff unlocked the cell door then guided Lee into the tiny space. Once he re-locked the door, he instructed Lee to turn around and to put his hands between the bars. He then took the handcuffs off and placed the key in his pocket as he walked away. Without turning his head toward Ellison he said good morning as he passed by.

"Mornin', Sheriff," Ellison replied, lying on his bed, staring at the ceiling.

Deadly Affair

Ellison watched the new kid in town from the corner of his eye. Lee was checking out the thin little pad that lay atop a worn out cot. Ellison was kind of glad to have some company for awhile.

Finally Lee stretched out on his bunk and placed his hands behind his head. He knew that Ellison had been watching him the whole time and without taking his gaze from the ceiling he asked him what he was being held for.

"Murder..." Ellison said flatly.

Lee quickly turned his head, "Murder! Who did you murder?"

Ellison sighed. "I'm charged with the murder of my wife."

"Dang!" Wait a minute... Are you that fellow who shot his wife in her kitchen?"

Ellison sighed again. "Allegedly..." he said, annoyed. "So did you do it? Did you kill your wife?" Lee was now propped up against the bars of his cell. Ellison just stared at him as if he were as dense as firewood.

Realizing how stupid he sounded, Lee apologized. "Sorry... sorry, man!" He threw his hands in the air. He walked back to his bunk and sat down. "Wow, man... How long you in here for?"

"Until my trial in September. Unless, of course, you would like to bail me out!" Ellison said jokingly. "I can't afford to bond myself out... What are you if for...? Ellison asked, needing to change the subject.

"Oh, you know... drunk and disorderly. So, when is your trial again?" Lee asked, changing the subject back.

"September 10th or 16th sometime in there." Ellison answered him.

"Wow... How do you think it will go, man?"

"Probably about like my hearing went."

"What do you mean?" Lee was seriously engaged.

For the lack of anything better to do, Ellison proceeded to tell the complete story of his affair with Arlene and how that pretty much ruined his reputation, and his 'innocent' standing in the community. He went on to say... "If the Pittsburg incident had not occurred, no one would know of my relationship with Arlene, and I'd be sitting pretty at my trial."

Those words would later come back to slap him hard.

~CHAPTER FOURTEEN~

Jury selection got underway the morning of September 17th. The first venire of jurymen was soon exhausted, and Judge Gates immediately sent out a call for more prospective jurors. Virtually everyone questioned for jury service had formed an opinion about the murder and of Ellison's guilt or innocence. It took two days to select from over one hundred people to sit on the jury. All but two jurors were farmers, bankers, or businessmen. The trial itself got underway on Thursday, September 20th. People once again poured into an uncomfortably warm courtroom, wearing their curiosity on their sleeves.

Once Judge Gates entered the courtroom and sat at his bench, the people began sitting down and getting comfortable for the day's events. Judge Gates once again commanded anyone under eighteen years of age to leave the courtroom due to delicate subject matter. People looked around, but no one left.

Attorney Edeburn had enlisted the help of Frank Sheridan of Paola, Kansas and assistant Attorney General of Kansas, W.A. Smith, to help prosecute this case. In opening statements, Attorney Smith set out to prove the motive for the murder of Mrs. Ella Scott was the intimacy and affection between her husband and her niece, Arlene.

Ellison sat, only half listening to Attorney Smith's statements. He was dressed in a nice suit, yet he looked disheveled. He had a growth of whiskers on his face and had made a poor attempt at combing his hair. He slouched in his chair with a look of utter defeat on his face.

Arlene sat in the same chair as she had during the hearing, however her father and mother were the only people sitting next to her. The rest of the Holt family sat across the courtroom from Bertha and her family.

The opening statement of Attorney Smith lasted only a few minutes and immediately Attorney Edeburn called Edward Lee to the witness stand. There was some commotion in the room, enough to cause the judge to strike his gavel and demand order. Edward Lee was not considered a model citizen in Linn County and it was curious that he was being called to testify. Hall and Trinkle looked hard at Ellison, wondering what Edward Lee would have to say. Ellison felt total betrayal and was angry at himself for even talking to the man. He just sat staring at the table.

Edward Lee, was dressed in a nice suit also, but his hair was combed back and his face was clean shaven. He walked up to take his oath, a very cocky man. He knew he had the goods on Mr. Scott, and he liked it. Once he was sworn in, and seated in the witness chair, Edeburn asked him how he knew Ellison Scott.

"I met Mr. Scott while I was recently incarcerated in the county jail," he said with a sarcastic smile on his face. "We both became kind of friendly and told each other some personal things about ourselves." He winked at Arlene, but she wasn't looking at him. Lee testified that Ellison confessed to having an affair with his niece, and had said that if the incident in Pittsburg had not happened, he would be sitting pretty and wouldn't have to worry about a trial.

Gasps filled the courtroom. Again the gavel came down hard.

Arlene sat indifferent, staring straight ahead. Ellison sunk a little deeper in his chair.

Trinkle jumped out of his chair in objection to Lee's testimony, but was immediately overruled. He shot a hot angry look at Ellison and whispered in his ear, "What else are you holding back, because this man just cooked your goose!"

"Ellison shook his head, conceding any control he might have ever had.

Once the prosecution was finished questioning Edward Lee, Hall jumped right up to cross examine. He was ill-prepared to question the man since his client had told him nothing about his conversation with this witness. In cross examination, Hall attempted to impeach Lee's testimony on the grounds that Lee's general reputation for telling the truth and for veracity were bad, but he was afraid the damage was already done.

It was the State's intention to continue the testimony in this trial to reflect the indecent relationship between Ellison and Arlene, thus providing a motive for Ella's murder.

Gus Clark, a friend of Ella and Ellison was called to the stand by Attorney Smith to testify about his observations as to Ellison and Arlene's behavior toward each other.

"My wife and I had gone to a social gathering at the home of Rob and Maude Rogers. This occurred about eleven months ago, or so. Mrs. Rogers and Ella are sisters and enjoyed planning "get-togethers. Several married couples were there and Arlene was also there. All the people there were well acquainted. We were visiting, cutting up, and having a good time. Some of us were in the dining room, eating ice cream and cake, some were in the sitting room with the door open between. My wife and I were in the sitting room and Ellison and Arlene were there sitting on the floor near the window. They were scuffling and tickling one another and he was grabbing

a hold of her knees. A little later they were scuffling and he had his arms part way around her.
Gasps and mumbling from the courtroom.
Thank you, Mr. Clark. No more questions, Your Honor, Attorney Smith said.

The defense had no questions. They sat silent and stunned.

Leona sat next to her mother, fanning herself with a paddle fan. She looked at her mother after Mr. Clark's testimony and they rolled their eyes at each other. They both certainly remembered the occasion and Arlene and Ellison's conduct. When Arlene came to her house, when there was a party, Leona usually enjoyed spending time with Arlene herself. That evening, however, Arlene was acting like a little fool, and Leona soon decided to spend the evening in the company of her mother and her aunts.

The next witness to the stand was Tom Peters. He testified he had witnessed an incident between Ella and Ellison in their home. Arlene was there, but she didn't say anything, she just sat crying. Tom testified that Ella had called him to her house to witness their dispute. "She said to her husband," 'Ellison you are not treating me right!' "Then Ellison said to her, 'Ella, I have done all I could for you and bought you everything I can. I went as far as I could... everything you asked for.' 'I know that this is true, Ellison,' she went on to say, 'but you crush me down and I can't do anything about it.'" Tom went on to say she showed him bruises on her leg and arm.

Ellison buried his face in his hands and quietly sobbed.

Attorney Edeburn asked one more question of Tom before finishing. "Refreshing your recollection, was there anything said about "if you caught me in the shape I caught you, you would kill me?"

"Objection! Your Honor!" Hall yelled out.

"Overruled!" the judge yelled back.

"Yes sir, Tom spoke up, "she did say that. Let's see... how did that go..." 'If you had caught me in the position I caught you in, you would kill me.'"

"No more questions, Your Honor."

Hall rubbed his hand down his long face, which was now red with anger. He had realized by now he and his partner, Trinkle, had not done a very thorough job getting to know their client and who he really was. It was a mistake that made them look very foolish in their defense of him.

More whispers and gasps broke out in the courtroom, and once again the judge demanded order.

The next witness called to the stand was Leona Rogers. She reluctantly walked up to the stand and swore to tell the truth on the same well-worn

Deadly Affair

Bible everyone else swore on, before sitting down. Arlene shot Leona a disturbing glance, fearing what she might say. Leona adjusted herself nervously in the chair. She decided not to look at Arlene at all while on the stand. She testified that a short time before Arlene's graduation from high school, in May, she was visiting Arlene at her parents' farm, on a Sunday. Ella and Ellison were also there. After dinner, Arlene asked Ellison if he would take her to see the members of the school board to try to engage employment at a school after she graduated teachers college.

"However," Leona went on to say, "Arlene had already been hired to teach at Cemetery School this fall." Arlene shot her another hot ugly glance. Leona didn't see it, but she felt it. "Anyway," Leona said," After Arlene asked Ellison for a ride, Aunt Ella looked rather angry. Uncle Ellison went over and had a private talk with her for a few minutes," Leona cleared her throat. "After that Aunt Ella was not as jovial as usual. However, we did get in the car and all of us went to look for a school for Arlene. Aunt Ella rode in the front seat with Ellison, and Arlene and I sat in the back seat. Arlene stated to me while we were riding, referring to our aunt and uncle, that they had a little trouble between them these days. She further stated it was like living in Hell over there with them, meaning in La Cygne."

"I believe..." Leona added, I believe Aunt Ella turned back with a stern look as if she had heard the remark."

Attorney Edeburn asked Leona if she remembered the evening of the party at her parent's house that Tom Peters referred to, and she said she did. " I pretty much remember the evening going just the way Tom remembered it. Attorney Edeburn also asked Leona if Arlene ever told her at anytime about her relationship with their uncle.

"Not really," Leona said delicately. "She has at times hinted at behavior with Ellison that I thought she was teasing about, but I guess now it wasn't a joke after all," her voice trailed off.

"No further questions, Your Honor, Attorney Edeburn said as he walked back to the prosecutions table. Again the defense had no questions.

Leona carefully left the stand. As she walked back to her chair, she glanced briefly at Arlene who was staring bullets at her. Leona realized she had probably just severed a lifetime friendship she shared with her favorite cousin. She decided to just walk on out of the courtroom, where she might cry freely without being disturbed.

*   *   *   *   *   *   *   *   *

Sarah Holt, mother of the murdered woman, was the next witness called to the stand. The State offered into evidence a letter known as exhibit

'G' written before school dismissed in May. For the most part the letter was a chatty one, such as a daughter would write to her mother, but contained a concerning paragraph at the end.

"Mrs. Holt..." Attorney Smith started respectfully questioning. "Would you please read aloud the last paragraph of your daughter's letter to the court?"

With her hanky in her hand, ready if she needed it, she cleared her throat, and shifted in her chair. She briefly looked over the room, recognizing family, friends, and neighbors. All who looked back at her, did with sympathy on their faces. Her heart was heavy as she read the words of a daughter she would never hear from again.

"....Well, school will soon be out and I'll be glad. Arlene is getting homesick, don't know how she will stand it to go to Pittsburg. But I won't have to worry about her anyway. Believe me she sure gets on my nerves sometimes. Don't say anything about it to anyone. But she sure won't mind a thing hardly we want her to do. But thank goodness it will soon be over.

Well, I'll quit and get to work. Write when you can. We will be down sometime this summer! Ha ha.

Love to all

Ella

Burn this up!

Sarah slowly folded the letter and handed it back to Attorney Smith, as she dabbed her right eye.

Arlene hung her head slightly. She would not be disrespectful to her grandmother by giving her a dirty look. She knew that her Aunt Ella's feelings toward her were justified, and by May her relationship with her aunt had become more than strained. She knew that she was responsible for bad behavior, thus destroying her aunt's trust and affection toward her. She just didn't want the whole world to know about it.

When her Grandmother was dismissed from the stand, Arlene only looked at the floor as she passed by.

Three days into the trial, the prosecution continued calling witnesses who could testify as to Ellison and Arlene's illicit affair.

They called Mary Carnegey to testify as to Ellison and Arlene's improper behavior in her home after Mrs. Scott's murder. And of course the Kansas City detective was called to testify about the meeting at the Wick Hotel in Pittsburg.

Deadly Affair

On the fourth day of the trial, feeling they had established motive for murder, the State redirected their questions as to the events in the Scott's home shortly after Ella was murdered.
Testimony was given by Ellison's neighbors, Dr. Morrison, and Dr. Kennedy as to the events of the night of June 19th, 1923.
The courtroom was once again packed with curious onlookers. The Ella Scott murder trial was the sensation of the century. The history making trial was not only on the minds and tongues of Linn county citizens, but also a curiosity in the entire state of Kansas, and surrounding states.

* * * * * * * * * *

Hall and Trinkle were relieved the questioning of the prosecution was shifting to the night of the murder, and away from their client's indiscretions. Ellison himself let out a relaxed sigh on the fourth day of testimony.
Arlene was not in attendance on the fourth day. She had been told she would not be called to testify, so she decided she would rather be teaching school. Her young students didn't know why their teacher had been absent a few days and needed a substitute, and Arlene meant to keep it that way. She only hoped their parents would be discreet. She so wanted the trial to be over and for the whole incident of her aunt's murder to die down in people's minds. She only wanted to get on with her life and her teaching. Her parents, Bertha and Clarence had decided to also forgo court that day. They were physically and emotionally spent and needed a break from it all. The rest of the family, however, were all there, except for John who had not attended even one day of the hearing or the trial. Sarah kept him informed of each day's events.
John was so heart sick about Arlene and Ellison that he had become irritated with company or visitors. He wanted and sought only to be alone. Sarah was worried about him, but she didn't have the strength to deal with her own grief, much less his.

* * * * * * * * * *

The judge took the bench around 8:30 the morning of the fourth day of the trial.
Several neighbors testified to hearing screams after the first two shots fired that night.

Mr. P.B. Leivy testified: "About a minute after the shots rang out, I went to the north door and looked about to see if I could discover what caused the shots and the dog to bark. I looked across to the Scott home. The blind on the south window of the sitting room of the Scott house was down only half way. Through this window I could see through the sitting room into the dining room of the Scott home where there was a light, and there saw Ellison Scott rush across the dining room to the west side, then back in a stooped position. I heard him call, 'My God, Ella, help me!' Then Scott moved quickly to the west side of the room. I turned and spoke to my wife about what I saw and hurried across toward the Scott home and heard a commotion west of the Scott house. Scott ran out of his house toward Dr. Morrison's house yelling to anyone and everyone that Ella had been shot and please come help"

Dr. Morrison testified after Mr. Leivy. "I heard Ellison yelling that Ella had been shot as he was running down the street. I jumped in my car and quickly drove to the Scott house. Mr. Leivy and Mr. Helms, along with Reverend Molesworth were already there trying to tend to Ella. I went to her, felt her pulse, which was very weak. I observed her countenance, pulled her dress down from the neck and saw a bullet wound in her right breast, which I thought would not cause death. I hastily gave her a hypodermic. I examined more closely and found a bullet wound in the left breast. While I was working with her, Scott came in, went to his wife and was making exclamations asking me to help her. Someone in the room directed Ellison to a chair and he sat down mumbling, 'I should have come in with her! What am I going to do' I saw a drawer from a chest in the dining area on the floor, but nothing seemed to be missing or disturbed. Mrs. Scott died about five minutes after I arrived."

About mid-day the prosecution rested and Judge Gates called a recess until Monday morning.

* * * * * * * * *

During that weekend, Ellison was allowed to meet with his attorneys in the small conference room in the sheriff's office. They spent several hours Saturday morning going over new strategy for his defense.

"You have to be up front with us about everything!" Trinkle firmly ordered Ellison. We looked like a couple of clowns out there trying to defend you without any information to go on.

Ellison sat at the small table in his shabby jailhouse clothes. He hadn't been allowed to shave for several days and had grown a short scruffy beard. His hair was in need of a cut and groom. It was tangled and overgrown. He was no longer the handsome confident man who had come to Trinkle and Hall a few short months ago for help in his defense.

Trinkle felt compassion for the man, but realized he needed all the information Scott had, good or bad, concerning his wife's murder if he was to defend him.

Hall entered the room with a tray of coffees for each of them.

"All I know..." Ellison straightened in his chair taking the coffee being handed to him.

"... is there had to have been a burglary in my home that night and the intruder shot my wife." He sipped some coffee and thanked Hall for it.

"Okay... okay..." Trinkle said impatiently, "Scott, there was no evidence that an intruder was in your house, so what would make you think your wife was murdered by an intruder?"

Ellison cleared his throat and shifted in his chair. He was afraid what he had to say would sound like words from the mouth of a desperate man. Mainly because they were. He let out a sigh then spoke.

"There was a rail rider in my store earlier that day. He looked forlorn. He was dirty, and ragged. He really looked like a menace to me.

"Did he act menacing?" Hall asked him.

"No not really, but he looked like a man who hadn't been around civilization for awhile.

I just had a bad feeling about him, that's all. And some of my neighbors thought they saw a stranger on the street the night of the murder. It had to be him!" he insisted. He avoided eye contact with either man. He stared straight ahead, sipping his coffee, as if in deep concentration.

"Who thought they saw a stranger?" Hall asked him.

"Well, I heard Laura Rowley say she saw a stranger on the sidewalk that night."

"Yeah, great... A twelve year old girl caught up in the chaos, wants to feel important. Just great!" Ellison shot Hall a fiery glance. "She's as good a witness as anyone!" Ellison snapped in defense.

Trinkle scratched the back of his neck, and opened his folder of papers, and let out an impatient sigh.

"Okay," he said. "I've looked into this 'stranger' concept. Some people think, if there was a rail rider in town, it might possibly have been a man by the name of Fred Slavens. From what I've learned, Mr. Slavens is from Pleasanton, and has an extensive criminal record, mostly theft. Ellison stared hopeful at his attorney as he spoke. "However," he went on to say, "No one has seen Mr. Slavens in a very long time. The sheriff investigated the man's whereabouts, and his family claims he hasn't even been in Kansas for the past year or so. He had been serving time in Nebraska for auto theft, and that had been a couple of years ago. They hadn't seen him since. It would be very hard to prove he was in La Cygne on a warm June night of this year just to burglarize your home, and shoot your wife." He was looking at Ellison sarcastically.

Ellison let out a sigh, and slumped back in his chair. "I didn't kill my wife," he said under his breath.

I've heard tell the brakeman on duty the night of the murder thought they saw a man jump the train," Hall spoke up. "But how do you prove it? I mean, it's speculation... hearsay."

"Pretty much all we have here is hearsay!" exclaimed Trinkle. "This whole trial is based on circumstantial evidence. We have nothing solid to go on here." He was truly angry at this case. "I guess we can play up the story of a stranger and hope for reasonable doubt."

The three men sat sipping their coffee in silence, deep in thought.

Hall and Trinkle didn't know if their client had murdered his wife. They never asked him, and they never would. They didn't want to know. "That may be all we have... hoping the jury believes there is reasonable doubt," Hall said absently.

* * * * * * * * *

John Hall sent a barber to the jailhouse, late Saturday afternoon to give Ellison a shave and a haircut. He looked like a civilized man come Monday morning when court took back up.

It was Hall and Trinkle's turn to try to mesmerize the jury and sway them to their point of view. They didn't realize, however, that some of their witnesses would turn their strategy on it's head.

* * * * * * * * *

Hall was designated to state opening remarks on Ellison's behalf. He spent a lot of time trying to bring home to the jury, the fact that Ellison Scott was a prominent, well liked citizen, Christian, and businessman in La Cygne. He was a man who loved his wife and very attentive to her. Hall never said a word about Arlene, but he did elude the fact there could have been a stranger in town who may have committed the murder of Ella Scott.

Miss Laura Rowley was the first witness called to the stand that morning by the defense. Her mother had made her a new green dress with a white crocheted collar especially to wear today. She had fixed her hair in a stylish French braid down her back. She smiled nervously as she walked to

Deadly Affair

the stand and took her oath. Hall asked her to tell the court what had taken place the night of June 19th from her point of view.

She testified that she was in bed, but not yet asleep when she heard gun shots and then Ellison's screams for help. She went to the front porch and saw a man walking along the sidewalk. "I asked him what the trouble was up the street and he replied that Mrs. Scott had been shot and killed."

Can you describe this man, Miss Rowley?"

He was tall, and was of dark complexion. He was a stranger to me," she testified.

No further questions, Your Honor," Hall said, on his way back to his table.

The judge asked the prosecution if they wanted to cross examine the witness, and W.A. Smith stood and walked to the stand.

Miss Rowley, you said the man you spoke to was a stranger to you. Is that correct?"

"Yes sir," she replied.

"Miss Rowley, was it very dark on the night in question? By that I mean, were the street lights in the area sufficient enough to see people around you?"

"Yes sir."

"Miss Rowley, you said the man you spoke to was a stranger to you... You hadn't seen him before, is that correct?"

"Yes sir," she replied.

"Miss Rowley, do you know most of the people who live in your neighborhood. For that matter do you think you know most people in La Cygne.

"Yes, sir." she said proudly.

"Do you suppose the people in your neighborhood would have known Ella Scott and her husband?"

"Probably so, sir, yes." she answered a little confused.

"Miss Rowley, you stated this stranger to you told you that Mrs. Scott had been shot and killed, is that correct?"

"Yes sir."

"Miss Rowley, if this man was a stranger to you, and probably everyone around you, how would he have known the name of the person who had been shot and killed?"

Laura Rowley tried to protest the question, as Mr. Smith said, "No more questions, Your Honor,"

on his way back to his chair.

Laura Rowley left the stand with tears of humiliation in her eyes.

* * * * * * * * * *

Mr. Walter Crow, conductor, and Mr. John Tucker, brakeman, both working on the Frisco freight train which passed through La Cygne the night of the murder, related to the court that a man answering the description of the stranger by Miss Rowley, was seen on their train after leaving La Cygne. The man refused to get off the train, but had disappeared before the train arrived at Pleasanton, or at least was not seen by the trainmen after that.

Mrs. Gladys Enloe, a widow, lived about four blocks from the Scott home in the direction of the stockyards. She missed her husbands company something awful, and had a hard time sleeping at night. She spent a lot of time sitting on her front porch late into the night and listening to the sounds of nature that only comes out after dark. She was an elderly woman, didn't move too fast, but still had very strong eyesight. She testified she had been sitting on her porch and saw a man running past her house in the direction of the stockyards. She had no idea what time it was, but she knew it must have been late as she usually came out to sit on her porch around 11 o'clock most evenings.

Mr. Hall thanked her for her testimony and even helped her down from the witness stand.

Lewis P. Bishop, who was not only a friend of the Scotts, but also a close neighbor testified that he had talked to Laura Rowley on the sidewalk the night of the murder, and it was he who had told her Mrs. Scott had been murdered. Testimony that, pretty much damaged a *stranger* theory. He was on the stand about five more minutes answering mundane questions Hall was throwing at him to try to save the idea of someone else committing the awful crime. He was finally excused and the last witness of the day was called to the stand.

Ellison Scott, who was called to the stand mid-afternoon on September 22nd, was sworn in and seated, among whispers and shuffling in the courtroom. The judge yelled 'order' but didn't strike his gavel. When Ellison had settled in his chair, Mr. Hall told him to recount the evening of June 19th, 1923.

"Ellison cleared his throat, and began. "I was in the garage oiling the clutch of my motor car, when I heard two shots. I walked to the front door of the garage and looked up and down the street. I saw no one. I went back to the car and then, feeling something was wrong, went into the house," he testified.

"What did you do when you saw your wife on the floor?" Hall asked him.

Deadly Affair

"I cried, 'My God, Ella, what has happened?' Then I knelt down beside her and asked her to talk. I could see that she was breathing, but her eyes were closed. I jumped up and went to the west door and called for help, and then went back and knelt down again. 'Tell me what happened?" I asked her, but she made no reply. Then I discovered the blood and saw that she had been shot. I immediately rose and ran out the door, calling for help, and went to the doctor's house."

Several times while testifying, it appeared hard for Ellison to speak. He seemed to be making an attempt to keep from sobbing, but he couldn't help it, he finally broke down, and for a few seconds sat in the witness chair with his head in his hands, crying.

Scott related that it was the custom of his wife to go in the house before him after coming home in the car. His wife complained to him the day before the murder that the clutch on the car was sticking. That night, after returning from the tent show, he drove into his garage and turned out the lights of the car. His wife turned on the lights of the garage and prepared to go in the house. He however, popped the clutch of the car out and started to oil it.

"When are you coming in?" he said his wife asked him.

"I'll be in pretty soon," he said.

"Those were the last words that I heard my wife speak," Ellison said hanging his head.

After arousing the doctor, who lived a block away, he ran back home, Scott said, and found several men in the house. One of them put his hand on Ellison's shoulder and told him they had plenty of help, for him to go sit down.

After Ellison gave his testimony, Attorney Edeburn cross-examined him before he was allowed to step down.

Attorney Edeburn again asked Ellison about his relationship with his wife's niece, Arlene Scott. Ellison wanted to leap from his chair, grab Edeburn around the throat and choke him to death! He was so sick and tired of being asked about Arlene.

"I have never had improper relations with Arlene Scott," he lied staring straight ahead.

"Is it true, Mr. Scott, that you registered as man and wife under the name of BOWMAN?"

Ellison didn't answer right away.

"Mr. Scott...?"

"Yes sir, he croaked. "Yes sir... It's true."

"Why would you do that, Mr. Scott?"

Ellison stared at him, as if he didn't understand the question.

"Why would you register yourself and Arlene as man and wife under the name of Bowman?" Attorney Edeburn asked patiently.

"I wished to avoid publicity, sir."

"Well, Mr. Scott, did you even think about what effect that would have on Arlene's reputation if it became known that she was registered at the Wick Hotel as the wife of some man she wasn't married to?"

"I never thought about that," was all Ellison could think to say, looking down at the floor.

"And you are saying that you did not have relations with Miss Scott at the Wick Hotel?"

"I had a headache. I needed a place to lie down... and that's all," he said flatly.

The judge adjourned court until the next morning when the prosecution started their closing arguments. The case against Ellison was purely circumstantial and was hard to try either way. After the defense made their closing arguments, Judge Gates directed the jury to consider the defendant guilty of murder in the first degree or innocent on all charges.

The jury left the courtroom around 5 o'clock that afternoon and filed into the small jury room to the left of the judge's chambers. They started deliberations at that time, and by Thursday morning, they sent a message to the judge that they were hopelessly dead locked, at eight for acquittal and four for conviction.

The courtroom had started filling up early that morning with everyone hoping that a verdict would be announced sometime that day. When the jury announced they were dead locked the courtroom broke out with a shocked eruption of disapproval. By now people of the county had come to a solid belief within themselves one way or another, and they wanted this case to be settled.

As people filtered out of the courtroom, Ellison was put back into handcuffs by the sheriff, and led back to the jailhouse across the street. Ellison was still being held on twenty thousand dollars bond and he still had no resources to pay for his release. No one wanted a verdict that day more than Ellison Scott himself.

Upon reaching his cell, he sat on the edge of his cot and wailed. The sheriff could hear his loud cries as he descended the stairs and walked out the front door.

~CHAPTER FIFTEEN~

On October 5th, Judge Gates held a short session in the district court. When he realized that Ellison was still in custody of the sheriff, and his bond had not yet been given, he decided to reduce the bond from twenty thousand, to ten thousand.

Ellison was being held for appearance for trial at the December term of court, and Judge Gates felt he need not sit in jail for the next two months.

However, even after the bond was reduced, it wasn't until October 12th that Ellison's bond was signed. Two of his uncles, Lee and George Scott, along with John Teagarden, W.F. Shattuck, and once again Dr. S.D. Morrison bonded Ellison out of jail.

* * * * * * * * * *

Charles Scott provided a ride home for his son upon his release from jail. The two men rode in silence for most of the trip. They were both broken men, with not much to say to each other.

After awhile, as if addressing no one in particular, Ellison spoke up, "I need to sell my motor car... I should get a good price for it. I guess tomorrow I will look into selling the market... and the house." He was staring out the windshield voicing his thoughts aloud. He shook his head, "I hope I can get it all done before December.

Charles' heart broke for his son. He realized he had given up all hope, and even though Charles knew Ellison was probably wise to sell his property and pay his debts, it still broke his heart.

I'll do what I can to help you, son" Charles promised, as he turned the car into the driveway to his farm.

* * * * * * * * * *

The following day, Ellison got up early, bathed and shaved, and dressed in a nice suit before heading down to breakfast. His mother was so impressed she had a huge smile on her face when she saw him come into the room.

"You look very nice this morning, son!"

Ellison cringed. He didn't look nice because he wanted too. He was on his way to selling his life, and he didn't feel like being complimented for it. He grumbled at her, then, realizing she didn't deserve that, he immediately apologized.

"I'm sorry, Ma... I'm not looking forward to today, that's all."

She looked concerned. "What's going on today?" she asked wearily.

He told her his plans to sell his assets and pay off his debts. She listened to him as she made his breakfast.

"Ellison," she set a plate of food in front of him and poured him, and herself, a cup of coffee. "I know the past few months have been so hard on you, on all of us, and if I could make it all go away, I would in a minute." Her eyes started tearing up as she sat down at the table next to him with her coffee. "I reckon you are probably doing the right thing, but I know it's hard for you."

He leaned over and kissed his mother on her forehead, and tried to smile at her. He knew this was hard on his folks, and that made him feel even more depressed. Sometimes he didn't know what kept him from just hanging himself.

After breakfast, he drove his Studebaker into La Cygne and parked in front of his meat market and grocery. He sat there for a minute, lost in thought about all the time spent here making a life for himself and Ella. It had been his dream. He loved this market and he couldn't imagine life away from it. He had to remind himself that he was now living without Ella, so living without the market couldn't be any worse.

He stepped out of his car, and onto the sidewalk. Several people, he knew well, were passing by, but acted like they hadn't seem him. He was now a hated man by most of the community, and that was unbearable for him. He walked into the store, and the little bell rang out as he stepped in. Clyde McCullough was standing at the register helping a customer when Ellison entered. No one spoke. Clyde was counting out change to the customer, and she left the store with her bag, but without saying anything.

Clyde looked startled at Ellison as he hadn't realized he had been bonded out of jail.

"Morning, Ellison...." he said, graciously.

"Morning Clyde. I was hoping the store wouldn't be too busy yet this morning, as I need to talk to you, privately."

"We can go back to the... uh... your office, if you like. Tom can take care of customers for a little while."

Ellison nodded his head, and the two men walked to the back of the store. Clyde motioned to Ellison to sit in his own chair behind the desk, but Ellison sat in the small chair near the door.

Deadly Affair

I won't take up too much of your time, Clyde. This is something I don't want to do, and never thought I would have to do..."

Clyde sat paralyzed not knowing what Ellison was going to say.

"I'm going to have to sell my store, Clyde, pay off all my debts that I can. I can't think of anyone who knows the workings of this market any better than you do, and I was wondering if you would be interested in purchasing it from me. I would be very reasonable about it." Those words were very hard for Ellison to say, as even now he had negative feelings for Clyde McCullough. But he felt he had no choice but to offer the market to him. He didn't feel Clyde would have a problem getting a loan from the bank, under the circumstances.

Clyde let out a huge sigh of relief, and smiled. "Really? Really, Ellison?"

Ellison had not looked Clyde in the eye the whole time they had been talking, but now he looked him in the eye. "Really."

"Well, yeah... I mean, I have to look over my finances and see what I can do. But yes, I'm very interested in buying the market from you." He tried to wipe the smile off his face a couple of times, but it didn't work.

Ellison rose from his chair, and excused himself. He shook Clyde's hand and told him he would be anxious to hear from him in the near future about making a deal. Ellison left the office and walked to the front door of the store, all the while feeling the stares of customers who used to be his friends. When he reached his car, he laid his head on the steering wheel and sobbed.

A few days later, Ellison put an ad in the La Cygne Journal to sell his Studebaker, and within a couple of weeks a man from Kansas City purchased it from him. Ellison was right, he did get a good price for it.

By the end of the month, Clyde informed Ellison he was ready to purchase the market. He had talked extensively with a cousin of his about going in with him on the store and the bank had granted the two men a business loan. Ellison met with Clyde and his cousin on a cool, crisp Friday afternoon in La Cygne to settle the transfer of property.

He never went back to the market after that. He didn't even clean out his old office, or return to get the paperweight Ella had given him. He told Clyde to throw away anything he didn't want to keep. Ellison just didn't want to look back.

He had borrowed his father's car to come to town and after meeting with Clyde and his cousin, he decided to drive by his old neighborhood... his old house. He drove slow as he realized not much had changed, except the house he had shared with Ella. The grass had not been mowed all summer, and there were tree limbs down on the north side from a summer storm. He never thought about having someone take care of the place. With all he had to deal with, it never crossed his mind. Vines near the kitchen door and the well were over grown and out of control. He parked in the street in front of his house for a few minutes. He felt he had died and come back to life in a different time. His store now belonged to someone else, so did his car, and his home was desolate and over grown. After a few minutes, he shook his head to come to reality, and slowly drove off on his way back to the farm.

The house in La Cygne, that Ellison Scott shared with his wife, Ella, never did sell. No one wanted to live in a house where such a heinous murder had taken place. Ellison couldn't meet the payments on it, so it went back to the bank. Over the years, it fell in on itself, and the wood and fixtures were eventually sold for scrap.

Ellison became a man with no property, but he was now a man with no debt.

* * * * * * * * *

During the weeks between the end of the first trial on September 28th and the first of November, Kansas Attorney General, Charles B. Griffith not only recommended the retrial of Ellison Scott, but also issued a warrant for the arrest of Arlene Scott as an accomplice in the murder. He felt strongly that she was involved in some way.

~CHAPTER SIXTEEN~

Friday, November 23rd, started out unusually warm, although the dark, black clouds in the western sky were threatening a severe weather change by the end of the day. The children at the Cemetery County School were excited that it was so warm, and asked their Teacher, Miss Arlene Scott, if the could eat their lunches outside later. The children were so restless, with the weekend right around the corner that she decided to allow them the privilege as long as they settled down and got to work on their arithmetic problems.

* * * * * * * * * *

There was a stack of mail laying on the sheriff's desk when he arrived at his office that Friday morning. He had not worn his jacket into the building, but did bring it to work that day.

Morning', Sheriff," the deputy greeted him as the sheriff was pouring himself a cup of coffee.

"Mornin', Lindsey, how are things going this morning?"

"Pretty quiet." Lindsey replied.

"Good then, the sheriff said, sipping on his coffee and sitting in his big leather chair. He reached for his mail, as he usually did first thing in the morning and started going through the pile.

Somewhere in the middle of the pile, he saw an envelope from the Kansas Attorney General's office, marked ,URGENT. He set his coffee cup down, pulled out his pocketknife and ran it across the top of the envelope flap. He pulled out the papers, sat back in his chair and started to read. After several minutes of reading, and re-reading the papers, he slammed them down on his desk.

"Damn it all!!" he exclaimed, rubbing his face. "I don't think this Scott case will ever be resolved!"

"What's going on, Boss?" the deputy asked cautiously.

"Now I have to arrest Arlene Scott in connection to Ella's murder!" he said loudly. He was really angry. "This letter is dated a few days ago, so I'm going to have to go arrest her today. Damn it!"

"Do you want me to go along?" the deputy asked.

"Yes, I want you to go along! I'm going to call Etta Wright and see if she can substitute Arlene's class this afternoon. If she can then we'll drive by there and pick her up."

"Why can't you arrest her this evening when she is at home?"

"Because, he said waving the papers at the deputy, The Attorney General wanted her arrested for murder several days ago, which means immediately, and I don't intend to disobey the Attorney General!"

He set the paper on his desk and picked up the receiver on his telephone and asked the operator to ring Miss Etta Wright's number for him.

* * * * * * * * * *

The morning sky grew darker, and loud claps of thunder and flashes of lightning released pouring rain from the sky. Some of the younger children at the school were frightened, but the older students and their teacher comforted them and assured them everything would be okay. The plans for lunch outside, however, had to be cancelled. The children were disappointed, but made the best of the situation. They sat on the floor in a circle, and pretended to have a picnic, and while they ate their lunches, Miss Scott read a couple of chapters of their favorite book,

Tom Sawyer by Mark Twain. When lunchtime was over and everything put away, she let the children play a couple of indoor games to burn some energy.

By the time the children settled back at their desks, the rain had stopped and the sky had lightened. But the wind started howling around the little schoolhouse, rattling the long tall windows on both sides of the room. Arlene handed out test papers on the states and their capitals and soon the children were hard at work writing down the answers. The smaller children were working on writing their letters and numbers.

Arlene sat quietly grading arithmetic papers. The room was quiet except for the sound of the roaring wind, when suddenly there was a loud knock on the door in the back of the room. Everyone was startled and jumped at the sound. No one had heard a car drive up, because of the wind. Once Arlene collected herself, she walked to the door and opened it. She was startled by the coldness of the air that hit her face, after such a warm morning. She was even more startled to see the sheriff on the other side of the door. Standing next to him was Deputy Lindsey.

Sheriff Ellington had about had his fill of Arlene and the Ella Scott murder case. He was not happy about being here, and after his last encounter with Arlene, he was determined to get this arrest done without incident.

Deadly Affair

The sheriff tipped his hat to her, "Miss Scott, I need to speak to you about something urgent," he said in a low voice.

"Of course, Sheriff. Come in, please," she said, opening the door wider so he and the deputy could enter. Sheriff Ellington stood with his back to the classroom, and faced Arlene, hoping the children couldn't hear their conversation. He didn't want to scare them, but at this point he was in such a foul mood about the whole affair of this arrest, he didn't feel the need to comfort them either.

"Miss Scott, I'm sorry to say, I have been given a warrant for your arrest in the matter of your Aunt Ella's murder, by the Attorney General of Kansas."

Before she could react, he pulled a pair of handcuffs from his back pocket and cuffed her hands behind her back.

Arlene was *mortified!* So totally embarrassed in front of her students, she nearly fainted.

The children were stunned. Some of the older students had heard whispers of the murder, but weren't really aware their teacher was involved in any way. The smaller children were frightened about the sheriff being there, and handcuffing their teacher was upsetting to them.

None of them understood the grown-up problems that plagued their teacher.

Little Emma Emerson started to cry aloud, as she was the teacher's pet and didn't understand what was happening to Miss Scott. Some of the older boys were making quiet jokes to each other. They cupped their hands over their mouths, thinking they wouldn't be heard.

"Why couldn't you do this at my house after school?" Arlene asked under her breath, her eyes shooting bullets at the sheriff.

He didn't answer, only took her by the arm and opened the door. A cold blast of air rushed into the room. Arlene was wearing a white cotton blouse and a black skirt, not appropriate apparel for the cold air.

"It's so cold out, may I please get my sweater?" Arlene asked, with a broken voice, and tears welling in her eyes.

She couldn't believe this was happening to her.

The sheriff asked one of the older girls in the front row to grab Arlene's sweater off the back of her chair. The young girl fearfully walked to her teacher's chair and grabbed the sweater. She cautiously walked toward the sheriff and reluctantly handed him the sweater, as if she thought he would bite her.

The sheriff thanked the girl, who was already rushing back to her seat, and then placed the sweater over Arlene's shoulders. He then escorted

Arlene to his car. Deputy Lindsey stood in the back of the classroom waiting for the sheriff to return. The children sat silently staring at him.

When the sheriff returned, Miss Etta Wright was with him. He walked to the front of the classroom and she followed him. He explained as best as he could that Miss Scott had to leave the class for the day, but that Miss Wright would be with them until school was out at the end of the afternoon.

Miss Wright smiled at the children and tried to bring order to the class. She assured them that everything would be alright. It took a little time for them to settle down and relax after all the commotion, but it didn't take to long for Miss Wright to take control of the class. However, most of the older students had lost their ability to concentrate on any studying, as they couldn't wait to get home to tell their parents what had happened at school that day.

By evening, nearly everyone in the county knew Arlene had been arrested for involvement in her aunt's murder. By now, interest in the case of Ella's murder had started to wane until it was hardly discussed any longer. However, with Arlene's arrest, rumors and speculation would once again run wild in the community.

~CHAPTER SEVENTEEN~

Rob Rogers pulled the chair away from the kitchen table and sat down to put on his work boots. He sat for a moment, elbows resting on his thighs as he closed his eyes and hung his head.

He was so tired. He had not been sleeping well for the past few months. Not since the murder. It was hard to sleep in the summer heat anyway, but it became practically impossible when his mind wouldn't shut down. The nights were cooler now that the autumn winds were blowing northern air, but sleep was still hard to come by.

The sun had started to glow in the eastern sky as he grabbed his old sweat-stained straw hat and headed out the kitchen door. He adjusted his suspenders over his heavy flannel shirt as he leaned down to pick up two milk pails setting on the back porch. He had only two milk cows these days, Bessie and Olive, but they gave plenty of milk for his family. Once he got to the barn he set the pails aside and picked up the pitchfork standing next to the door and started filling the 'girls' trough with hay. They mooed in appreciation, which in turn woke the hogs on the other side of the barn.

"Hold on!" he hollered their way. "You'll get yours!"

After giving the cows their hay, he walked over to the other side of the barn and opened an old wooden bin filled with field corn. He placed several ears in the trough for the hogs then watched for awhile as they grunted, climbing over each other to get to their share of the breakfast.

Finally when he was done, he shook his head, and turned around to head back to his cows.

"'Mornin', girls," he said, as he grabbed a pail and his small stool. He set them both under Bessie and went to work. Bessie didn't seem to mind, she was preoccupied with her breakfast. When Bessie had given up her last drop of milk, Rob moved his stool over to Olive and grabbed the other pail. Olive wasn't giving as much milk these days, so it didn't take as long to milk her.

Once he had finished milking, he let his livestock out in the barnyard for the day. He pumped water from a nearby well and filled the water troughs before grabbing his pails as he headed for the house.

The sun was still very low on the horizon. There was a chill to the morning air, and goose bumps covered his arms.

"We need some rain so bad!" he said to himself, on the walk back to the house. The rain that had poured on the Cemetery School a few days before, didn't hit much of his land, and it was still pretty dry. He looked up at the cloudless sky and shook his head.

When he stepped onto the porch he could smell the mouth watering aroma of breakfast cooking. He set his milk pails down long enough to take off his boots, then picked them up to take in the kitchen. By this time Maude had heard him on the porch and had come to hold the door open for him. She kissed his cheek as he passed by her.

"Good morning," she said.

He said good morning back to her as he set the pails on the table.

"Would you like a cup of coffee?" she asked him.

"Sounds good. Breakfast sure smells good!"

"It will be ready in a few minutes."

Leona and Wilma never woke up in time for morning chores, but they could never resist the smell of breakfast floating upstairs. They both came pounding down the stairs hollering 'good morning' as they ran outside to use the outhouse. Maude and Rob just smiled at each other.

"Is it your turn today to go help your folks?" Rob asked as he sipped his coffee.

"Yes it is." She spooned him a plate of food and set it down in front of him. Then she poured herself a cup of coffee and sat down next to him.

"Rob, I am so worried about Papa." Tears filled her eyes, and he reached for her hand. Papa told me the next time we came over, he wants to have a serious talk with you."

A tear stole down her cheek. "He..." she wiped her eye. "He looks so bad," she whispered.

"Did he say what he wanted to talk about?"

Maude shook her head and walked back to the stove to fix plates of food for the girls and herself.

"I win!" Wilma shouted as she ran into the kitchen, letting the screen door slam in Leona's face.

Leona didn't care. She wasn't racing. She had outgrown such childish games long ago.

"Slow down!" Rob yelled, and not too kindly. "Since you *won* missy, you get to put the milk in jars and put it away."

Wilma started to throw a tantrum, then thought better of it when she saw the way her papa was looking at her. Her tantrums were usually more effective when her papa wasn't around.

Leona smiled at her as she walked past to get her plate of breakfast.

Be careful not to spill any," Maude warned, as Wilma reluctantly, but carefully, poured the milk into jars her mother had set out for her.

* * * * * * * * *

It was about 7:30 that morning when Maude and Rob set out for the Holt farm. The girls had been instructed to feed the chickens, and gather eggs after cleaning the breakfast dishes.

There was very little conversation as Rob drove his Ford on the rough and dusty gravel roads to Maude's childhood home. He could tell his wife was exhausted with worry and grief. He noticed new lines that had recently appeared on her face. Sprigs of gray hair had cropped up around her hairline that hadn't been there a few short months ago. He wished he could say something to her to offer real comfort, but he didn't know how to process his own grief, his own loss in the matter. They rode in silence on the twenty minute drive.

The house looked deserted and vacant as they pulled into the long driveway. Even on a wind chilled morning such as this, a stronger, healthier John Holt would have been sitting in his rocker on the front porch, taking in the morning air.

Maude released a huge sigh and gently closed her eyes as she reached for the car door handle. She sat motionless for a few seconds. Rob knew she was probably praying. Praying for the strength to get through this day. A big gust of chilly air greeted them as they stepped out of the car. Multi-colored leaves raced and chased each other across the yard as the wind had it's way with them. The front of Maude's coat flew in the gust and flipped her around and into the back of the car before she had time to react. Rob ran around the car and grabbed her arm before she fell. The gust seemed to subside a little, as another one started to increase.

"The wind has really picked up since we left home!" Rob shouted.

"It's gotten a lot colder too!" Maude shouted back as she grabbed her coat tight around herself.

They walked arm in arm to the porch and into the house.

The front room was dark. Sarah was napping in her rocking chair and John was asleep in his bed. The smell hit them first. The house reeked of body odor, and body waste, mixed with dust and a hint of death.

Maude raced to the little bedroom off the kitchen, stripping off her coat as she ran. Sleeping soundly in the small bed was Maude's niece, Glenora. Glenora was older than Leona and Arlene, yet she did not work at a paying job. Her mother, Mary had Glenora help her folks once in awhile to give her sisters a break from the burden of caring for their father. It was almost 8 o'clock and the house was cold and dark. Rob quickly checked the pulse of both Sarah and John and after feeling certain they were okay, he immediately started building a fire in the front room stove.

Maude grabbed the shoulders of the sleeping girl and shook her awake. Glenora wiped spittle from her mouth as her eyes rolled awake.

"Aunt Maude...." she said, confused. She worked at sitting up and tried to swing her legs off the bed in a hazy fog of sleep.

"Glenora, what's going on here? Is everyone okay?"

"When.... what?" she stuttered, scratching her head.

"Glenora, it's 8 o'clock in the morning. Why are you all still asleep? Why is there no breakfast?" Why is the house so cold?!" Panic ran deeper in her throat with each question.

Glenora quickly came awake as last evening's events started replaying in her mind.

"Oh... Aunt Maude...." she sighed as she rubbed her face in both hands. "Aunt Maude it was a... a horrible night! I didn't get to sleep until... until maybe 5'30 this morning... some time around then. I'm so sorry," she said rubbing her face.

"What do you mean, *horrible night?* What happened?" Maude was almost screaming at the girl.

"Grandpapa was sick all night," she said, as she stood and slipped into her robe.

"Grandmama and I tended to him all night, Aunt Maude. He vomited several times... soiled the bed sheets more than twice," her voice was low and soft, an octave above a whisper.

The girl had been through the most dreadful night of her young life and she was horrified at remembering just what she had needed to do to help care for her aging and fragile grandfather.

She looked into the eyes of her aunt with shame filled tears, for she also had *seen* her grandfather as no young lady should have to.

Maude, sensing her niece's despair, warmly put her arms around her and they wept together.

Let's get some breakfast started, and warm up this cold old house," Maude smiled, trying to sound cheerful. "Would you please get some water from the well?" Maude asked Glenora, as she gently wiped tears off her face. "Then you can come back to bed and rest for awhile."

Glenora nodded her head.

They rose from the bed and Glenora grabbed her sweater from the back of a small chair. She picked up the water bucket next to the kitchen sink on her way out the door to the well off the back porch.

Deadly Affair

Maude walked to the box phone on the wall and rang the operator in Centerville. After exchanging 'hellos' and small talk, she asked the operator to connect her to her sister, Mary's number. She explained to Mary what a rough night it had been for their folks and for Glenora. She told her she was going to let the girl sleep for awhile and she and Rob would bring her home later.

Mary understood, but she was very disappointed. She was counting on Glenora's help with the laundry and watching kids that day. But she didn't complain to Maude, as she felt guilt enough for not being able to do her part in helping her folks, and sending her daughter instead. She also felt very sorry that her daughter had such a rough night.

Within a half hour the stove in the front room started to warm the house. Rob had started a fire in the cook stove as well. Maude made a pot of coffee, but waited to start any breakfast.

Sarah startled awake after awhile, in her rocking chair, and was confused for a time at the activity going on around her. She slowly unwrapped herself from the two warm quilts she had bundled up in. Maude came to her mother's aid when she realized she was awake.

"Mama?"

Sarah's eyes filled with tears when she saw her daughter. Her emotions were tender, her energy spent. Sarah raised a hand to her as Maude helped her out of the chair.

Oh...." she groaned, "What a horrible night!"

"That's what I've heard, Mama."

Tears were streaming down Sarah's face by now. Maude helped her mother to a chair at the kitchen table, handed her a handkerchief, then poured them each a cup of coffee and sat down next to her mother. Maude sipped her coffee while her mother tried to collect herself.

Then she got up and made her mother a piece of toast as she listened to her sobbing her way through the story of the 'around the clock' care of her husband, she and Glenora had been devoted to do. Maude listened intently to her mother, all the while noticing that she had lost too much weight in these past months. She noticed the dark circles under her eyes that had become more prominent lately. Her hair was now almost white. Maude handed her mother the toast and sat beside her again. She gently put her hand in her mother's hand as she listened to her story.

* * * * * * * * * *

Rob had gotten the fire roaring in the front room and the cook stove, and when he was satisfied the fire would burn safely, he closed the doors on both stoves, and brushed himself off.

He grabbed the little broom leaning against the wall in the front room near the stove and swept the area around it. As he returned the broom to it's resting place, he looked into his father-in-law's bedroom. As he walked toward the room the air became heavy... thick. The room seemed so much smaller than it should be. As he approached the door the stench took his breath away. He took his handkerchief out of his pocket and covered his nose so he could inhale a couple of decent breaths of air. The room was so dark. Rob could hardly make out the figure of the dying man lying on the small bed.

He walked to the window closest to him and lifted the shade just enough to let in a little light. He thought about opening the window about an inch to let in some fresh air, but decided not to. The wind would perhaps only make the room colder.

Rob noticed in the corner of the room, a large pile of soiled sheets and blankets, most likely the main source of the horrible smell. He tied his handkerchief around his face and carefully carried the pile of bedding to the front porch. It took a couple of trips, and even though the smell lingered with him, he felt better about the bedding being out of the house.

John Holt was slightly stirring in his bed when Rob re-entered the room. He stood still a moment, hoping the old man wouldn't vomit... or much worse, mess his sheets again. Rob watched him for some time. John had been good to him over the years. They had a mutual respect for each other, one that could be considered friendship, beyond father and son-in-law. Finally, when he felt the old man was stable, he picked up a chair and set it closer to the bed. He sat down next to John.

As if knowing he was there, John turned his head toward Rob and slowly opened his eyes. He sluggishly reached out his hand to Rob. A pained and knowing smile tried to cross John's face as he recognized Rob sitting there.

"Glad you came by, Boy," a term of endearment, John spoke as he coughed and wheezed. Rob reached for a clean handkerchief lying on top of the dresser and handed it to John.

"Could you help me sit up a little, Son?"

Rob got out of his chair to help John sit up and was surprised at how fragile the old man really was.

"Had a rough night, last night... thought I wasn't going to make it 'till morning"

John's breathing was labored and interrupted by strong painful fits of coughing. Once in awhile he would spit into his clean handkerchief as he tried to collect himself.

Rob just sat next to the bed, partly wishing he was anywhere but here. Rob was a good man to help anyone with almost any chore or errand, but he was not good with emotions, with death and dying and broken hearts. He couldn't fix broken people the way he could fix a broken fence or a squeaky door. Transgression and misconduct had been offensively forced on this family for so long now, the weight of it was destroying them all.

"What can..." he cleared his throat. "What can I do for you, John?" Tears were filling his own eyes by now.

John let out a huge sigh and laid his head back on his pillow.

"You can sit and listen to the rambling of an old soldier, Rob. "That I can do, yes," he settled back in his chair.

For a moment, the old man lie there with his eyes closed as he collected his thoughts. Finally, out of the blue, he opened his eyes and looked straight at Rob.

"You've heard Arlene was arrested for Ella's murder, haven't you?" asked the old man.

"Yes, unfortunately. But she was arrested as an accomplice, not as the actual suspect who shot her." John waved his hand, as if indifferent. "I know who killed my Ella. I know where the gun is that ended her life. I need to tell you." he coughed.

Rob sat shocked. He didn't know if the old man had dreamed this up, if he was losing his mind, or really did know something. He sat there stunned and said nothing.

"Ellison killed my baby. I know it for a fact, now," he said breathlessly as he started another coughing fit.

"John, would you like a cup of coffee? Warm your bones up a little."

John thought for a moment and then decided that sounded good.

Rob hollered at Maude to bring a cup of coffee for her papa, and she hollered back that she would.

When John had calmed down after his coughing fit, he went on with his story, "I haven't seen Ellison much since Ella died, but the times I have his behavior is shifty. He was always sweaty and nervous. I tried to ignore my intuition about him until the truth came out about him and...." He sighed another huge sigh. "About him and Arlene," he whispered. Tears ran down his face, which he wiped away with his handkerchief.

Maude entered the room carrying a tray with two cups of coffee and set the cups down on the nightstand. She felt good about her father sitting up in the bed, and she smiled at him as she walked out of the room.

"But how?" Rob started to ask, as John held up his hand to stop him.

"I've had a gut feeling Ellison killed Ella since the wake," he choked through his words.

Rob again said nothing.

There was a pitcher of water on the nightstand and Rob poured some in a glass and offered it to John. With a shaking hand John reached for the glass.

"I'll do it," Rob said, as he helped John with the glass.

John laid his head back on his pillow, feeling a little refreshed and grateful for it.

"Ellison came in late that night... the night of the wake. He should have been there early with the rest of us to greet people. He looked disheveled, sweaty and nervous. He hardly said anything to anyone unless someone came up to him, making him feel obliged. He was carrying a wooden box and was headed to the viewing room. He stopped in the doorway where the undertaker was standing. Mangold... Mr. Mangold?"

Rob nodded, offering John more water. John took a sip or two and waved his hand when he had enough.

"I watched Ellison as he talked to Mangold. He seemed agitated... nervous. He kept wiping sweat from his forehead as if he couldn't wipe it dry. The room was hot that night, but not that unbearable. I watched him, as he seemed to be referring to the wooden box in his hand. He told Mangold something about the box and then handed it to him. Mangold acted like he didn't want to take it…but I think he did anyway."

John let out another long sigh. "I was distracted for a few minutes and when I noticed Ellison again, Mangold was no where around. Ellison was talking to a gentleman I didn't recognize... and his whole demeanor had changed. He seemed calm and much more relaxed than before. And he no longer had the wooden box. I found his behavior very curious. Did you notice his behavior, Rob?"

Rob shook his head, trying to think about that evening. An evening that seemed to take place a lifetime ago. He stood up and placed a large pillow behind John's head, making it easier for him to sit up. Then Rob offered him a cup of coffee, figuring by now it wouldn't be real hot.

Again, he helped John hold the cup, and John took several sips before Rob set the cup back on the table.

"That's good coffee. I probably shouldn't have a lot, but it sure is good."

"John, I really don't remember Ellison that night, I guess my attention was elsewhere. I just really don't remember much about how he was acting."

John lie still with his eyes closed for a minute before going on.

"When Ellison approached me that evening, I asked him what was in the box. He seemed startled by the question, but then became thoughtful and said, 'Some of Ella's favorite things.'

'*Some of Ella's favorite things.*'" Tears welled up in John's eyes again and his voice was full of emotional pain. "What he said has haunted me everyday since then."

Rob looked confused, "Why?"

"Because there was nothing of Ella's in that box," he choked. "I believe that son of a bitch hid his gun in that box and buried it with my daughter. He broke down in uncontrollable sobs at this point.

Rob sat paralyzed. He had no words for reply. He just couldn't wrap his mind around this idea. He took a long deep drink of his coffee, trying to think how to process this.

"John... John do you realize what..."

John held his hand up in protest.

"I have not thought of much else since her murder." he sobbed. And now that it seems Arlene is involved in this mess, I'm *sure* Ellison shot her! The son of a bitch! My son-in-law with my own granddaughter! My heart is so broken. He turned his body away from Rob and sobbed into his pillow until he fell asleep.

Rob sat with him until he was sure the old man would sleep quietly and restfully. The longer he sat there watching John's chest rise and fall with each labored breath, the more an intense anger welled up in his very soul. He quietly stood from his chair and walked to the front door. He needed to clear his mind, breathe some cool fresh air into his lungs. As he stepped outside he heard the muffled voices of his wife and her mother coming from the kitchen.

He inhaled three or four huge lungs full of air before he broke down and cried. He had been the strong one for everybody else for so long now, he could no longer hold the burden. Through wet blurry eyes he noticed the pile of soiled bedding he had thrown out on the porch. In his anger, he started kicking the pile of sheets and blankets until they were off the porch in a pile in the yard. In his rage he walked around gathering sticks and debris and piling it on top of the bedding. When he was satisfied that his pile was complete, he took a book of matches from his shirt pocket. The flame from the first match he struck instantly disappeared, and suddenly he realized the wind was too strong to safely burn his pile.

"Just as well." he said to himself as he slowly walked back to the porch where he sat down in John's chair and began to rock back and forth.

Some of Ella's favorite things.... Ellison hid the gun in Ella's casket.... Just what was he supposed to do with this information?! He took a small can of chew from his pants pocket and put a pinch of it in his mouth. He rocked and chewed. Chewed and rocked. Every once in awhile he would spit off the side of the porch.

Maybe, just maybe... he wasn't supposed to do anything with this information.

Two days later, John W. Holt fell asleep in his bed... and never woke up. On that day Rob burned the pile of bedding and wept.

* * * * * * * * * *

Each and every member of the Holt family was exhausted from strife and grief and no one had the interest or energy to go through another funeral. Most of the sisters, however, were, in their own way, relieved that their father's suffering had come to an end. They all felt Ella's murder, and now Arlene's arrest, had hastened his demise. They each tried to deal with their own anger and grief privately for the sake of their mother, and also for the sake of their own sanity.

Bertha perhaps suffered the most. Because of all the scandal, even her own daughter couldn't come to her grandfather's funeral. She knew her sisters and their families blamed her in a small way for their sister's murder. *If she had been a better mother, Arlene wouldn't have become such an immoral, permissive young lady. If it wasn't for her daughter, Ella might still be alive.* The dirty looks and whispers behind her back were ripping her heart out. She did not want to lose her family, but could do nothing about it.

The family had a small private funeral for the Holt patriarch in the living room of their childhood home. The service was held by Reverend L.E. Dixon and the interment was made in the Oakwood cemetery, a short distance from the Cemetery County School. John Holt's funeral was the last time his children would ever all be together again. The family ties had been broken.

* * * * * * * * * *

After Arlene's arrest on Friday morning, Ellison was re-arrested on the same charge of murder on Saturday afternoon. They both were held in the county jail until their preliminary hearing, Friday, November 30th.

~CHAPTER EIGHTEEN~

KANSAS CITY STAR, MONDAY, NOVEMBER 23, 1923

ARLENE SCOTT BLAMES GOSSIP

La Cygne, Kans., Nov,26 - Country town gossip was blamed today by Arlene Scott, 19 year old school teacher, for charges of murder against her and her uncle John. E. Scott. They are accused of killing Mrs. Scott last June.

"Stories of love affairs between Uncle John and myself are false," Miss Scott said. "As soon as Mrs. Scott was killed, all the gossips in La Cygne were whispering. Authorities have not a bit of evidence to show I knew anything about the murder, but I was humiliated before my pupils because of waging tongues."

There was a chill in the air and the sky was overcast the morning of the Scott preliminary hearing. There was a huge interest in the case again, now that Arlene had been arrested along with Ellison. The courtroom was again full, but only a handful of Holt family members were in attendance. Arlene's parents were there to support her, but Robert Rogers and his daughter Leona were the only other family members there. Charles and Mollie Scott were always at every hearing and trial for their son, but they sat as far away from the Holt's as they could. Out of respect mostly.

Hall and Trinkle were charged with Arlene's defense as well as Ellison's. Both Arlene and Ellison sat stoically at the defense table, with their attorneys sitting between them. Arlene wept bitterly as Attorney General Griffith summed up the testimony presented by the prosecution. Scott twitched nervously in his chair, as the prosecution attacked Arlene's moral character. The hearing was entirely centered around proving Scott was intimate with his wife's niece.

Bertha, appearing aged and worn, sat motionless as her daughter's reputation was being destroyed. She had buried her father the day before, and her sisters and mother no longer supported her. Her small world had been destroyed.

Leona quietly got up from her chair and walked out of the courtroom and down the hall to the ladies room. She turned on the cold water tap, and filled the sink. She splashed some on her face. Before she knew it she was sobbing. She knew Arlene and Ellison flirted with each other all the time, but she really had not known, or realized the extent of their relationship until her aunt's murder. Maybe she hadn't wanted to know, but the facts brought out today could not be ignored. Leona's emotions were also raw from having just lost her grandfather, and the months of grief leading up to today. Her anger overwhelmed her and it took several minutes to get herself under control. When she had finally collected herself, she walked back into the court- room and quietly sat down next to her papa. He could tell she had been crying and he put his arm around her shoulder and patted her arm.

* * * * * * * * *

Throughout the day, witness after witness testified against Arlene and Ellison. The proprietor of the Wick Hotel testified that Arlene and Ellison had registered at his Hotel in July under the assumed name of Mr. and Mrs. Bowman.

Pauline Potter, Arlene's roommate at teachers college, testified that when the telephone rang at the time Arlene was told of the death of her aunt, she said before answering the phone, 'I'm afraid that's for me and it's bad news.' Arlene was quoted as saying that she had been expecting bad news.

A La Cygne doctor told the justice's court that he had made a hasty physical examination of Miss Scott, and he believed her to be virtuous. Two other physicians, however, testified that they had made a through examination and arrived at conclusions directly contradicting those of the La Cygne doctor.

Neighbors of Scott in La Cygne testified that though they were awake and were attracted by the noise of the fatal shots, they saw no one leave the Scott house until Ellison ran out on his way to the doctor's house. Mr Leivy once again testified that he recognized Scott in his home after the shots, and that he passed before the window several times before running out of the house.

Tom Peters once again testified that he had heard Mrs. Scott say to her husband, 'If you had caught me as I caught you, you would kill me.'

Deadly Affair

Clyde McCullough testified Scott had confided to him before the murder that he owned a .32 caliber revolver. Mrs. Scott was killed with a .32 caliber bullet, and the gun which killed her has never been found. Scott, however, has said he had no such revolver.

McCullough said that after the murder he told Scott that the sheriff was preparing to send for bloodhounds to trail the murderer. 'They need not do that,' Scott replied to McCullough, 'They will not find anything.'

"Objection, Your Honor!" Trinkle leapt out of his chair. "Why hasn't the witness mentioned this before?"

"Mr. McCullough..."

"Nobody asked me about it."

Trinkle slapped the palm of his hand on his forehead as he sat down hard in his chair. He glared at Scott, who did not respond to him.

* * * * * * * * * *

BLUE MOUND SUN, DECEMBER 6, 1923

DOUBT FOGS SCOTT KILLING

Mound City, Kans., Dec. 2 - Sherlock Holmes, that famous detective of fiction, was never involved in a plot shrouded in deeper mystery than that which surrounds the murder of Mrs. Eleanor Scott at La Cygne, in the county one night last June.

Kansas has had murder cases that have created more general interest than the murder of Mrs. Scott, because she was unknown outside the county in which she had lived from her childhood. But in all the annals of crime in this state a murderer never has covered his tracks so cleverly.

John Ellison Scott, husband of the slain woman, is held on the charge of having committed the murder and Arlene Scott, her niece, was bound over yesterday by a justice of the peace for the trial on the charge of being an accessory. Yet little light has been thrown on the murder itself.

Behind the arrest of Arlene Scott, the people believe, there is a legal move only to find another way to unfold evidence the officers believe exists against Scott. Sufficient evidence was introduced against the young girl to cause Justice Ed R. Smith, himself an old time court officer, to hold her for trial on the murder charge.

It is understood Scott's attorneys, who are also Miss Scott's attorneys, will go to the supreme court immediately and ask for a writ of habeas corpus. The Scott defense fought every inch of the way against the holding of Arlene Scott and the attorney general fought as hard to have her held. It was an extraordinary legal battle for a simple preliminary hearing. That adds to the mystery of the case, for there was the impression at all times, in every move, that the attorneys for Arlene Scott were fighting to save Mr. Scott, and that the state was waging its fight, not to convict the girl, but to draw an invisible net tighter about the man.

From the public viewpoint, there still remains grave doubt as to who murdered Mrs. Scott.

Little evidence was introduced against Mr. Scott at the last hearing that was not placed before the jury at the first trial, except for the unfolding of the account by Arlene Scott of the Pittsburg incident.

* * * * * * * *

 The preliminary hearing lasted two days and wrapped up on Saturday afternoon. Ellison was re-charged with Ella's murder, and Arlene was charged with being involved. The date of the trial had not been set, however Attorney General Griffith, who had taken over the prosecution of this case, stated it probably would be after the first of the New Year.
 Ellison had some money left from selling all his possessions and gave bail for ten thousand dollars for appearance for trial, and Arlene gave bond for five thousand. Several farmers from the county helped her post her bond. One of those farmers was W.B. Ferguson. The father of a young man Arlene had gone to country school with and had known all her life.

* * * * * * * *

 Ellison and Arlene's freedom was limited to living at the homes of their parents. Arlene was allowed to teach at the Cemetery School every day, but could go nowhere else but her childhood home. Ellison spent most of his time in his bedroom either reading or sleeping. He did help his father with morning chores once in awhile, but mostly stayed to himself.

Deadly Affair

The holidays, Thanksgiving and Christmas were hardly celebrated by either family. Sarah spent both holidays with her daughters and their families. Except for Bertha and her family, of course.

Mollie Scott begged her oldest son, Walter to come home from Kansas City, for either or both occasions. But he declined, stating he was too busy to travel.

Cold, gray, snowy winters in Kansas are usually always depressing, for the most part, but for Ellison, Arlene, and their families it was nearly unbearable.

* * * * * * * * * *

THE MOUND CITY REPUBLIC
THURSDAY JANUARY 10, 1924

BOTH SCOTT CASES FEBRUARY 4

Judge Ed C. Gates has set February 4th as the date for the Scott trial. Both cases, one in which Scott is charged separately with the murder of his wife, Ella Scott and the other in which he and Arlene Scott are jointly charged with the murder, are set for the same day.

Of course, both cases will not be tried at the same time. It is generally supposed that the second case will be tried at that time, though officials have given no indication of their plans. The attorneys for both Scott and Arlene entered objections to setting the date.

* * * * * * * * * *

By the end of January, Arlene's temper and emotions were set on a short fuse. Her own small bedroom was the only place she felt comfortable and safe.... *and trapped!* She taught at school everyday, but she felt scrutinized by her students and it was hard for her to feel in charge.

The older students, by now, knew pretty much everything about the trial, even though their parents had tried to shelter them from the real truth about their teacher.

She was growing more impatient day by day with her situation, and decided to consult Mr. Trinkle as to how she might get her life back. Of course, due to her bond agreement, she couldn't leave her house and had to ask Mr. Trinkle if he could meet with her at her home. He agreed and made an appointment with her toward the end of the week.

Arlene and her mother were still not on speaking terms, and her father kept himself busy with non-existent chores. For someone as social and self-absorbed as Arlene was, her every day was made a living torment for her. She could read only so many books, grade so many papers, and write so many letters before going mad. She tried to take walks occasionally, but the January wind and cold made it unbearable to enjoy being outside for long. She longed to call Leona and ask her to come visit, but never did. She would have loved an afternoon of laughing and joking with her like they used to do. She, however, assumed her cousin most likely didn't want anything to do with her anymore, anyway. Arlene decided that was probably okay. She merely yearned for company.

She was so relieved when Saturday rolled around, and Mr. Trinkle came to visit. Bertha served hot tea and cookies at the dining table before leaving Arlene alone with her attorney. Arlene voiced her concern to him about going through a trial for something she had nothing to do with. There was no evidence she was guilty of murder and she was afraid she could not stand any more public scrutiny, especially being a school teacher in the county.

"I will apply for a writ of habeas corpus on your behalf, Arlene, on the grounds of insufficient evidence," Trinkle promised her, biting into a cookie.

"What would that do?" Arlene sighed, rolling her eyes dramatically. She had heard all this before.

"I will appeal to the State Supreme Court and hopefully they will drop all charges against you," he said with genuine hope in his voice.

"How long will that take?" Arlene asked anxiously.

"Well, these things can't be predicted, Miss Scott."

"What do you mean?" she snapped impatiently.

"The courts work on their own schedules and their own terms. If we file at the beginning of the week then I'm pretty sure you will not go to trial on February 4th. You and Ellison will most likely not be tried together, and hopefully you will be released, and not tried at all."

Arlene quickly clapped her hands together in a very juvenile way. Her mood quickly lifted and she believed she could finally see the light at the end of the tunnel.

Deadly Affair

Arlene visited with Mr. Trinkle for perhaps another half hour as they ate cookies and drank their tea.

The next few weeks were a little easier for Arlene to get through. She felt more focused on her job and in more control of her classroom. She even tried to engage in conversation with her parents once in awhile. The trial date had indeed been postponed for both her and Ellison. Nothing would be scheduled until after the Supreme Court ruled on Arlene's writ.

* * * * * * * * * *

Throughout the cold winter days at the end of 1923 and the beginning of 1924, Sarah Holt worked daily at cleaning out unwanted and unneeded possessions she and John had accumulated over their lifetime together. She needed this cleansing to revive her soul. Many days, Rob would drive Maude and her twin sister, Mabel over to the old farm and they would help their mother go through all her things. They had a great time together reminiscing, laughing and sometimes even crying about years and events gone by.

Sarah and John had purchased and planned for sometime before Ella's murder, to move to a small house in Centerville, and Sarah decided that she would move there in the spring. She hoped moving to town would be a refreshing diversion for her, and a hopeful new start.

She read the newspapers daily, and followed the events of her granddaughter and former son-in-law, but she had stopped trying to care. She had grown weary of the drama and gossip and chose to stay away from Bertha and her family.

She wanted to heal, needed to heal. She had lost her youngest daughter, became estranged from her oldest daughter, her granddaughter, and a son-in-law. Also she watched her husband wither to his death, all in the same year. She needed relief, and was determined to get it.

Toward the end of March, when a warm dry day would blow through once in awhile, Sarah decided she felt ready to make the move. Rob, along with Mabel's husband, Earl, and Blanche's husband, George all pitched in and had her moved in no time. Maude, Mabel, and Blanche had fun wiping down cabinets and closets and helping their mother put her things away.

Sarah had regained most of her strength back by spring and was enjoying making changes in her life. While she was enjoying making changes, her granddaughter, Arlene, was receiving some really bad news....

* * * * * * * * * *

In the middle of March, word was sent to Arlene that the State Supreme Court had ruled against her writ of habeas corpus, and stated she was to stand trial along with Ellison for Ella's murder.

Of course Arlene was devastated, and quickly became melancholy and felt hopeless. A couple of days after hearing this news, her mother started feeling a little compassion for her. Upon returning home from church one Sunday morning, she stopped at Arlene's bedroom door and knocked gently.

"Arlene, may I come in?" Arlene was laying on her bed reading.

"Yes," she said softly, throwing her legs over the side of the bed.

Bertha walked slowly in the room with apprehension, and sat down in the chair next to the window. She stared helplessly at her daughter.

"I'm really sorry you are going to have to stand trial for Ella's murder," she cleared her throat, as a tear ran down her cheek. "I'm worn out with the coldness between us, child," she said, wiping her nose with her Sunday hanky.

"Oh... Mama!" Arlene leaped into her mother's arms.

"Both women sobbed for sometime in each others embrace. After they wiped their tears, and blew their noses, they relaxed some in each other's company. They both realized their relationship was damaged, but hopefully not destroyed.

"Arlene... you didn't...." her mother started with caution.

"NO MAMA! NO!" Arlene cried. "I have been such a fool, but I've never meant to hurt anyone... NEVER!" she started crying again.

Bertha started calmly rubbing her daughters arm, as she stared out the window, as if looking for answers in the sky.

"I have been such a fool," Arlene moaned. "I'm so sorry, Mama. I'm so sorry any of this has happened. But I had nothing to do with Aunt Ella's murder."

"Do you think Ellison murdered her?" Bertha asked boldly.

Arlene shook her head slowly. "I don't know, Mama. I really do not know." Arlene buried her face in her hands and continued to cry.

"Well...." Bertha sighed. "Hopefully this will all be over soon," she lied to herself.

~CHAPTER NINETEEN~

Arlene headed off to the school house early Monday morning, feeling better after having reconciled with her mother the day before. The morning air was crisp and very cold, but the sky was blue and there was a chance the day would warm up later.

She cleaned the blackboards of chalk, once she had built a small fire in the stove. By the time the children started to arrive, she felt prepared for the day's lessons. She always let the children visit with each other for a few minutes before getting started on lessons. While they were visiting, Arlene started writing arithmetic problems on the board. Easy problems for the smaller children, and more difficult problems for the older students.

The morning hours went by quickly and by noon the weather had warmed enough that Arlene let the students go outside to eat their lunch and play for awhile. She sat on the porch steps and ate her sandwich and watched the children play. It was a good day, and so wonderful to feel the warm spring sun on her shoulders. Every once in awhile she would think of the trial hanging over her head, but for the most part she dealt with each day as it came along, and tried not to dwell on it.

As she was sitting on the porch, eating an apple she noticed a black sedan driving slowly by the schoolhouse. Two men were in the front seat, and even though she couldn't tell who they were, they were staring hard at her. A chill ran down her back. She watched as the car drove down the road, and out of sight. She then hollered at the children to start putting their trash in the barrel and picking up their things to go inside. She had been unnerved. She wanted to get the children inside as soon as possible. When she did, she locked the door behind her.

When everyone had settled in their seats, she decided to start the afternoon reading another chapter of *Tom Sawyer* to the class, while they settled down from playing outside. She leaned on the corner of her desk where she could look out the window as she was reading. Half way into the chapter, she was distracted by the same black sedan driving slowly be the school. She kept reading the story, hoping the children didn't notice the concern in her voice. Once she was done with the chapter, she put the book away and decided to have a spelling bee. The class loved participating in a spelling bee. It always lightened the atmosphere in the room. The children enjoyed being able to laugh and talk out loud and this was almost the only time they were allowed to do so. Everyone was having fun, all except the students who misspelled their word and had to sit in the chairs by the wall.

At about 1:45 that afternoon, there was a loud knock at the door. The classroom erupted in pandemonium at the interruption. The last time there had been a knock at the door the sheriff had taken the teacher to jail. The children were truly frightened, and so was Arlene, even though she tried not to show it for the sake of the children. She calmed the children down and told them to take their seats, as she walked slowly to the window to see if she could tell who it was. She was shocked to see across the school yard there was a man dressed in Ku Klux Klan regalia standing next to a small cross he had stuck in the ground. She let out a small scream before she could cover her mouth. At that moment there was another, even louder bang on the door. She opened the door slowly, and encountered another man dressed as a Ku Klux Klan member standing on the other side of the door. Arlene was startled and let out another quick scream. She closed the door slightly so the students would not be frightened, but not before some of the students sitting by the wall had caught a glimpse of the man. A couple of the boys gasped at the sight of him and Arlene was terrified. How was she going to protect her classroom?

The man at the door said nothing, he only handed her a letter signed 'The Ku Klux Klan' and walked away.

Arlene briefly looked out the door and watched the two men walk back to the black sedan, get in and drive away. She quickly closed and locked the door and walked back to her desk and sat down hard in her chair. She was visibly shaking, and the students became quiet, as they were scared as well. She called Susan Moore, a shy eighth grade student to come to the head of the class and continue with the spelling bee. She then excused herself and walked to the hallway that entered into the water closet where she broke down and sobbed.

She reluctantly opened the letter and read the contents. Her face turned white, and her hands were shaking. *How much more can I take!*

When she was able to get herself under control, she splashed cold water on her face and ran her fingers absently through her hair. When she walked back in the classroom, the children were engaged with the spelling bee, and she sat down at her desk and watched. She told Susan to go ahead and finish the words, that she was doing a great job. Arlene didn't trust herself to be able to take over. She sat at her desk, trying to quit shaking. She had a half hour left in the school day to try to stay composed and professional.

As the children left the school house that afternoon, they couldn't help but notice the wooden cross standing on the far end of the schoolyard.

Deadly Affair

Arlene was once again horrified of what her students and their parents would think of her and the situation.

* * * * * * * * * *

Mr. Hall arrived as soon as he could Monday evening at the home of Arlene's parents. Arlene had calmed down some by the time he arrived. By now she was just angry.

"What's going on?!" he asked, when Arlene opened the door for him.

"Come on in, Mr. Hall. I received an interesting letter today, from a very interesting person, in a very interesting way." she said leading him to a chair in the living room. She wasn't really trying to be sarcastic, but it came out that way anyhow.

Mr. Hall opened the letter and began reading. The letter was typewritten, and had been signed by representatives of the Ku Klux Klan. The letter stated the Klan organization represents law abiding citizens and warned Miss Scott, that being a person of ill repute, she should not set her foot inside the school house again, or her punishment would be such she wouldn't forget it for fifty years. There were more empty threats written as well, plus the claim that the letter was backed by sixty thousand members of the Klan.

Mr. Hall read the letter over and over, before speaking a word. He cleared his throat. "Miss Scott... I'm so sorry you have to deal with such things," he said sincerely.

Arlene was staring at something across the room, totally disengaged.

"Arlene...?" Mr. Hall gently touched her forearm as he watched a single tear fall down her cheek.

She slowly turned her gaze to her attorney. "What am I supposed to do now?" she said with defeat in her voice. "I wish I could just wake up in my little room at Aunt Ella's house and I could run into her kitchen and give her a huge hug, laughing about the most horrible dream I had," she whispered.

"Miss Scott," Mr. Hall patted her arm, "I'll talk to the sheriff immediately and make sure there are guards at the school. We'll make sure no harm comes to you or your students," he tried to assure her.

She tried to smile, but only made a halfhearted attempt. "What are my children going to think?" she shook her head.

"I'm going to leave now, Arlene, and head over to the sheriff's office. We will make sure you and the children can come and go from the school house safely."

She nodded her head slowly, and rose from her chair and walked him to the door.

"Thank you, Mr. Hall," she tried to sound sincere, as she closed the door behind him. She begged off supper and went straight to her room for the night.

* * * * * * * * *

THE LA CYGNE JOURNAL
FRIDAY APRIL 11, 1924

THE SCOTT CASE AGAIN

The Scott case was called in the district court at Mound City Tuesday and after motions and arguments by the attorneys the original charge against Ellison Scott was set for trial on Tuesday, April 22, and the charge against him in which he was charged jointly with Arlene Scott was dismissed although the charge against Arlene Scott remains on the docket as a separate case.

Thursday's, Kansas City Journal had a story to the effect that the case against Arlene Scott had been dismissed, but this was a mistake as the original charge against Miss Scott still stands.

As the case now stands the defendants are to be tried separately.

* * * * * * * * *

THE LA CYGNE JOURNAL
FRIDAY APRIL 18, 1924

THE SCOTT TRIAL NEXT WEEK

The trial of the case of the state vs. J. Ellison Scott, in which Scott is charged with the murder of his wife in La Cygne last June, is set for next Tuesday, April 22, in the district court at Mound City. Scott will be tried on the original charge, instead of the one in which Arlene Scott is charged jointly with him in the crime.

The date for the trial of the case against Arlene has not been set and it appears now that whether or not the case ever comes to trial depends on the outcome of the trial of Ellison Scott next week.

* * * * * * * * * *

THE KANSAS CITY TIMES, THURSDAY, APRIL 24, 1924

Mound City, Kans., April 23 - A jury of young farmers, all married, will hear the testimony in the murder trial of Ellison Scott.

The jury was finally completed at 5 o'clock this afternoon and adjournment taken until 9 o'clock tomorrow morning when the first witnesses will be called. It was chosen from a regular and special venire of 75 men.

In the examination of the talismen, it was revealed a great many had formed opinions and were dismissed for that reason. It took two days to choose the ultimate twelve.

~CHAPTER TWENTY~

Finally, on Thursday, April 24th, Ellison's second trial began. The day was overcast and a steady rain had been pouring for hours. The courtroom was full of spectators as with the first trial, and Ellison felt just as nervous and anxious today as he did then. The state proceeded to break down Ellison's recollection of the night of Ella's murder according to the witness of neighbors.

Mrs. L.P. Bishop, Mrs Laura Rynerson, Mrs. Charles Anderson, and Mrs. C.E. Hesser all testified they heard the shots the night of the murder, and simultaneously heard the scream of a woman. Lucy Rynerson, Laura's daughter, and the other women also testified the screams appeared to be cut short by the second shot.

The importance of this evidence, being the contradiction with Scott's story of the shooting. Scott said he was at work in his garage, when he heard two shots; that he could not determine where the sound came from; that he heard no screams.

The state contended that if the neighbors heard the screams, then Scott himself must have heard screams. Equally important was the evidence as to the time that elapsed between the time the Scotts reached their home the night of the murder and the time the shots were fired. The state produced a witness who said she saw the Scotts come home and drive into their garage, and that it was more than ten minutes afterwards that the shots were fired that killed Ella. This testimony was for the purpose of destroying Scott's alibi. The testimony showed he might have done the work on the car and then entered the house and fired the shots that killed his wife.

The state, having produced all this testimony to break down Scott's defense, then proceeded to the second phase of their theory - that Scott murdered his wife because of his infatuation for Arlene Scott. Witness after witness testified, as in the preliminary hearing, as to the relationship existing between Ellison and Arlene. The state had traced this infatuation and produced witnesses to prove Mrs. Ella Scott, several months before her death, had complained of the relations. It also showed the relationship continued after Mrs. Scott's death.

The state produced evidence and witnesses, for the most part, that were rendered in the preliminary hearing and rested their case by Friday afternoon. Judge Gates adjourned court until Monday morning, when the defense would begin their rebuttal.

* * * * * * * * * *

Come Monday morning, April 28th, before a packed courtroom, Hall and Trinkle put into evidence the bulk of the testimony.

Seven witnesses testified they heard the shots that killed Mrs. Scott, but did not hear screams of a woman.

Members of the Carnegey family, living across the street from the Scott home, testified they heard shots, but no screams.

Hall and Trinkle spent most of the day trying to dispute the state's accusations of their client's guilt. Their only strategy was to try and explain away the state's charges and they did the best they could to keep their heads above water.

First thing Tuesday morning, Ellison went on the stand in his own defense. For the first time, the courtroom was crowded to capacity. Standing room only. It had rained for several days in the county, and by now the roads were beginning to dry, allowing vehicles to pass on them easier. Hundreds of farmers from miles around came to town to attend the trial. Court-room attaches made improvised seats with planks to accommodate as many people as possible.

As Ellison walked to the stand to take his oath, a solemn hush fell over the courtroom. Hall had made sure that Ellison had once again had a haircut and a clean shave, Monday afternoon after court recessed. Ellison's shirt and pants were smartly pressed, and he looked the part of a law abiding citizen.

Ellison took the stand and wiped his forehead with his folded handkerchief.

John Hall walked to the stand and calmly asked Ellison to tell the court, as he waved his hand toward the jury and on around the crowded room, his recollection of the night of June 19th, 1923.

Ellison cleared his throat and proceeded to tell his side of the story... *again.* His account of Ella's murder read almost word for word as his testimony in the first trial.

"I was in the garage oiling the clutch of my motor car, when I heard two shots. I walked to the front door and looked up and down the street. I saw no one. I went back to the car and then, feeling something was wrong, went into the house. I saw my wife on the floor and cried out, 'My God, Ella, what has happened?' Then I knelt down beside her and asked her to talk to me. I could see she was breathing, but her eyes were closed. I jumped up and went to the west door and called for help, and then went back and knelt again. 'Tell me what happened,' I asked her, but she made no reply. Then I discovered blood, and saw that she had been shot. I immediately rose and ran out the door, calling for help, and went to the doctor's house. After arousing the doctor, who lived a block away, I ran back home and found several men in the house. One of them put his hand on my shoulder and told me they had plenty of help, and I should go sit down."

"Mr. Scott," his attorney asked, "did you ever at anytime have improper relations with your niece, Arlene Scott."

"No. Never," he stated emphatically.

"Mr. Scott, do you own, or have you ever owned a .32 caliber revolver?"

"No, sir." was his reply.

"Mr. Scott, did you fire the two shots that killed your wife?"

"I did not, sir."

"Mr. Scott, do you know who did fire the shots?"

"I do not." was all he said.

"No further questions, Your Honor," Hall said, as he walked back to the defense table.

"Does the prosecution wish to cross examine," the judge asked.

"Yes, Your Honor, I have one question to ask Mr. Scott," Attorney General Griffith stated, as he walked toward the stand.

"Mr. Scott, you stated that when you realized your wife had been shot, you ran from the house calling for help as you rushed to the doctor's house. Is that correct?"

"Yes, sir...." Ellison replied.

"Mr. Scott, why didn't you step to the phone and call the doctor so you could stay and attend to your wife?"

Ellison Scott sat stunned. At first he didn't understand the implication of the question, that he would have had an opportunity to hide a gun in the bushes along the way to the doctor's house.

"I was in shock, sir. Getting the doctor was by first thought. I wasn't thinking straight," was all Ellison could think to say.

"No further questions Your Honor," the Attorney General said, walking back to the prosecution table.

Ellison was dismissed from the stand, and Reverend M.C. Molesworth was called as the next witness. Ellison almost fell as he left the stand. His legs were weak and barely held him up. As he walked toward the defense table, Hall noticed he was having trouble and jumped up to meet him halfway. Hall grabbed his arm and supported him back to the table. He then poured a glass of water, and handed it to Ellison. He drank heartily from

Deadly Affair

it and seemed to recover some. There were whispers in the courtroom as Reverend Molesworth was being sworn in.
"What a great effect to display before the jury!"
"I wonder if he is really upset, or if he's putting on a show?"
"I don't feel sorry for him."
"I do."

Once on the stand, the Reverend testified as to Ellison's overall good character. He spoke of his constant church attendance, his willingness to help out in the community, and that he had been a good neighbor for several years. He testified as well, that he never witnessed any strife between Ellison and his wife.

The last witness on the stand was Dr. S.D. Morrison, the physician who attended to Ella the night she was murdered. Dr. Morrison was by no means a combative witness, but he was indeed a reluctant one. He cared a lot about Ellison and had an arrant need to believe he was innocent. He had set through all the hearings and the first trial, listening to all the testimony, good and bad, and had been broken hearted to hear things about Ellison he didn't want to believe were true. He, himself had testified more times than he had wanted to, and did not wish to testify again at this point. He did, however tell of the events of the night of Ella's murder and what he had done to try to help the dying woman.

Before he was allowed to leave the stand, however, Attorney General Griffith cross- examined him vigorously to try to show that he, Dr. Morrison, had a special interest in Scott's behalf. He attempted to draw from the physician an admission that he had tried to induce witnesses to change their testimony, but Hall objected and the court sustained his objection. The defense rested.

* * * * * * * * *

After the opening argument for the State by W.A. Smith, the defense announced they would waive their argument. This was Trinkle's idea, the strategy being to prevent the Attorney General from too strongly arguing the case before the jury.

When the defense rested, the case was immediately given to the jury. Judge Gates instructed the jurors that they must be fair to Ellison Scott, but that if they believed him guilty beyond a reasonable doubt, it was their duty to find a verdict against him.

"Certain punishment is the surest remedy for lawlessness." Judge Gates finished.

The jury was also instructed they might find a verdict of first or second degree murder or manslaughter, in the first, second, or third degree. After the instructions were given, the jury exited to the small room next to the judge's chambers. They were out all night, deliberating their verdict. It was a long and bitter night for Ellison Scott. He could not fall asleep, even though his body was crippled from exhaustion. His mind would not shut down. Thoughts of the past, year, the trial, and the despair of his future prospects were shouting loudly in his head. He was upset that the possibility of a stranger burglarizing his home and killing his wife had not been presented during this trial. He felt the stranger, or the thought of a stranger, was his only hope for reasonable doubt. His attorneys, however, had been reluctant to play that card all along because it couldn't be proven.

A couple of hours after lying down, Ellison started developing a pounding headache that tortured him as he dozed in and out of shallow sleep during the night. By morning light he felt as though someone had been beating him for hours.

When Hall and Trinkle entered the jail to escort him to the courthouse, they were extremely concerned about their client's well being. They helped him dress, and Hall went downstairs to retrieve a cup of coffee for him. While Ellison was getting ready for what he hoped was his last day in court, Deputy Lindsey brought him a tray holding a light breakfast.

By the time 8 o'clock rolled around the sheriff was notified the jury was still out. He decided then that Ellison should stay in his cell until a verdict was rendered, only adding to Ellison's anxiety.

Hall and Trinkle decided to walk on over to the courthouse and wait for the verdict there.

The day had started out warm and sunny and the attorneys noticed that people were already gathering on the courthouse lawn. Many had laid out blankets and quilts on the grass to sit on while they waited to hear the verdict. Some had picnic baskets full of food, in case they would be there all day. County citizens from miles around wanted to be able to say they were there the day the verdict came down on the Scott murder case. As the morning dragged on and turned into early afternoon, people started growing impatient. Many loud arguments broke out as opinions of Ellison's guilt or innocence became vigorously debated.

About 2 o'clock in the afternoon the jury sent a note to the judge that they had reached a verdict. When Sheriff Ellington was notified the verdict had been reached, he walked over to the courthouse lawn and instructed the crowd to either settle in the courtroom or go on home, so Ellison could be brought to the courthouse in peace to learn his fate. People started moving quickly and with excitement into the building to find a good seat. Hall

Deadly Affair

and Trinkle, by now, had returned to the jail to escort their client to the courthouse. Before they got there, Ellison had thrown up his breakfast, and was once again heaving when they reached his cell.

"Are you going to be okay, Scott?" Trinkle asked with concern.

Deputy Lindsey quickly unlocked the cell door so the attorneys could enter then ran to find some rags and a mop to clean up the mess Ellison had made.

Hall rushed to Ellison, who had sat down on the edge of the cot with his head in his hands. Hall took his handkerchief out of his pocket and handed it to Ellison.

"Thanks, man." he whispered.

Trinkle took out his own handkerchief and ran cold water over it from the tiny sink in Ellison's cell. Ellison rubbed the cold cloth slowly over his face and around the back of his neck. He could see the genuine concern on their faces and worked at making half a smile.

"Just nerves, boys... just nerves. I don't know how much more of this I can take.

He shook his head slowly and began to cough. He carefully worked to put on his shoes and gradually tried standing.

"Are you sure you're okay?"

"No! I'm not okay!" Ellison choked, as he grabbed for the wall to steady himself. "But I will have to make it anyway, now won't I?" he said irritated.

He sluggishly walked to the cell door as Hall helped him on with his suit coat, and brushed at his hair with his hand. When Ellison stepped out of his cell the deputy cuffed his hands in front of him and bent down to cuff his ankles together with a sturdy chain. Ellison still had Hall's handkerchief in his hand and would wipe his face from time to time as they all walked slowly and carefully down the stairs. Sheriff Ellington was standing outside the jailhouse waiting when the men emerged. He had been watching the crowds of people disperse and had decided it was probably okay to bring Ellison across the street to the courthouse.

Once again, the courtroom was congested. A few people were even standing in the hallway waiting for the verdict, when Hall and Trinkle escorted their client in the room. Upon reaching the courthouse door the deputy removed Ellison's leg irons, but left the cuffs on his hands. When he sat at the defense table Ellison leaned over to Hall and asked him if he would pour him a glass of water, and he did.

A subtle hush fell over the crowd along with gasps and murmurs at seeing Ellison in handcuffs. The judge entered the room as the assembly rose and sat when he did. The jury was then allowed into the room from the deliberation room off to the judge's right side. When all the twelve men were seated, Judge Gates asked the jury collectively if they had reached a verdict, and the foreman spoke up and said they had.

The bailiff was ordered to take the verdict paper from the foreman to the judge. After the judge read the verdict he then passed it back to the bailiff to return to the foreman.

The whir of the ceiling fans became the only sound in the room.

On this day, the day Ellison's fate was to be revealed, the members of Ella's family were all in attendance, even Arlene. All except, of course, grandchildren under the age of eighteen. Arlene did not sit next to her parents. They sat on the southeast side of the room. She sat near the door, so she could exit the minute the verdict was read. Jonah Holt sat next to Sarah and her daughters, and their families. They all sat on the west side of the room, and without realizing it, they all reached out to hold one another's hands.

The judge asked the defendant to stand for the verdict to be read. The foreman stood to receive the paper.

"We the jury find the defendant, John Ellison Scott, guilty of murder in the second degree." The foreman stood stoic, looking at the far wall, so he wouldn't see any reaction from anyone in the room.

"So says all?" the judge asked the foreman.

"So says all," the foreman confirmed.

Ellison's legs turned to jelly and he sat down hard in his chair. He buried his face in his hands and silently wept. The courtroom erupted with cheers and boos and Judge Gates had to slam his gavel several times to quiet the room.

Tears immediately poured down Sarah's face. She couldn't get a hold of her emotions and started sobbing uncontrollably. For so long she had steeled herself against any bias concerning her daughter's murder. She wanted the murder solved but she didn't want to believe Ellison had shot her baby. She certainly didn't want to think Arlene had anything to do with it, yet her feelings for Arlene had changed so much.

Arlene herself was sobbing, but her concerns were not for Ellison, but for her own fate and what she might be facing. She quickly left the courtroom and the building before anyone could say a word to her.

Across the room, Charles and Mollie Scott, wailed, wrapped in each other's arms. They didn't want to believe their son was convicted of murder, and they didn't want to think about what might happen to him now.

The judge slammed his gavel one more time. Ellison's attorneys immediately filed a motion for a new trial and a hearing. The motion was to be brought before Judge Gates on the following Friday.

Deadly Affair

* * * * * * * * * *

Ellison's legs were again cuffed at the ankles before he was led away from the courtroom. Hall and Trinkle helped guide him out of the room, as Ellison's strength was spent.

Once he was on his way back to the jailhouse, the people in the courtroom were allowed to leave. People slowly and carefully exited the building. Some stopped on the courthouse lawn to discuss the event they had just witnessed. Most dispersed and headed to their homes or businesses.

The sheriff escorted Ellison back to the jail, but Hall was holding him up as he walked. Ellison didn't say anything on the way, only moaned and sobbed. He had finally broken.

Upon reaching the jail cell, the sheriff removed the cuffs from Ellison's wrists and ankles.

He helped him into his cell and steadied him as he sat on his cot. The sheriff started to tell Ellison to change his clothes back into his jumpsuit so he could take his dress clothes to hang up until the next time he needed them for court, but decided to wait. Ellison rolled over on his cot facing the wall, sobbing and trembling. Hall asked him if he needed anything, but Ellison did not respond so the attorney walked out of the cell. I'll check on him after while," the sheriff said sincerely. He knew the attorneys were genuinely concerned about their client.

* * * * * * * * * *

Saturday morning, the day after Ellison's conviction, Arlene was sitting in the swing on the front porch of her home, when a beat-up truck pulled off road into her drive. Her heart sank. The last thing she wanted was any company today. She had been very shaken by her uncle's fate, and wrestled constantly in her mind with how to deal with her own pending doom. As the truck approached, Arlene suddenly recognized the driver. She stood up from the swing and walked down the porch steps to greet her visitor.

The young man parked his truck under the shade of the old oak tree. The driver's side door popped and loudly screeched as he opened it to step out.

"Hi, Charlie!" Arlene called and waved from the sidewalk by the porch.

"Hey, Arlene! Young Charlie Ferguson hollered to her as he walked around the back of his truck. Arlene felt a sudden flutter of excitement when she saw Charlie. They had attended Cemetery School together before she went off to high school in La Cygne. As he walked toward her she remembered how she used to tease and flirt with him during recess in the schoolyard. The thought put a smile on her face.

"Whatcha' smiling 'bout?" he asked, smiling himself.

"It's good to see you, that's all," she said sweetly.

"Good to see you, too..." he said, as he produced a bouquet of flowers from behind his back and handed them to her.

"Charlie!" she exclaimed, "For me?!" she was truly thrilled and her eyes started watering. Nothing so nice had happened to her in a really long time, and she was genuinely touched.

"For you!" he said, as she reached out to take the bouquet.

Upon hearing voices outside, Bertha came to the front door to see what was going on. She was surprised to see Charlie Ferguson handing her daughter flowers, but she was pleased to see him.

"Well Charlie, what on earth brings you here?!" she said light heartedly, as she stepped out on the porch. She had been washing dishes and she was wiping her hands on her apron.

"Hello, Mrs. Scott," he said as he tipped his hat.

"Look, Mama!" Arlene cried, "aren't they just beautiful?!" She stuck her face in the middle of the flowers and inhaled vigorously.

Charlie was a little embarrassed by Arlene's reaction. He had planned to make her happy, but the flowers were some he had picked in the field before coming over to see her. Nothing really special.

"They sure are, Dear!" Bertha said, as she walked down the steps toward them. Realizing Charlie had come to 'call' on Arlene, she suddenly needed a reason to leave the two of them alone.

"How about I go put these flowers in a vase of water for you, while you two visit?"

"Thanks, Mama," Arlene said, handing the flowers to her. Bertha took the flowers and walked back to the house.

"Would you like to go sit on the porch swing for awhile?" Arlene asked, suddenly feeling a little awkward.

Charlie sheepishly took Arlene's hand. "How 'bout going for a walk instead?" he smiled.

"Yeah... well... okay, but I can't go far," she looked at her feet, a little embarrassed. "I'm under house arrest and can't leave the property."

"I know, Arlene. We won't go far."

"Okay," she smiled.

~CHAPTER TWENTY-ONE~

Rob and Maude drove Sarah home Friday afternoon after the verdict was read. They rode home in silence. There wasn't much to say. They all were relieved there had been justice served and hoped they could start healing now. No one was thinking of Arlene at this point. As far as they were concerned, Ellison's conviction meant the end of the whole affair. Even though Sarah had not mentioned Arlene for some time, most of the family felt Arlene would be on her own. Whether she would eventually be convicted was of no concern to Sarah at this point. She could not find a way to forgive her. She had chosen not to get involved in her granddaughter's future and without saying as much, so had everyone else.

Leona sat in the back seat, staring out the window, lost in her own thoughts. She hadn't spoken to Arlene since the day she'd testified against her, and she felt she would probably never have a reason to speak to her again. The two young ladies who were once so very close had been severely divided by a chasm of moral deceit that had changed both lives forever. They would never see each other in the same way again and Leona had decided moving on with their lives would be best for both of them. Well, for herself, anyway. She let out a sorrowful sigh, as she watched trees and telephone poles quickly fly by the window. Wilma sat quietly, oblivious to everyone's weariness. She was hoping her Grandma might have a piece of cake or pie for her when they got to her house.

Rob drove along the bumpy gravel road trying to steer as straight as the road would allow. In his own heart he was relieved the verdict had been rendered guilty. He had been wrestling in his mind what to do about what John Holt had told him about the gun last November. He had thought about going to the sheriff with this information, but he was afraid the sheriff would think him daft for listening to the rambling of a dying old broken hearted man. Then again, he was also afraid the sheriff might consider checking into the prospect and order Ella's grave exhumed. The idea of that happening terrified Rob and he didn't want to think about that. He knew his wife and her family would be horrified and never forgive him. The fact that Ellison had been convicted freed Rob's conscience somewhat, to keep what he knew to himself. He had not told a soul and didn't know if he ever would. He had spent a few sleepless nights between the first and second trials wondering if it was his moral duty to say something. If the casket had been exhumed and the gun was there, there would be no question of Ellison's guilt. He was glad he didn't have to think about it anymore.

In the middle of May, 1924, Leona headed to Pittsburg teachers college so she too could become a teacher. She had put in an application to teach at the Washington county school in the fall term. The Washington school was about a mile east of her parents' farm and was the school she and her sister, Wilma, attended in their elementary years. She didn't attend teachers college the summer before with Arlene because Rob needed her help working the farm. This summer she insisted on going to school, and after many arguments about it, Rob finally gave in and agreed to let her go. She was so excited to be on her own and free to make her own decisions. She was glad to be free from the dark cloud of her aunt's murder and the constant conversations around it by every family member nearly everyday. She was also glad to be free from her sister's constant persistence to tag along with her everywhere she went. She was happy to be away from the farm, and all the hard work she was expected to do daily.

* * * * * * * * *

Rob hired a couple of local farm boys to help him in the fields and for the most part, life in Linn County was back to a hum of familiar summer Kansas farm life. The men worked in the fields, and the women worked in their homes and gardens, and went to the Ladies Aid meetings. The thought of murder and trials were mostly forgotten.

Forgotten by most, but not by Arlene Scott. The first of July, she had been notified by her attorney, John Hall, that her case was on the docket in district court on July 14th.

Since May, Arlene had been seeing Charlie Ferguson on a regular basis, and he had become her whole world in the previous weeks. He told her he had always had a crush on her and she admitted she always liked him, too. They spent a lot of time together talking and making plans. He had saved her from a boring summer of doing nothing more than helping her mother with chores. She had allowed herself the fantasy of believing the nightmares of the past year were completely over and she was free of it all. However, when Mr. Hall had stopped by her house on July 1st with the news of her upcoming hearing, reality hit her hard once again.

Charlie had promised he would drive her to the hearing so she wouldn't have to go alone, and she was grateful for his support. He had become a solid confidant to Arlene, and he never judged her about anything. She needed that kind of friendship in her life right now.

Deadly Affair

It was a very hot and dusty morning when Charlie arrived to pick her up. She had chosen a light-weight yellow sun dress to wear, so she could feel as cool as possible on such a hot day. She had tied her hair back in a bun to try to keep it controlled on the windy ride to town. Before Charlie backed his truck out of the drive, she tied a scarf around her head to protect herself from the dust.

As Charlie pulled up to the courthouse, Arlene felt a flood of anxiety rush over her. She had not had to think about Ella and Ellison, or the trials for several weeks and really didn't want to be here again. After parking, Charlie jumped out of his truck and walked around to Arlene's side to open her door, and help her out of the truck. They both walked up the steps of the court- house together, through the double doors and down the hall to the county clerks office. Arlene announced to the clerk that she was present for her hearing, and was told to take a seat to wait for further instruction. Within a few minutes, Charles Trinkle walked into the office and walked over to talk to the clerk. Arlene tried to hear their conversation but was unable to make out their words from across the room. When he was finished talking to the clerk, she wrote something down in a book and walked back to her desk. Mr. Trinkle crossed the room to Arlene and put out his hand to help her out of her chair. She introduced him to Charlie before asking him what was going on.

"It seems your hearing has been postponed until a later date, Miss Scott."

"What do you mean?!" Arlene asked, both relieved and upset.

"What does this mean for me?" she asked, anxiously.

"Well, it isn't unusual for hearings and court dates to be postponed or cancelled on a moments notice, unfortunately. So I guess you go back home and continue on," Trinkle said apologetically.

Arlene sighed hard. "This whole thing is killing me!" she said, clenching her fists. "I'm so worn out, not being able to live my life without this murder trial hanging over my head!" Tears filled her eyes. "I just want my freedom back," she whispered.

"Sit down a minute, Arlene," Trinkle said, gently pushing her shoulders to guide her in a chair. He sat next to her.

"Arlene, I know this is hard for you, but now that Ellison has been convicted of murder, the case against you will probably, eventually, be dropped. They really have no evidence of murder against you, and I'm all but sure your arrest was to the benefit of convicting Ellison."

Arlene took a lacy handkerchief from her purse and wiped her eyes.

"Can I come and go as I please, then?" Arlene asked, hopefully.

"I'm afraid not, Arlene. Not until the court orders all the charges against you dropped. You are still under the conclusion of your bond."

"Mr. Trinkle," Arlene started timidly, "What should I do about teaching this fall? The superintendent has asked me to think about stepping down, so someone else could teach this fall semester. They don't want to deal with any more threats and they really don't want to hire armed guards to protect the children and me. Do you think this will all be over by the time school starts this fall?"

Trinkle shook his head slowly. "I can't even begin to think what the court plans to do, but I do know cases could continue to be scheduled before your case. Maybe you should take a year off teaching, and see if the superintendent won't contract with you for a future position."

She looked hard at Trinkle and realized he was being sincere. He might not know how long it would take for her trial to be over, but she trusted he know it would probably take longer than she would want to think.

"Okay," she sighed, with resolve. "Thanks." She shook his hand gently. "I guess I will just sit at home and wait." She tried to smile.

Charlie lightly put his hand on the small of her back and led her out of the room, after tipping his hat to the attorney.

Arlene sat silently on the ride home, and Charlie didn't try to talk to her. He could not begin to understand what she was going through, and what she had been through. He knew the story, but he couldn't imagine the depth of the emotions, and how someone's mental health could be affected. He felt bad for her, and wished he could make it all go away for her. On arriving at her house, he pulled the truck up to the front walk and started to get out and open her door, but she grabbed his hand and told him she would be okay. She opened her door, as it popped and squeaked, she climbed out to the walk and shut the door. She didn't really want Charlie's sympathy or even encouragement right then, she just wanted to be alone.

"I'll talk to you later, Charlie." She gave him a slight smile. "Thanks for the ride"

She turned and walked up the porch steps and into the house without looking back.

Arlene walked into the kitchen and set her purse on the counter. She picked up the receiver on the wall phone and flipped the handle a couple of times to signal the operator.

"Operator. How may I help you?" Mrs. McGee answered.

"Would you be so kind as to ring Superintendent Morgan for me, please..."

* * * * * * * * *

Deadly Affair

John Hall and Charles Trinkle spent the next several months working on appeals for a new trial for Ellison Scott.

The Linn county district court allowed Ellison to remain in the county jail rather than being transferred to Lansing prison, where he had been sentenced to serve his time.

In September, Scott's attorneys filed a motion in the Kansas Supreme Court, claiming that one of the jurors, in Ellison's second trial, David Johnson, was prejudiced against Ellison, and should have been dismissed. He had mentioned after the trial to many other jurors that he believed Ellison to be guilty and thought so all along. The jurors had signed affidavits claiming David Johnson had been angry that the jury in the first trial had not convicted Ellison, and he should have never been selected as a juror in Ellison's second trial. However, in early October the Supreme Court denied the motion of Scott's attorneys as a reason for a new trial. Trinkle and Hall kept working on an appeal strategy for a new trial. The attorneys decided to file a motion that the court didn't allow evidence of a possible stranger who might have killed Ella Scott in the process of burglarizing her house. It was such a long shot, and one that they were apprehensive about, as they still didn't have any proof of such an occurrence happening. They felt they had to try to build on that theme, as that seemed to be their only possibility of a new trial. They put in long hours every day working to get Scott an appeal, and sometimes turned away other possible clients because they were so involved with Ellison's case.

Finally their hard work paid off, when in December, the Kansas Supreme Court reversed Ellison's verdict and granted motion for a new trial.

~CHAPTER TWENTY-TWO~

THE LA CYGNE JOURNAL, FRIDAY, DECEMBER 12, 1924

Supreme Court Reverses Linn County Verdict

Last Saturday the state supreme court reversed the decision of the district court of Linn County in the case of J. Ellison Scott, charged with the murder of his wife, Ella on June 19th, 1923, and sent the case back to Linn County for a new trial. The reversal was on the ground that the district court should have allowed the defense to submit to the Jury the evidence that a stranger had been seen to board a train leaving La Cygne a few minutes after the time of the murder.

The decision of the court ordering a revisal was reached by five members, Justice Harvey wrote the opinion and was joined by Justices Burch, Mason, Marshall and Dawson.

Richard J. Hopkins, associate justice, wrote a dissenting opinion, assailing the majority opinion of the court, and in this dissent Justice Hopkins was joined by W.A. Johnston, Chief Justice of the Supreme Court. In his dissenting opinion Justice Hopkins detailed many of the circumstances of the murder. Following is the text of Justice Hopkins' opinion as printed in Saturday's Kansas City Star:

"The admitted actions of the defendant himself at the time of the tragedy, the things he did and the things that he failed to do must have had weight with the jury in its conclusion that he was the guilty party. First, he heard the shots, but no scream, although six witnesses testified positively that they heard the scream of a woman, either between the firing of the two shots or immediately after the last one, or that scream was cut off by a second shot. These witnesses lived north, east and west of the Scott home. Two of them lived north and beyond the garage where the defendant said he was at the time the shots were fired. Second, (and if the defendant is not guilty these things are so remarkable they pass understanding), the defendant, on discovering

Deadly Affair

that his wife had been mortally wounded, left her lying on the floor alone in the house while he went away. He met a friend in the street, told him to go to his wife while the defendant himself went a block and a half away from home to get the doctor. He could've stepped to his own telephone, called the doctor and remained to minister to the needs of his dying wife, or, he could have sent his friend for the doctor and himself remained. Third, he did nothing, nor asked anybody to take action to ascertain and capture the guilty party. Other people did that. Fourth, after returning to his home from the doctor's, when other people had gathered and were endeavoring to save his dying wife, the defendant sat down in a chair near the door with his back to her and the people administering to her.

"The defense makes much of the fact that a gun with which the shots were fired was not found on the premises. It was the most reasonable thing in the world that it was not found. Doubtless the jury concluded that when the defendant ran away through the darkness a block and a half from the scene of the tragedy, threw away the revolver. Anywhere on his journey of a block and a half in the darkness, he could have thrown the revolver 150 or 200 feet either north or south and so far away from his own premises that as a matter of course it would not be found there.

"It should not be overlooked that an able trial court had considered the matters presented in the case three times previous to the trial under consideration. First, in a preliminary hearing, when the defendant was charged jointly with Arlene Scott. With this situation the defendant offered testimony that within five minutes after the tragedy a strange man was seen across the street from the Scott home going toward the main street of La Cygne; that about the same time, or a little later, a man was seen running along the right-of-way of the Frisco railroad several blocks distance from the scene of the tragedy; that a man was seen by two trainmen on a Frisco freight train that came through La Cygne about 2 or 3 o'clock in the morning; that the train had been examined at Paola and nobody was riding it except the train crew; that from a photograph this man that was seen on the freight train was a man who had been in the penitentiary and had been convicted of petty larceny, and that his home was in Pleasanton and that he had a bad reputation.

"The defendant offered this testimony on the theory that once accused of crime may introduce evidence to show that it was committed by another and that, therefore, he did not commit it.

"Instead of there being a 'mysterious stranger', what happened is quite apparent. L.P. Bishop, a banker of La Cygne, who lives a block west and across the street south from the Scott home, was in bed. He heard the shots and outcries, got up and went to the Scott home, arriving immediately after the defendant had returned there from the doctor's. Bishop made some investigations about the house and decided he needed a flashlight. He went back across the street toward his home and was accosted by Laura Rowley, with whom he had some conversation concerning the tragedy. He went on to his house, got his flashlight and returned to the Scott home. This was all done within a very few minutes. Laura Rowley testified that she talked to some stranger, who came by her house, but that she did not see or talk with Mr. Bishop that night."

~CHAPTER TWENTY-THREE~

On a cloudy, gloomy, December Saturday, nine year old, Billy Hays and his best friend Tommy Mason were playing hide and seek outdoors in their neighborhood. They both had been driving their mothers crazy with their horseplay in the house and both boys were sent outside to run off some energy. They met up on the street corner between their houses. It was a very chilly, windy day, but the boys didn't seem to mind.

They decided to play hide and seek first, then do something different later. Tommy decided to do the counting first and Billy ran off to hide. He decided to hide behind a huge bush with a lot of dead brush around it, setting in the back of an alley. When Tommy had finished counting, Billy watched him go the opposite way from him when he called out "Here I come, ready or not." Billy watched as patient and quiet as he could. He knew it was going to take awhile for Tommy to come around, and he was starting to get cold just sitting there in the dry leaves. After awhile he lost interest in the game and started exploring his surroundings. He sat watching a thin stream of water run into a culvert across the alley and once in awhile it would carry stray leaves and debris along the way. He started concentrating on the stream, and on the culvert itself, when all of a sudden he saw something shining every once in awhile. Sometimes he could see it depending on how the water flowed. He was too curious to let a game of hide and seek keep him from checking it out, but he did look to see where Tommy had gone. He was halfway down the block, going in the other direction. So Billy half crawled, half scooted across the alley. When he got to the culvert he reached his hand in under where he thought the shining thing was and wrapped his hand around hard steel. He slowly drew his hand back and saw he was holding an old, partly rusted revolver. He just stared at the gun in disbelief.

Tommy had heard leaves rustling and caught sight of Billy out the corner of his eye. He couldn't believe Billy was sitting in the alley looking at something in his hand, when he was supposed to be hiding. Tommy went running to tell Billy he was now 'it'. But when he reached his best friend's side and saw what Billy was holding, he dropped to his knees to get a better look.

"Wow, Man! Where did you get that?!" Tommy shrieked.

"It was just setting up under this culvert here. I thought I saw something shining and when I reached in, this is what I found."

"Wow! What are you going to do with it, Billy? Can I have it?! This is so terrific!" Tommy was so excited he could hardly contain himself.

"No! You can't have it! I found it!" Billy barked at him, as he tucked the gun inside his pocket.

"Well, can I at least hold it for a minute?" Tommy asked.

Billy hesitated, then took the gun out of his pocket and slowly handed it to Tommy. His eyes grew as big as saucers. He turned the gun back and forth in his hand admiring it. "Wow!" was all he could say. "What are you going to do with it?" he asked looking at the gun.

"I don't know! Quit asking me that!"

Tommy looked around the alley and at the houses near them, as if someone was watching them doing something wrong. He noticed right away, a small faded, light yellow house next to where they were that had been overgrown in vines and weeds. Some of the windows were broken, and many shingles on the roof were missing. It was obvious no one had lived in it for a really long time.

"Hey, wait a minute, Billy," Tommy said quietly, as if not wanting anyone to hear him.

"What?" Billy asked.

"I think I know where we are." Tommy said, looking around. Billy just stared at him.

"This is the old Scott place, remember? The guy shot his wife and now he's in prison, or something!"

"Oh, yeah! Wow!" Billy said excited. "Do you suppose this is the gun? Do you suppose he shot her with this gun?"

"Yeah! Could be.... Wow!"

"What should we do, Billy?" Tommy asked, sincerely. "Do you think we better tell someone?"

Billy looked at the gun for awhile, turning it over and over again in his hand. "We probably should, Tommy. Maybe I should show it to my Mom. She'll know what to do. But first.... let's have some fun with it! Want to play cowboys?"

"Sure!" Tommy's eyes grew big.

The boys played with the gun until they were to cold to stay outside any longer, about an hour and a half, then took it to Billy's mother and told her they just found it in the culvert.

* * * * * * * * * *

Deadly Affair

Sheriff Ellington had been sitting at his desk all afternoon sorting through paperwork when the ring of his phone cut through the silence in the air, almost making him spill his coffee.

"This is Sheriff Ellington," he answered, and then listened for a few minutes to the voice on the other end of the line. Every once in awhile he would mumble and 'uh-huh', but mostly he just listened. "It will take me about forty minutes to get there, Mrs. Hays, but it does sound like something I should look into, alright." He listened a little longer then told her 'good bye' and hung up the phone.

"What was that about?" A very curious Deputy Lindsey couldn't wait to ask.

The sheriff stood from his chair and stretched his back before grabbing his coat from the back of his chair. "A call from La Cygne. Some boys playing out behind the old Scott place found a gun in the alley culvert. I think I'd better go check it out," he said adjusting his hat on his head.

"You don't say...." Lindsey said, totally surprised. "I sure would like to ride along, sheriff," he almost begged.

"Well...." the sheriff checked his watch, then the clock on the wall. "Probably shouldn't this time. Ireland isn't scheduled to come in for another couple of hours, and I really can't leave Scott unsupervised. Sorry, man."

"I know. It just sounds like an interesting change of pace." Lindsey stretched his arms over his head and yawned, emphasizing his boredom.

"You can leave as soon as Ireland gets here," the sheriff told him, as he checked his pockets for his car key. "Guess I'll see you tomorrow, if I run too late getting back tonight."

He stepped out in the cold December air and was grateful his police car had a heater in it.

* * * * * * * * * *

The next morning, Deputy Lindsey unlocked the office door and stepped in to find Night- watchman Ireland making a fresh pot of coffee.

"How's it goin' this mornin'?" Lindsey asked as he hung up his coat and hat. "That coffee sure smells good," he said rubbing his hands together and blowing on them to get warm.

"How's Scott this mornin'?" he asked pouring himself a cup of hot coffee.

"He's okay." Ireland said, indifferently. "Annie brought breakfast over from the café and I got him some clean clothes for the day. I've started waiting for him to change so I could take his dirty ones with me, instead of going back for them later.

Lindsey looked at Ireland, confused.

Ireland went on to say, "Scott has been so despondent the past few weeks, I don't want him tying his clothes together to hang himself or anything. He really doesn't care anymore, you know? I'm starting to feel sorry for the man... a little anyway," he said, shaking his head.

Just as Ireland headed up the stairs to check on Ellison one more time, Sheriff Ellington came through the door, shaking off the cold. "Mornin' boys, sure is a cold one today! Brrrr...."

"What did you find out about the gun, sheriff?" Lindsey asked, impatiently.

"Good morning to you too, deputy..." The sheriff teased with a wink.

"Well," he started, as he hung his coat on his chair and placed his hat on the edge of his desk. I took the gun from the boys, but I don't really think it's the murder weapon," he said, pouring himself a cup of coffee. "The gun's pretty rusted up and it's hard to tell but I don't think it's a Smith and Wesson and it for sure isn't the same caliber, so I don't know." He sounded really disappointed, as he sat down in his chair and sipped on his hot coffee.

Ireland came back down the stairs, and the sheriff motioned for Lindsey to keep quiet about the gun. "How's our prisoner doing today?" the sheriff asked as Ireland entered the room.

"Same as always. Sleeping." he said putting on his coat. "Is it really as cold out there as you guys are putting on?" he asked.

"Yes!" the sheriff and the deputy hollered at the same time, then laughed.

"Dang!" Ireland said, as he wrapped a thick wool scarf around his neck. "See you guys tomorrow," he hollered back, as he threw open the door and ran out in the cold.

The sheriff and deputy laughed again and then the sheriff returned his focus back to the gun.

"I brought the gun back and I plan to have someone investigate it. I don't know how it got in the culvert, and it's a hell of a coincidence, but I really don't think it's our weapon," he sighed.

* * * * * * * * *

The year 1925 rolled in with the bitterest cold weather Linn County had seen in years.

Snow fell every day for weeks. The only reason most farmers would even try to venture outside was to tend to livestock or to fix a fence now and then. Whenever they could get out to go to town they would stock up on as many supplies as they could afford to last awhile. Winter was a good time

Deadly Affair

for women to get sewing caught up on, and quilting, knitting and crocheting done. The men however went a little stir crazy.

Ellison Scott was beyond stir crazy. He felt he only had a passing relationship with his mind these days. He would sit on the edge of his small cot watching the snow falling in the one small window of his cell until he was almost hypnotized by it. He slept a lot, as there wasn't much else to do. Once in awhile the deputy would bring him a newspaper, and one day he even brought him a deck of cards so he could play solitaire now and then. His mother faithfully wrote him a letter every week, which he was grateful to receive, but there was never much news from home. Usually she just wanted him to know she was thinking of him.

On January 22nd, Ellison was visited by his attorneys, Hall and Trinkle. They were excited to share the news that the Kansas Supreme Court had granted a new hearing in his case. The hearing date had been set for March 2nd.

"This is a very rare instance for the state to seek a rehearing and the Kansas Supreme Court to grant such a hearing, Ellison!" Hall almost shouted, as he slapped Ellison on the back.

Ellison almost fell off his cot, but he was trying to smile. He was trying to be cheerful about the news, but as he was trying to take it all in, a wave of depression blanketed his mind.

"What difference does it make really?" he asked. "There's no different evidence than before; why would the verdict be any different now?" He rubbed the side of his face with the palm of his hand.

"Come on Scott! We're killing ourselves here trying to get you out of this mess! Show a little excitement and gratitude here, man!" Trinkle said, trying to tease Ellison into a better mood.

Ellison tried a stronger smile, for his sake. "March 2nd, huh?" Ellison asked, trying to participate.

"Yep. And when you think about it, it will be here before you know it!" Trinkle said enthusiastically.

"Okay, so what's our defense this time then?" Ellison asked, disheartened.

"The stranger who burglarized your house and shot your wife!" Hall said, a little sarcastically.

"Haven't we done this before?" Ellison seemed to be growing impatient with this conversation.

"It's pretty much all we have to go on." Trinkle said. "The 'stranger' theory was brought out in the first trial and the outcome was a hung jury. There was some reasonable doubt. We weren't allowed to mention a possible stranger in the second trial, and you were convicted. We received this appeal on the grounds you have a right to try and prove someone else *might be guilty* of your wife's murder. Try to present testimony that will produce reasonable doubt. We hope to get a change of venue as well."

"What does that mean?" Ellison asked.

"That means we are going to try to have the trial in a different county, where there is less publicity about your case. Too many people around here have already decided how they feel about you and they would probably hang you for sure here." Trinkle said, sincerely.

Ellison started to chuckle. "Are you guys kidding?!" Everyone in the state of Kansas knows about this murder case, and about me! What county are you going to pick, one next to the Colorado line?"

"Damn it, Ellison!" Yeah, the whole state knows the story, but they don't personally know you, nor do they know the case against you. It would be fresh news to someone who hadn't lived through two trials around here and are pretty sick of the whole thing." Hall jumped down his throat. "What, do you want us to just give up? Let you spend your life in this little cell? Huh? What do you want, Ellison?"

"Okay, then," Ellison said, shaking his head. "What do I have to lose?"

He stood and shook the hand of each attorney. "I really do appreciate all you guys do for me."

"We know." Hall said. He had calmed down some. "Try to stay strong, man."

He and Trinkle picked up their briefcases and rang the bell for the deputy to come let them out of Ellison's cell. Once the attorneys were gone, Ellison lie back down on his cot and fell back to sleep watching the snowflakes pour from the gray sky, out the small window of his cell.

~CHAPTER TWENTY-FOUR~

Winter turned to spring early, in 1925, and after such a harsh winter, the community seemed to come alive from their hibernation during the winter months. Leona had taught at her old elementary school, Washington, and was enjoying being a teacher. She was kind of looking forward to having a break in the summer, but she didn't really want to work for her father in the fields. She was hoping she could find a summer job somewhere, maybe even tutoring.

By May, the days were very warm, and the crops were growing in the fields and gardens, and people were hopeful for a productive summer.

Clyde McCullough, had made a few small changes to the store, but he left the name as Scott's grocery and meat market. He felt it was the least he could do. Ellison had given him a good deal on it, and he had all the business he could handle since taking it over. Tom continued to work for him, full time over the winter, and part time now that the weather was warmer so he could help his dad on the farm. Clyde had to hire another young man also part time to fill in for Tom when he couldn't be there.

For Ellison Scott, the days ran together and life outside his cell didn't matter much to him.

March had come and gone and he had not heard a word concerning a new trial. He would occasionally get a letter from either Hall and Trinkle encouraging him that things were going well.

It would just take time to get through the legal process. That being true, Ellison refused to allow himself to be very hopeful.

* * * * * * * * *

Arlene had spent a rough winter fighting depression and boredom. Even though she had the company of Charlie now and then, the snowy, icy roads made those visits few and difficult. She had spent a lot of time helping her mother stitch together a quilt and after both women spent an afternoon, just before Christmas, framing it out, she spent many hours a day working her needle on making fine stitches on the colorful fabric. Quilting, and helping her mother with household chores kept her hands busy, but her mind was very discontent.

In spring she helped her mother plant flowers around the house, and hoe and plant the garden. She tried to be outside as much as possible. She enjoyed the warm sun and fresh air. She had missed teaching and getting out of the house for a few hours a day, but was sort of glad she didn't have to deal with the harsh winter weather. Besides, she really didn't miss being around whispers and ugly stares as well.

On a very warm sunny day in the middle of May, Arlene was busy weeding the flower beds around the front porch when she heard a vehicle slow down and turn into her drive. She immediately recognized the car to be that of her attorney, John Hall. For a moment her heart stopped.

"Oh…no," she said under her breath. She just knew he had come to inform her of her next hearing date and she did not want to know.

Mr. Hall was stepping out of his car when Arlene stood up to brush the dirt off her apron.

"Miss Scott!" he greeted her cheerfully. "How are you doing today?"

"I'm okay," she said reluctantly. "What brings you out this way?" Her heart was beating way too fast.

"Well, you do, Miss Scott! You do!" He walked over to her with a smile on his face and handed her a sealed envelope.

"What's this?" she asked, cautiously.

"Good news, my dear. Good news!" he was trying to keep from laughing right out loud.

She grabbed the envelope and ripped the sealed flap open and quickly began reading the paper that was inside. As she read the letter inside, a big smile crossed her face and she began to giggle like a little girl.

"Mama! Mama!" she shrieked. "Mama come quick!" By now she was jumping up and down.

Bertha busted out the front door, thinking someone had been hurt until she saw her daughter laughing and jumping up and down.

"Mr. Hall," she acknowledged him politely. "What's going on Arlene? You scared me to death, child!

"Mama, read this! Read what this says!" she said, waving the paper in her mother's face.

The letter stated in legal terms that the case of 'the state vs. Arlene Scott' was dismissed on motion of the county attorney, who had been advised to do so by the attorney general of Kansas.

Bertha started smiling, then started letting out short spasms of laughter. "Does this mean what I think it means, Mr. Hall?" She looked him in the eye hopefully.

"If you think it means that Arlene is free from any further legal obligation, then, yes it means what you think," he laughed.

Deadly Affair

"I'm free of all charges!" Arlene exclaimed. "Oh, Mama!" Arlene blurted out as she hugged her mother, crying.

Bertha grabbed Mr. Hall's hand and vigorously started shaking it hard, as she thanked him over and over again. "We'll try to get you paid as soon as we possibly can. We just really appreciate what you have done on Arlene's behalf."

"Don't worry about it, Ma'am. All in due time. I'm just happy to bring good news for a change! You ladies have a nice afternoon," he said, tipping his hat as he walked back to his car.

Arlene and Bertha hugged each other one more time, laughing and jumping.

"Lets bake a cake!" Bertha exclaimed. "Let's have a party!"

"Can I invite Charlie over for supper and cake?"

"Sure, Honey! Won't your Papa be surprised?!"

Arlene ran into the house to call Charlie and tell him the good news, and to invite him over for the celebration.

Bertha stood there for a minute. All at once her joy turned to melancholy when she realized that she wouldn't be able to invite her mother and sisters to celebrate with them.

* * * * * * * * * *

On a warm, summer morning, a few days after Arlene's case was dismissed, her grandmother, Sarah had gone out on her porch to rock in her chair as she drank her morning coffee. Her front porch faced the west side of the house, so the early mornings were a perfect time to sit outside and relax. Sarah enjoyed living in town and was glad she made the move. She realized she would have been so lonely on the farm, but in town there were always people to talk to and she could walk to the stores on her own. She felt a sense of freedom she had never had.

She was grateful to Rob and Earl for taking care of the farmland, and with selling off the livestock, especially since it would all be theirs one day anyway.

As she gently rocked in her chair, she watched as Elmer Marsten slowly approaching on his old International Harvester tractor. He usually always stopped at her house to see if she needed anything.

"Mornin' Miss Sarah!" he hollered over the noise of his tractor motor. He was afraid if he shut it off, he might not get her started again. He jumped off the tractor and briskly walked up the sidewalk. Elmer was the youngest of five children, and at the age of twenty-nine had the capacity of a young child. He had a good heart, but he wasn't smart about most things and needed help thinking things through. He loved driving his tractor, and he was able to help his dad on the farm some, but someone always had to be near him just in case he would have an accident. He liked to visit with people, and when Sarah moved to town, they became instant friends.

"Morning, Elmer," she hollered back. "How you doin' this morning?"

"I'm real good, Miss Sarah, real good." he said with his big smile. "Do you need anything today, Miss Sarah? I'm driving my tractor uptown, be glad to get something for ya, if ya need something."

"Would you mind getting my mail this morning, dear. I didn't get to the post office yesterday."

"No problem, Ma'am. Need anything else?"

"No, I don't believe so, but thank you so much."

"I'll be back shortly, then," he said, waving as he walked back to his tractor.

Sarah had finished her coffee and was dozing in her rocker when she heard the roar of Elmer's tractor coming back from uptown. She stood up from her chair and walked to the edge of the porch and down the sidewalk to greet him when he pulled up at her house. He handed her the mail, tipped his hat and slowly drove off.

There were a couple of letters and a Mound City Republic newspaper. She walked back to her porch and laid the mail on the little garden table next to her rocking chair. She picked up her coffee cup and walked to the kitchen to refill it. Once she was back on her porch she sat down and started reading her mail. She read her letters as she sipped on her coffee. When she finished her letters, she unfolded the newspaper and immediately she was hit with the headline that charges against Arlene Scott had been dismissed. Sarah smiled at this news. She knew in her heart she would probably not see Arlene again, nor speak to her again for the sake of the family. But she was glad to know her granddaughter was liberated from the courts, even if not from the public.

* * * * * * * * *

While John Hall was delivering good news to Arlene, Charles Trinkle was working out the final details with Assistant Attorney General W.A. Smith for Ellison's new trial. The state Supreme Court had decided to reverse it's opinion and ordered the case to be retried in district court in Linn County.

Charles Trinkle delivered this news to Ellison in the middle of May, and pleaded with Judge Gates to once again lower Ellison's bond from twenty thousand to ten thousand dollars. Judge Gates decided to grant

Deadly Affair

Trinkle's motion for a lower bond the third week of May. Trinkle expected Ellison to be thrilled with this news upon hearing he could go free, but Ellison merely grumbled at him.

"I've been through this so many times before." Ellison waved his hand at his attorney.

"First of all, I don't know anyone who has any money left to put on my bond, much less anyone who cares about my sorry ass enough to pay my bond. Second of all, I don't have anything to get out of jail for anymore. I have no life outside of this cell. I sold my every possession, and I have no prospects for a life outside of jail. I personally am pretty tired of going home to mommy and daddy's house every time I leave here. I really wish they would just send me to Lansing and get it over with. At least there would be inmates there, someone to talk to once in awhile." He shook his head.

His hair was standing straight up in places and his beard was matted. He looked like someone who had just walked out of the woods after being lost for days. Trinkle also wondered when the last time was the man had taken a shower.

"You really have lost your hope, haven't you, man?" Trinkle asked with compassion.

"Pretty much. I don't even know if I can come up with money for a ten thousand dollar bond, and as I said, I doubt anyone else would care to. Shoot, I don't even know if I can pay you and Hall for your services, by now, much less bond." Ellison laid back on his bed and stared at the ceiling.

"Well, I'll keep in touch and make sure you're updated on everything," Trinkle said, discouraged. He put his hat on his head and pushed the buzzer on the wall to signal the deputy to come and unlock the door.

* * * * * * * * *

Trinkle walked out of the sheriff's office feeling angry and defeated. He knew Ellison had a right to feel despair, but he also knew he and Hall had put a lot of time, money and hard work in on defending their client. He was growing tired of this case and he was pretty sure Hall probably felt the same way. Trinkle's office was located in La Cygne, and Hall's office was located in Pleasanton. They both spent a lot of time on the road and on the telephone, and Trinkle was beginning to wonder if Scott wasn't right. *Maybe they all ought to give up.*

The next morning Charles Trinkle called his legal partner and asked him if he would have a little time in the afternoon to get together, maybe at

Mabel's Café and discuss their future strategy on the Scott case. John Hall agreed, and they decided to meet around 2 o'clock.

Mabel's Café was pretty empty by 2 o'clock in the afternoon. The lunch crowd had come and gone. The two attorneys felt they could speak their minds with out being over heard.

Hall and Trinkle each ordered a cup of coffee and a piece of cherry pie, from Sally, the waitress, then Trinkle started telling Hall about his visit with Ellison. He explained how angry and annoyed he had become with Ellison's attitude.

"Why should we work so hard on the man's case, when he doesn't seem to care anymore?"

Hall listened intently and nodded his head from time to time.

"Maybe it is time we moved on." Hall concurred, as Sally set two plates with generous portions of cherry pie on the table. She then filled their coffee cups, asked if they needed anything else, and walked away with a smile when they said they were fine.

"You know, in a way it's kind of hard to let it go, without seeing it clear to the end. But on the other hand, you do have a good point. We have been able to do some remarkable things for Scott, even with such a flimsy case as his is. How many times has the Kansas Supreme Court turned a murder conviction around for a new trial! I guess in that regard, I would like to see it through, and if he were found innocent we would be the famous attorneys who pulled it off!"

Trinkle smiled at him and his delusions of grandeur, as he shoved a bite of pie in his mouth.

"Ah, well, truth is, I have been thinking about this for some time as well." Hall said, sipping his coffee. "You know, now that Arlene's case has been dismissed and we've been able to get Scott a new trial, maybe it is time to move on. He'll probably be good with new representation. Heck, maybe even better with a fresh pair of eyes looking at the case, and a new and fresher attitude," Hall said, taking a huge bite of his pie. "I don't know about you...", he said with his mouth partially full of pie, "But I have turned away some really good cases and well paying clients over the past couple of years because of this case.

"I have too!" Trinkle exclaimed. "Now that I think about it, I don't know if I really want to work through another Ellison Scott trial," he said, frustrated. "I've been wondering how hard it would be to present a plausible case about a 'stranger' on a level of reasonable doubt," he said, shoving another bite of pie in his mouth. "Maybe the only glory we could ever hope for is that we were able to get him a new trial after he was convicted. Maybe we should let someone else take the fall representing him in a new trial."

"Perhaps you are right." Hall said, finishing his last bite of pie.

Sally came by with her coffee pot, and refilled both cups with fresh coffee.

"Getting Ellison a new trial is one thing, but we would still have a lot of work to do to get him a new venue for trial," Hall said.

"Yeah, no kidding," Trinkle agreed. "That would be something I wouldn't mind turning over to someone else to do," he said, stirring sugar into his coffee.

"John, have you ever wondered if Scott really did kill his wife?" Trinkle asked.

"Every day." Hall answered.

On June 25th, John Hall and Charles Trinkle announced in open court that they were withdrawing from the murder case they had fought so hard to win. Neither attorney gave a reason why they were leaving, only that they desired for someone else to take the case.

~CHAPTER TWENTY-FIVE~

Charles Scott was devastated to learn that his son's attorneys had dropped him as their client. Now that a new trial had been ordered, his son needed good representation. He couldn't imagine who could take the case and do a better job than Hall and Trinkle. Upon hearing this news, however, Charles telephoned the office of Judge Gates and asked for the court to appoint new council for Ellison.

* * * * * * * * *

Ellison could hear the heavy footsteps of the sheriff's boots plodding up the stairs in the early morning hour. He sat up on the edge of his cot, running his hand absently through his hair.

"Good morning, Scott," the sheriff said pleasantly, as he turned the key in the lock of Ellison's cell door. "And how are you doing this morning?" he asked, as if he cared.

He didn't walk into the cell, but merely stood by the door. "You need to get what little belongings you have together. Your Pa is here to pick you up to take you home."

Ellison shot him a confused look.

"Guess someone posted your bond. You're free to go, until your next new trial, anyway," the sheriff said with a touch of sarcasm.

He really didn't care one way or the other. It was less work for him and his deputies if Scott was at home. He turned and walked away, leaving the cell door open.

"You're on your own for breakfast!" the sheriff hollered back, as he plodded back down the stairs.

* * * * * * * * *

The new trial had been set to start in the July term of court, but since Ellison would not have time to counsel with a new attorney, the trial date had been postponed.

A few days after Ellison had returned to his parents' farm, he received a telephone call from a Robert Sawver, announcing he had been court

Deadly Affair

appointed to take over the case. Sawver told Ellison he had been studying his case and felt like he had some different options for his representation, and wondered if they could meet soon to discuss a strategy for his upcoming trial. Ellison liked the upbeat attitude Mr. Sawver displayed on the telephone, but he still didn't put too much stock in his new trial. However he agreed to meet his appointed attorney the next morning around 10 o'clock at his office in Paola.

* * * * * * * * * *

Ellison hadn't expected to feel better after going home, but he was surprised to realize he did. He had not really seen the light of day for a long time and he found the warm sun on his pale face extremely refreshing. He had gone for a couple of really long walks since he had been out of his small, stuffy jail cell, and enjoyed the sun and exercise. He decided he was looking forward to driving again as well, and cherished the thought of driving to Paola the next morning.

It had rained during the night, which helped keep the dust down on the road as Ellison drove to his appointment. He had to drive his father's truck, since he had sold his Studebaker, and the ride was a little rough and bumpy, but he was grateful for the transportation.

A small bell rang over the door as Ellison entered the attorney's office. Robert Sawver's office waiting area was small, but very comfortable and well decorated. Ellison was impressed with all the filled bookcases lining one whole wall of the waiting room. He wondered to himself if Mr. Sawver had read all of them.

Mr. Scott, good morning!" Mr. Sawver said, walking down a short hallway to meet his new client.

He reached out his hand, and Ellison graciously shook it. Robert Sawver was a young man, or perhaps he just looked young, but he wasn't what Ellison expected. He was very handsome, and very well dressed. What surprised Ellison the most was the man was instantly likable. He had an air of compassion and friendship that not every person possesses. He was charismatic. He asked Ellison to follow him down the short hallway, into his even smaller office.

Please have a seat," he motioned to a chair. "Would you like a cup of coffee?"

Ellison thought for a moment. "Yes, I believe I would, please, that sounds good."

Ellison decided right away he was going to like working with this gentleman. A carafe of coffee and a few mugs set on a small table between

Sawver's desk and the chair Ellison was sitting in. Robert then poured a cup of coffee for Ellison, and then a cup of coffee for himself. There was cream and sugar on the little table, and Robert scooped a spoonful of sugar into his cup and stirred it as he sat down in his overstuffed chair behind his desk, and got to work.

"As I mentioned on the telephone, I have been studying your case thoroughly and I have a suggestion or two I would like to run by you, if you don't mind."

"No, not at all," Ellison said, sipping his coffee.

"First thing, I feel we need a change of venue for your trial."

"One of my other attorneys mentioned that to me," Ellison said.

"Well I think it would help your case immensely if we can get the court to allow you to be tried in a different town, in a different county, by a different judge, and in front of a jury who hasn't been saturated with your case. A totally fresh start, in other words. What do you think?"

"I... uh. Wow! I think that would be great!"

Ellison was excited at the thought. He tried to imagine what it would be like to sit in court and look around at people he didn't know and wouldn't be intimated by.

"Great then!" Mr. Sawver went on, "we will have to get affidavits signed from citizens of La Cygne and Linn County, stating they believe you would not get a fair trial in a county that had an exhausted jury pool. I don't know how long all of this will take for the footwork, and to convince the courts of a change of venue, but I'm sure it can be done. Now that you are out on bond, perhaps the wait won't be torture for you."

"I have to admit, I'm a little encouraged by this prospect," Ellison said, truthfully.

"Well, it's usually the case when someone's been on trial for the same crime more than once in one court. The public pretty much has their minds made up, and want to be done with the matter. If your case is tried in a different place altogether, you're likely to find less knowledge of the case, and less prejudice toward you."

Ellison nodded his head and added 'uh-huh' when appropriate.

I have a partner, as I'm sure you saw on my sign outside, Dexter Lane. He, of course, is not on your case, but advises me from time to time. He suggested we look into one county over, Anderson County, and hopefully hold the trial in Garnett. That will be just far enough away, hopefully, the citizens from Linn County will be too tired of the whole thing to make the extra trip to watch your trial again.

Ellison nodded is head and gave a crooked smile. "I agree with everything you've said, and for once I feel kind of hopeful."

Deadly Affair

* * * * * * * * * *

Mr. Sawver was very fascinated with Ellison's case and had been enjoying working on every detail of it in the past few weeks.
Ellison certainly felt encouraged by his new attorney's positive attitude and it even helped him get out of bed in the mornings. In the few weeks since he met Mr. Sawver, he had gotten into a routine of getting up early to help his Pa with chores and eating breakfast with his parents. He had fallen into such a depression in jail that he had forgotten that even the small things in one's day could be inspiring. He tried not to think too far ahead. However, once in awhile he would catch himself daydreaming about a future far away from prison.
Mr. Sawver had filed a motion for a new venue for Ellison's upcoming trial, which was denied by Judge Gates. He then immediately took his case to the Kansas Supreme Court and after much pleading on behalf of the many affidavits he had acquired, the court granted a new venue for Ellison's trial.
The trial was scheduled to begin in October, however, like most things involved with the court system, Ellison's trial was rescheduled on the docket for March 10th, 1926 in Garnett, Kansas.

* * * * * * * * * *

The winter between 1925 and 1926 had not been as harsh as the winter before. It snowed and was very cold, but there were days in between bad weather that allowed people freedom to come and go. Even though Arlene had been released from all charges surrounding her aunt's murder, she had decided to wait one more year to go back to teaching. She hoped by then the gossips would have something else to talk about besides her.
She had a wonderful winter. The holidays were fun for her, especially because Charlie Ferguson was now a major part of her life. She missed spending time with her extended family, but she was getting used to it all the same.
She had not followed Ellison's circumstances for months, and didn't know anything about a new attorney or a new trial. She was only concerned about her own life. She would go shopping at towns where the people didn't know her or didn't realize it if they did. Sometimes Charlie would take her dancing, and usually they would go not only to a different town, but a different county as well. She felt for the most part, her life was back on track. Until one morning in late February, 1926.

Arlene sat at the breakfast table, finishing her morning coffee, and thoughtfully reading the day old copy of the Mound City Republic newspaper.

"Oh, no!" she said, loud enough to get her mother's attention from the living room.

"What is it, dear?" Bertha walked in the kitchen carrying her crocheting in her hands.

"Oh, Mama!" she said, exasperated, dropping the newspaper on the table. "Ellison has a new trial starting on the 10th in Garnett! I thought he was in prison in Lansing! Why can't he just.... just go away!" She threw her hands in the air. "What am I going to do? I can't... No! I *won't* go through any more public humiliation!" she cried.

Bertha set her crocheting down on a little table by the doorway and calmly walked to the counter and poured herself another cup of coffee. She sat down next to her daughter, picked up the newspaper and read the article about Ellison's new trial. When she was done reading, she set the newspaper down and stared out the window sipping on her coffee. Arlene sat quiet, as she knew her mother was thinking, and she didn't want to disturb her.

"You haven't been subpoenaed yet," Bertha said, as if to herself. "If you aren't here you can't be subpoenaed, and if you haven't been subpoenaed, you can't testify." she said smiling at her daughter. A mischievous grin suddenly crossed Bertha's face.

"What are you thinking, Mama?" Arlene asked.

"How would you like to go visit with Aunt Bernice in Oklahoma for a spell. Say, long enough to be gone for the whole trial?" Bernice Holmes was Arlene's great aunt, on her father's side, and it had been awhile since anyone had visited her. Bertha was thinking that maybe Bernice would not mind if Arlene stayed with her for awhile.

"Shame on you, Mama," Arlene giggled. Then after a minute, put on a sober face. "Really, Mama, do you think she would want me to come?"

"Well, honey, I don't know, but when your Pa comes in from the fields for dinner, well talk to him about it. Maybe he'll drive us in to Blue Mound to the operator's office so we can call his aunt and see if she's up to having long term company."

"Oh, I really hope so!" she rolled her eyes. "I really hope so!"

~CHAPTER TWENTY-SIX~

On March 10th, in the court of Judge Hugh Means, of Lawrence, Kansas, Assistant Attorney General W.A. Smith, along with Linn County Attorney Reeve, and Anderson County Attorney Bert Woods, selected a jury of men by noon of that same day. Attorney J.Q. Wycoff of Garnett assisted Robert Sawver in Ellison's defense.

The layout of the Anderson County courtroom was very different than Ellison was used to, but he soon became familiar with where he was supposed to be.

The next morning his trial began with opening statements to the jury by W.A. Smith, followed by the calling of the first witness. There were only a hand full of people in the court- room from Linn County and there were many seats in the gallery left empty. The interest in Ellison's third trial certainly did have a different atmosphere to it. However, the witnesses were the same, the story was the same, and most of the testimony was the same.

The state stuck to it's conviction about Ellison and Arlene's love affair being the reason for the murder, but it was very apparent Arlene was absent and would not be testifying.

In this trial the defense was determined to play up the concept of a 'stranger' who could have burglarized the Scott home and murdered Mrs. Ella Scott.

Attorney Robert Sawver had his work cut out for him, as the idea of a 'stranger' being the guilty culprit in this case had been debated many times and in many ways.

It seemed every witness's testimony confirmed Ellison's guilt and the idea of a 'stranger' seemed no more than a fantasy.

The state spent the whole day re-questioning witnesses from the previous trials and coming up with the same testimony as in the former trials.

One of the last witnesses of the day was L.P. Bishop, who testified Scott expressed no grief a few minutes after the murder and there were no signs of a burglar's entrance into the house. Ellison watched his one time friend, Lewis Bishop, as he coldly testified as if he never knew Ellison at all.

Tom Peters again testified that he heard Mrs. Scott tell her husband, "If you caught me as I caught you, you would kill me."

Tom's testimony was one of the most damning to Ellison. However, the most outstanding testimony that day, or any other day in any of the previous trials, came from Clyde McCullough at the end of court that afternoon.

Clyde was sitting next to his wife, holding her hand until his name was called to take the stand. When he was summoned, he squeezed her hand, kissed her cheek and told her he loved her. She smiled at him. He slowly walked to the stand and stoically took the oath to tell the truth. He sat down and adjusted his body in the chair to get comfortable. He looked out into the room and was relieved to see that the courtroom was practically empty. He was not looking forward to his testimony today, and he really wished his wife wasn't here. He was not happy about Ellison having a third trial. He had hoped this case had been put to rest when Ellison had been convicted. But he guessed all bad deeds must be revealed and paid for.

W.A. Smith started his questioning by asking Clyde if he knew whether Ellison Scott owned a gun.

"Yes sir, he did." Clyde answered.

"Did you ever see this gun, Mr. McCullough?"

"Yes sir. I did on one occasion."

"What kind of gun was it, do you know Mr. McCullough?"

"Yes sir. It was a Smith and Wesson revolver... I believe a .32 caliber," Clyde said calmly.

"And you said, you yourself have seen this gun. Is that correct, sir?"

"Yes sir, it is."

"Mr. McCullough, it is true that you worked for the Scott's Grocery and Meat Market in 1923?"

"Yes, sir."

"Were you friendly with Ellison Scott, Mr. McCullough?"

Clyde looked confused. "What do you mean, sir?"

"Well, did you get along. Did you have a good working relationship with each other?"

"Yeah, I guess so." Clyde answered, shifting in his chair. He felt uncomfortable.

"How about Ella Scott? Did you have a good relationship with her?"

"Excuse me?" Clyde choked.

"Mrs. Scott. Did you have a good relationship with her?"

Clyde cleared his throat. "Yes sir, very much so." Clyde, had by now removed his handkerchief from his pocket and started wiping his forehead.

"What do you mean by, 'very much so,' Mr. McCullough?"

"Sometimes," he cleared his throat again, truly nervous, "sometimes I would catch her in the storeroom crying, and I would try to comfort her. Sometimes Ellison could be unreasonably harsh toward her, and she was sensitive."

Ellison shifted in his own chair, and felt very uncomfortable.

"Did these occasions of 'comforting Mrs. Scott' happen often, Mr. McCullough?"

Clyde was visibly shaken and was very reluctant to speak.

"Mr. McCullough?" Smith asked him.

"Yes sir... yes sir, they did. Clyde wiped his forehead and the back of his neck.

Sensing something more needed to be revealed, Attorney Smith decided to push him a little. The question was definitely off script, but the attorney's curiosity had been aroused.

"Mr. McCullough, I want you to tell this court what your relationship was to Ella Scott, and remember sir, you are under oath."

Ellison sat on the edge of his chair, with his elbows on the table. He was shaking one leg up and down nervously, as he anxiously listened to what McCullough had to say.

Clyde was very nervous. He had been afraid, at some point he would be asked about Ella, but he thought he was free and clear after Ellison's conviction. He felt like he had been caught off guard with this question, even though he wasn't totally surprised it had been asked of him.

Clyde sat very still for some time. He glanced at Ellison briefly and saw confused contempt on his face. Clyde then looked in the middle of the courtroom, where his wife sat at the end of her row. Her face looked so sweet, so beautiful, and so trusting. He could hardly stand himself for what he might be asked to say.

"On Tuesdays," he started, clearing his throat. He took a long drink of water from a glass setting on the stand. "On Tuesdays, I would go to the train depot to pick up supplies for the store. Also on Tuesdays, I would deliver groceries to some of our customers, along with ice deliveries. I was driving in the truck most all day." He let out a long sorrowful sigh. "Sometimes Ella didn't work at the store on Tuesday mornings. Most Tuesday mornings she would work, but some Tuesday mornings she didn't." He was so nervous now. He was starting to ramble.

Ellison's eyes became very narrow with anger. He was just waiting for Clyde to say it.

"It didn't happen often, but when I delivered ice to her house, she sometimes invited me in for a cold iced tea, and we became good friends. She confided her feelings to me." Clyde looked at his wife, who was by now fanning herself with a paddle fan, and looking down in her lap.

Ellison could hardly contain himself. He wouldn't look in Clyde's direction, but he sat clenching and unclenching his fists in his lap.

"Did your relationship with Ella Scott ever become more than that of 'good friends,' Mr. McCullough?"

Tears started welling in his eyes. At that moment, if he could take it all back he would, but he knew he had taken an oath to tell the truth.

"Yes sir. I'm afraid it did," he whispered. He held his head down, running his hand through his hair.

There were gasps and murmurs from the spectators and a single light scream from a woman running from the courtroom. The tears started falling down Clyde's cheeks, and he hoped someday his pretty little wife would forgive him.

"Mr. McCullough," W.A. Smith went on soberly, "did you ever have intercourse with Ella Scott?" Smith couldn't believe he was asking this question. No one had ever held the slightest thought of Ella being unfaithful, only Ellison. What did this mean now?"

"Yes sir, I'm afraid I did." Clyde hung his head.

Ellison almost came out of his chair, but his attorney grabbed his arm tightly before he could move.

"Son of a bitch! I knew it!" Ellison said loud enough to be heard. "I knew they were messing around the whole time!" he said, as he pounded his knee with his closed fist.

"There will be order in my court!" Judge Means struck his gavel a couple of times, and ordered Mr. Sawver to get his client under control. The Judge then dismissed court for the day after the bombshell testimony no one had expected to hear.

* * * * * * * * * *

The state made a few statements the following morning and then rested its case.

It was now Attorney Sawver's turn to try and take this case in a different direction. He didn't know what to think of Clyde McCullough's testimony. He realized the fact he had testified that he had seen Ellison's .32 caliber Smith and Wesson revolver was not helpful. Before court got underway that morning, Sawver asked Ellison if he knew about his wife's affair.

Ellison only smiled wickedly, and said he wasn't surprised about it. He had thought all along it might be going on.

Sawver was a little unnerved with Ellison's reaction to his question, but he hoped Clyde and Ella's affair would be neither here nor there concerning

Deadly Affair

Ellison's guilt in the eyes of the jury. Even though Sawver had studied Ellison's case thoroughly, he had not grown to know the man personally through the process of trials. He was beginning to wonder if Ellison *did* kill his wife after all. He was relieved when the state rested its case. Perhaps it meant that Clyde's testimony wasn't as damaging as it had sounded, although Tom Peters' testimony could have pounded a nail in Ellison's coffin. It sure didn't sound good to Mr. Sawver, anyway.

The defense spent the day calling witness after witness, who saw, or thought they saw, a strange man at the murder scene, running down the street, hiding in the stockyards and eventually hopping a freight train out of town. When the defense finished questioning a witness, the state was allowed to cross- examine.

Attorney Wycoff called Sheriff Ellington to the stand. Once sworn in and seated, Attorney Wycoff began by asking the sheriff if he had ever heard of a man by the name of Fred Slavens. The sheriff said he had, and Attorney Wycoff asked if he knew Fred Slavens.

"I know *of* him," the sheriff replied.

"Did you ever investigate the whereabouts of Mr. Slavens the night Ella Scott was slain?"

"I did, sir."

"Would you please tell the court about your investigation, Sheriff?"

"When it came to light that Fred Slavens might have been involved with the crime of burglary and murder at the Scott home, I then went to his family home in Pleasanton to talk with him."

"And *did* you talk to him, Sheriff?" Wycoff asked him, a little condescending.

"No sir. I talked to his mother."

"What did she tell you?"

"She told me her son was incarcerated in Nebraska at the time of the murder of Mrs. Scott, and would be incarcerated until sometime this year, sir."

"Did you investigate this?"

"Of course I did, and she was telling the truth." the sheriff was irritated.

"Is it possible, Sheriff Ellington, that another strange man to the community could have committed this crime?"

"Objection, Your Honor!" Attorney Smith jumped to his feet.

"Sustained," the Judge too, was irritated.

"No further questions," Attorney Wycoff stated as he walked back to the defense table.

" Mr. Smith, do you have any further questions?"

"No sir, not at this time."

Sheriff Ellington was dismissed, and he stepped down from the witness stand and walked right out the door. He had work to get to.

Sawver was a little distressed. He was beginning to realize the difficulty of *proving* there could have been a stranger. Just because Fred Slavens had an alibi, didn't mean there wasn't someone else who committed the crime.

In the defense's closing statements, Mr. Sawver worked hard to convince the jury that it was very possible that a stranger had committed this horrible crime. Many people had testified they had seen a strange man that night at many different times and places that would concur with him being the culprit in this case. He went on to say that Ellison Scott loved his wife and had no reason to kill her. He was hoping he was not lying about that.

He reminded the jury that if they had even a shadow of a doubt that Ellison was guilty of murder, they should render a not guilty verdict. When he was finished with his statements, he sat down in his chair, poured himself a glass of water, and realized his client would be heading to Lansing prison soon. He felt he hadn't made a dent in the evidence against Ellison Scott.

Twelve jurors took twelve ballots to the jury room around 6 o'clock that evening for deliberation, once again, for the fate of Ellison Scott. By 11 o' clock that same night a verdict had been reached. Ellison and his attorney were petrified with fear. The courtroom was vacant except for Ellison's parents, the attorneys for the state and defense, the judge and of course the jury. The judge asked the jury foreman if they had reached a unanimous verdict.

Ellison sat numb in his chair. All of a sudden he felt sick. The room started to slowly spin around him. It was hard for him to grasp that this was the third time he was living this nightmare. A nightmare where someone he didn't know would tell him where he would be spending the rest of his life. His anxiety almost got the better of him. The facts of the case had been pretty much the same as throughout all the trials, and even to Ellison, reasonable doubt seemed to be a stretch. He was beginning to feel foolish for once again having hope for his future. He sat with his hands clenching the sides of his chair as he heard the foreman exclaim, "We have Your Honor."

"Will the defendant please rise?" the judge remarked. "Would you please go ahead and read the verdict?" He summoned the foreman.

"We the jury in the above titled case, the state of Kansas vs. Ellison Scott find the defendant not guilty of murder in the first degree."

"So says all?" the judge asked.

"So says all." the foreman answered.

Ellison stood stunned. He couldn't move his arms or his legs. He didn't trust that his ears had heard a 'not guilty' verdict. Mr. Sawver was beside himself! What a case to win for such a young attorney, just starting out. He threw his hands in the air and whooped for joy as he grabbed Ellison by the shoulders and gave him a big hug.

Ellison started laughing, slowly at first, then almost uncontrollably. He hugged his attorney several times and thanked him profusely. He knew that his attorney's advice to change the venue had made all the difference in the world.

Judge Means struck his gavel a couple of times and announced court was dismissed and the defendant was free to go.

It is doubtful two such opposite verdicts, under practically the same evidence, were ever before recorded in a Kansas Court. The error committed by the court in the second trial was really almost immaterial and could not have changed the verdict.

Ellison's parents ran to him after the verdict was read and hugged their son. His mother smothered him with kisses, and they all laughed and cried at the same time.

After a few minutes, in the middle of his little celebration, Ellison realized he was now a free man, but with no place to go. He had no money, he had depleted his parent's wealth, and his reputation would not allow him employment for miles around. What was he going to do? For nearly three years he had been a man with no hope, at the mercy of the courts. Now he had the world at his front door, but no resources to help himself. A wave of confusion blanketed his new found happiness.

* * * * * * * * * *

In the days that followed his third trial, Ellison grew restless in his state of oblivion, not knowing what to do with himself. Since selling his car and his market, he really never believed he would be a free man again. He knew he couldn't move back to town and try to start over. No one would accept him. He didn't really want to stay in La Cygne anyway.

One morning, after eating breakfast, he took a cup of coffee, and the newspaper out to sit on the porch. While reading, his mother walked out to the porch with her own cup of coffee, and sat down in a chair across from him.

"You know, dear, I've been thinking some about your situation." She said, sincerely.

Ellison smiled at her. She looked so much older sitting here than he had ever remembered her looking. Grayer hair, more wrinkles on her face. Yet it still had the same sweetness he had always known.

"Really," he said, "and what conclusions have you come to?" he asked, with a smile.

"Don't be smart with me," she smiled back. "I know you have been struggling with what to do with your future, and I think we all know you have no future here," she said.

He nodded his head as he sipped his coffee.

"I have a suggestion to make, if I may." She said, with tears in her eyes.

"Sure Ma. I need all the suggestions I can get," he was being sincere.

"Your Pa and I have been talking a lot about what you might be able to do, and what you might enjoy doing. We all know there's nothing here, so we took the liberty to driving in to the Centerville telephone office, and putting a call into your Aunt Jennie, in California. Your Pa told her of your situation and how lost you were about your future here, and she invited you to come live with her in California for awhile until you get on your feet. She said she would love to have the company. No one would know you there or what has happened here in Kansas, and you could get a fresh start." She sipped on her coffee, and let him think about it for awhile. She looked at him from time to time, hopefully. He sat quiet, staring into space, sipping on his own coffee.

"California, huh." he said, finally. "That might be a great adventure, Ma. You're right, no one knows me there. I could get a fresh start, maybe. Starting all over again sounds really good to me. And she really said she would be glad to have me there, Aunt Jennie?"

"Yes she did, son, she was excited for the opportunity to see you again. You were just a small boy the last time she saw you. She would love to have family stay with her!"

"Thanks so much, Ma! This gives me something to look forward to, something to plan for. When should I plan on going?"

"Anytime you feel like it. The ticket has been purchased, and can be used whenever you want."

"Thanks, Ma!" Ellison jumped out of his chair, kissed his mother on the cheek, and ran upstairs to start packing his meager belongings.

He didn't know it, but his Aunt Jennie had paid for his train fare out to California. She realized, after talking to Mollie, that they were all strapped for money, after the many years of court fees, and bonds. Jennie offered, and Mollie was grateful.

The morning before Ellison was to leave, he helped his Pa with the morning chores for the last time. His heart was heavy. He saw the age on his father's face the same way he saw age on his Ma. He knew he had been a terrible burden to both of them and he was sincerely sorry. His parents had at one time been securely well off, and because of him, they were struggling financially at an age where it would be hard to make the money back.

He and his Pa had just finished milking the cows and were walking back to the house.

"Pa," Ellison started. "I can't tell you how sorry I am for the last three years, and for causing you and Ma so much grief." He was quiet for a moment. "I remember when you finally offered to help me buy the meat market, I told you I would be rich one day and buy the farm so it would stay in the family."

Charles looked at his son with some degree of despair. He had remembered the conversation well. He never counted on his son becoming rich, but he hadn't counted on Ellison depleting his wealth either. The irony was almost funny. He looked at his son with a crooked smile.

"I'm not a young man anymore, Pa, but maybe I can find good employment in California and send back money now and then. It probably wouldn't pay my debt to you, but maybe it would help out some." Ellison was making a plea for forgiveness.

"You go find a life for yourself, son. Do well. Do something that makes you happy. If you have enough money left over and want to send some home, I won't turn it down. But on the other hand, don't feel obligated. I would ask that you settle your debt with Mr. Hall and Mr. Trinkle before anything else. Your Ma and I, we'll manage."

Ellison nodded his head, but didn't say anything.

When they reached the house, Ellison said, "I've never said this before, but I love you, Pa." Tears were standing in his eyes.

Charles smiled. "I love you too, son." he said, placing his hand on his son's shoulder. They both walked into the kitchen to help Mollie separate the milk.

Later that afternoon, Charles, Mollie and their son, Ellison drove into La Cygne's train depot. They arrived there about a half hour before Ellison's train was to head out. They sat on the benches outside and visited with each other for perhaps the last time. Ellison had become very excited about going out west. At least out west there might be prospects. His parents were sad to see him go, but yet so relieved he was not going to spend the rest of his life in prison.

When it was time to board the train, Ellison picked up his small suitcase and boarded the train, after kissing his Ma goodbye, and shaking hands with his Pa.

Lorraine Robinson

* * * * * * * * * *

Rob had been up all night occupying a small space in the barn, waiting to help one of his mares give birth. It had been a long, hard night for the old girl, she had been in labor for hours.

Finally the small colt was born as the sun was rising blood red on the eastern horizon. Once Rob cleaned up some and watched the new mother and son bond, he decided he could leave them for awhile so he could go eat some breakfast. If nothing else, he would love a cup of coffee.

As he walked out the side of the barn, he noticed his brother-in-law, Earl driving his truck out of the drive onto the road. He waved at Rob once he noticed he was there. Rob waved back, wondering what on earth Earl was doing here so early in the morning.

He walked into the kitchen and gave Maude a kiss on the cheek before going to the washroom to clean up.

"What's Earl up to so early this morning?" he hollered at his wife, while pouring water in the wash basin.

"He brought yesterday's newspaper over. Thought we might like to read it." She had her back to him stirring eggs on the stove.

"Something interesting in it?" he asked drying off his hands and arms, as he stepped out of the washroom.

She nodded her head toward the table, still with her back to him. She had been crying, and didn't want him to see.

He saw the newspaper lying on the table, next to a cup of coffee. He took a sip, opened the newspaper and read:

THE KANSAS CITY TIMES, WEDNESDAY, MARCH 17, 1926

Garnett, Kans., March 16 - John Ellison Scott, La Cygne grocer, was acquitted tonight of charges of murdering his wife, Ella, in June, 1923.

Scott was tried three times on the same charge. The first jury failed to agree and the second pronounced him guilty, but the Supreme Court set aside the second verdict. Scott was tried here on a change of venue from Linn County.

Twelve ballots were taken tonight by the jury, which deliberated three hours, returning it's verdict at 11:15 o'clock.

Prosecution counsel attempted to show that Scott slew his wife because he wished to marry her niece, Miss Arlene Scott, who lived

Deadly Affair

at their home. Miss Scott appeared at the first two trials, but went to Oklahoma shortly before the third trial and therefore could not be summoned again.

Rob sipped his coffee as he read the article under the headline. When he was finished he folded the paper, and let out a heavy sigh. He stood up from his chair and walked to his wife and gave her a hug. He then climbed up the stairs to a bedroom now used only for storage. In the far corner set an ornate glass display case about three feet tall.

Years before, when his girls were very young, Rob had been called out in the middle of the night to help put out a fire at the general store in Blue Mound. By the time most of the farmers called to help, had reached the store, the fire had ravaged the building, and very little was left. The owner of the store told all the men who came to help, that they could take anything that was salvageable. Rob took the glass display case. He really didn't have a purpose for it, but liked the way it looked.

Since the murder of his sister-in-law, he had been putting the newspapers chronicling her story in the case. As he stood and looked at it, he realized the newspapers filled the case almost halfway up.

He opened the door and placed this newspaper on top of the many others that told Ella's story. He gently closed the door on the glass case, and thus on the story of Ella's murder. He stared at it for a moment before closing the bedroom door on his way back down the stairs.

~CHAPTER TWENTY-SEVEN~

It was a cool, crisp autumn morning as the freighter pulled into the depot of a small mountain farm town, somewhere in Colorado. The yard workers had their work cut out for them these days. Due to the depressed economy there were an abundance of rail riders traveling across the country looking for work. Most of the riders climbed to the roof of the boxcars so they could scatter quickly when the train rolled to a stop. But some, mostly the old timers, still rode inside the boxcars and the yard workers still had to check each car.

Tom Hagerty had worked this job for many years and didn't mind checking the cars, except when he ran into a drunk, aggressive rider. He started at the back of the train and slid open the door of the third car from the back. At first all he saw were a few boxes stacked in a corner in the back of the car. Then he noticed the man propped up against the wall.

"Come on, buddy. Rides over, time to go." Tom hollered, as he hopped in the car.

"Mister...time to get off the train!" he said loudly, as he walked toward the immobile body.

"Buddy?" Tom touched the man's shoulder. There was no response.

"Come on man," Tom said irritated, as he pushed the man gently, and the body fell over on the floor.

"Oh Jeez! God bless him!" Tom moaned, as he realized this rider was dead.

Tom was shaken. In all his years working the yard he had never encountered a dead rider. He noticed a well-worn leather bag lying next to the man and he picked it up and started rifling through the contents. He was looking for some sort of identification, but there wasn't much of a clue in the man's bag as to who he was.

Tom pulled out a small photo case from the bag and opened it. Inside was a photo of a young girl, perhaps about eight years old. Tom put it back in the bag and pulled out a tattered coin purse with nearly two dollars in coins. There was a change of clothes wadded in the bag, but no sign of anything that would identify the man lying next to him. He cautiously patted the pockets of the rider's coat, and the only thing he found there was a pouch of tobacco, matches and rolling papers. Tom stood up, took his hat off and ran his arm across his forehead. Putting his hat back on, he walked back to the door, jumped to the gravel and headed to the depot to report his find in boxcar number three from the end.

    The man had passed away in the middle of the night. He had been suffering with fever for several days, and finally succumbed to the illness his body was carrying. He died a lonely man, and he died alone. He had lived his life riding the rails, working here and there, and never connected to anyone. He died not knowing what had become of his little sister he had loved so much, the only person in the world he did love. The one person he had sacrificed his life for.

    He also died not knowing the impact he had made on the people of a small farm town in Kansas years before.

    He died not knowing, that because of him, a young man who had been convicted of murder was allowed to go free.

~ AUTHOR'S NOTES ~

    The events of this story happened nearly a century ago, but for many years now, I felt it was a story that needed to be told.
    My Mother, Kathryn Jean (Williams) Sims, was Leona (Rogers) oldest daughter. In the early 1990's she was deep into genealogy research, and wrote two major books on her great- grandmother's (Sarah Vinton Holt) family, The Vintons and also her great-grandfather's (John Wesley Holt) family, The Holts. In her research, she of course came across this story of Aunt Ella's murder. Kathryn was born in November of 1926, after the saga, and it was never talked about in her presence. Growing up, she would over hear her elders talk about the murder, but when she would enter the room, the subject would be changed.
    In the early 1990's, Leona was close to 90 years old, as was Arlene. There were a few cousins that were alive in the early 1920's and had some memory of the story. Kathryn asked many questions of her mother, her aunt (Wilma Rogers) and cousins, mostly children of Mabel Cox, Maude's twin sister. All of the information that my mother Kathryn, collected was fascinating. However, it was usually vague and incomplete. She spent hours researching accounts of the trials written in the old newspapers in libraries and research centers. It's ironic that she would have had all those resources available to her tucked away in that glass display case, (now in my possession) had those newspapers not somehow disappeared by the time she was old enough to read.
    She wrote a 50-page outline of the events of the murder, and I pleaded with her then to write a book, but she refused, mainly because there were still people alive at that time that this story might hurt. I have been through a lot of activities and experiences in the past twenty years, but I have thought about this story off and on since my Mother's research.
    In 2007, I decided I was going to write this book, and it has taken me seven years to get it done. Some of the reasons why it has taken me so long to write this is because of life's little interruptions that happen to all of us daily. The main reason is because I was scared to death, and had no idea where to start.
    There are many unanswered questions in this story, because there are no answers to be found. For instance, did Ellison hide the gun in Ella's casket? It was a major family rumor. Was Ella pregnant? That too, was

a rumor, (outside the family) but it was interesting, so I made it part of the story. What about the Ku Klux Klan? What I wrote about them really happened, but is that all there was to their encounter with Arlene? I really do not know. I have tried to follow the facts of this story, and the people involved as closely to the truth as I possibly can, because that was my purpose, to tell Aunt Ella's story. However, I had to fill in some blanks at different times in order to make it flow. This is my first attempt at writing anything outside of a letter, and it was a major challenge to me. It was difficult for me to make all the pieces fit together, but I did have some help with putting facts together with a story line and make it work. For that I am grateful.

Ellison Scott really did move to California for a fresh start. Linn County history doesn't mention anything more about him, until his father, Charles', death in 1934. The obituary mentions him attending the funeral.

Arlene married Charlie Ferguson and settled on a farm in Linn County. I have no idea if she ever went back to teaching.

Leona also married, taught school for several years, was a farm wife, and raised a family near Blue Mound, Kansas.

The one event in the lives of many of the farm wives, was attending the Prairie Valley Ladies Aid Club once or twice a month, to spend the day quilting and visiting. Many ladies of Linn County loved to quilt and the Holt sisters, daughters, and granddaughters were among the group. The ladies made casseroles or desserts to take for dinner. They would spend the morning quilting, stop around noon to eat, and continue quilting and talking in the afternoon.

Sometimes the quilts they worked on would belong to one of the members, sometimes it would belong to someone in the community. They would charge a little money for their time and thread, which went into a fund to help families in need.

Club day was sacred. It was the only day the ladies had to do something they wanted to do. Being a farm wife was full time, no days off normally, and the ladies loved to sit, quilt and talk without worrying that they should be doing something else.

After Ella's murder, and the split in the family, club day became a little uncomfortable. No one was going to give up 'their' day out. Bertha stopped going to club, but Arlene did not. She was determined to be a part of the Ladies Aid, no matter what anyone thought. For many years, Maude, Leona, Kathryn, Maude's sisters Mary and Mabel, went to club, as did Arlene. During those many years there was not one word spoken between them. Once upon a time Leona and Arlene were best friends, but every club day for years, they treated each other worse than if they didn't know each other.

The irony is: Leona and Arlene spent the last years of their lives in the nursing home in Mound City, sitting across from each other during meal time. Sometimes life can be so cruel.

* * * * * * * * *

I lived on a farm two miles straight east of my grandparents, near Blue Mound, Kansas until I was seven years old. I loved to go play at my grandmother's house, and many days I would have a playmate. Chester and Frances Herrmann lived across the country intersection from my grandparents, and they had a daughter two years younger than me, Keitha Ann. We loved to play together, and always got along. My family moved to central Kansas when I was seven, and I only saw Keitha in the summers when I would come back to spend time with my grandma. Keitha has lived in Linn County all her life, and knows almost everyone in the county and they all know her. We have been friends all our lives, we don't remember ever not knowing each other. Our families were meshed together as neighbors and friends. Keitha's mother and grandmother were also members of the Ladies Aid Club. We would have so much fun playing together on club day, because we knew the 'ladies' would be so involved in quilting and talking they would pretty much ignore us. And they did. Except when we would sneak under the quilt and flip the thread in the air with our fingers, then giggle as if we were getting away with something.

Keitha remembers Arlene. I do not. She went to club with her mother and grandmother for years after we moved. I remember only a few of the ladies, but she remembers them all. When I decided to write this book, she was a wealth of valuable information to me. Her mother was as well. Keitha and I have spent hours hashing out the facts of this story, and she has helped put the people and families in the right places for me. I feel this is her book as well.

My thanks goes to her, Keitha (Herrmann) Brown for helping me see this through, and proof reading for my many mistakes, but mostly for being a true friend.

My thanks also goes to my cousin Rebecca (Thyer) Fawcett, who also ran a fine toothed comb through my many mistakes, and I really appreciate her time, effort and interest in helping me make this book the best it could be.

I wish also to thank Susie (Wolfe) Mahon, of La Cygne. I met her years ago through Keitha and realized through conversation that she is related to Ellison Scott. Her grandfather was a brother to Charles Scott, Ellison's father. She had some valuable information that helped me in so many ways.

I want to thank my son, Ian, for the design layout of the front cover so it would be easier for me to draw. I have been an artist for years, but he's so much better than me. I depend on him a lot.

I want to thank my family for putting up with my devotion to this book, when I probably ignored their needs. Especially my wonderful husband, Robin.

Last but not at all least, I wish to thank my brother-in-law, Allan Robinson for all his help to me with my computer. There were so many times I was ready to quit, but he would always be able to help find the problem and fix it. What a life-saver! It wouldn't be a book without him!

This book has been a valuable journey for me. The experience of writing it, and the experience of living through the eyes of some of my family members has been a real adventure for me. I hope reading it was an adventure for you.

Lorraine Robinson
August 2014